MEANS OF CONTROL

MEANS OF CONTROL

HOW THE HIDDEN ALLIANCE OF
TECH AND GOVERNMENT IS
CREATING A NEW AMERICAN
SURVEILLANCE STATE

BYRON TAU

CROWN
NEW YORK

Copyright © 2024 by Panopticon Project LLC

Published in the United States by Crown,
an imprint of the Crown Publishing Group,
a division of Penguin Random House LLC, New York.

CROWN and the Crown colophon are registered
trademarks of Penguin Random House LLC.

Hardback ISBN 978-0-593-44322-4
Ebook ISBN 978-0-593-44323-1

Printed in the United States of America on acid-free paper

crownpublishing.com

2 4 6 8 9 7 5 3 1

First Edition

Book design by Elizabeth A. D. Eno

To Barbara Anne, my mother.

May every child have a parent who never says no to buying a book.

Once the technical means of control have reached a certain size, a certain degree of *being connected* one to another, the chances for freedom are over for good. The word has ceased to have meaning.
—Thomas Pynchon, *Gravity's Rainbow*

And in this sense, all Americans are Marxists, for we believe nothing if not that history is moving us toward some preordained paradise and that technology is the force behind that movement.
—Neil Postman, *Amusing Ourselves to Death*

CONTENTS

AUTHOR'S NOTE

What follows is a work of nonfiction. Like all journalism, it's the best possible approximation of the truth. It is based on more than 350 interviews and tens of thousands of pages of documents. The narrative is supported with extensive documentation in the endnotes whenever possible. But because this is a book about intelligence and law enforcement—in some cases, classified intelligence or sensitive law enforcement methods—a full recounting of every source is not possible. Most people spoke to me only on the condition that their words not be attributed to them. The U.S. government has not always taken kindly to its employees and contractors speaking to the media and has often found ways to visit professional or reputational consequences on those who do. When sources have asked to remain anonymous, I have always tried to weigh the motivations of these sources; to evaluate what they have told me with a skeptical eye; and to seek corroboration for anything and everything in any way I can.

For those willing to speak on the record, I am eternally grateful. But I'm also grateful for those willing to speak at all. Journalists and intelligence officers are alike in some ways—except spies ask their foreign recruits to commit treason and reporters ask their sources to commit acts of transparency. Most people who cooperated seemed to do so out of a belief that the public should know more—more about their government's activities, more about their technology, and more about a shadowy industry that arose with scant public notice or debate. At the same time, my highest obligation is to the truth as I found it. Not everyone who appears in these pages will like what's said about them. I pulled no punches and did no favors.

The reader should not assume that because a person appears in this narrative, they were a source for this book. In many cases, people in the following pages refused to cooperate, and what is attributed to them was drawn from written accounts, documents, or other people familiar with the events described. Even when someone has refused to speak to me, I have sought to be fair, to seek their perspective in any way I can, to try to see things their way, and not to assume the worst about them or their actions.

I have tried whenever possible to cite emails or documents. I have tried to take copious and contemporaneous notes. A small amount of dialogue is a reconstruction from memory. I have sometimes lightly cleaned up quotations to fix grammar or syntax but never in a way that altered the meaning of the quotation. I have tried to visit locations in person whenever possible. I have very occasionally based short anecdotes or fleeting scenes on a single account, but only when it comported broadly with what could be checked and only when the source had an extensive track record of being reliable. Nothing of significance in this book is based on a single source. Every major claim is supported by numerous sources and documents, oftentimes dozens of sources and thousands of pages.

I have aimed to be transparent with the reader about what I do not know, and I have always tried to approach every story with an open mind and with the possibility that I am wrong. As the reporter and press critic Jack Shafer once said, a journalist should "follow a hunch with reporting that could undermine the hunch, address possible criticisms, remain open to criticism and refutation, correct meaningful errors of fact, abandon dry wells instead of pretending they're gushers."

One note on the use of the word "anonymized" as it relates to data sets. Documents or people may be quoted or paraphrased saying that bulk data sets were "anonymized," or stripped of personal information. As a factual matter, I dispute in most cases that data at issue can truly be "anonymized" and have rarely, if ever, used that characterization in my own writing. Stripping data of personal information and replacing it with a random identifier should be properly described as "pseudonymization." There is ample evidence that individuals can be re-identified in nearly all of the data sets covered in this book.

One of the challenges of reporting a complex story filled with technical details about technology and government is keeping track of acronyms and language that comes across as jargon. I've done my best to explain the technical developments covered in the book in plain English. I've also included a list of key concepts and definitions in the back of the book, and I encourage you to consult it frequently.

As a matter of full disclosure, my partner worked for a short time as a lawyer representing a company, Booz Allen Hamilton, that is briefly mentioned in this text. Her work was on an antitrust matter that is not at issue in this text or any of my other reporting. She has never provided me with nonpublic information regarding her work, nor has she been a source for this book or any of my other journalism. A final note to disclose: Until the fall of 2023, I was employed by *The Wall Street Journal*, whose parent company, Dow Jones, owns Factiva, which is a competitor to some of the data brokers mentioned in a very limited sense. However, Factiva largely competes against those brokers in the media monitoring and corporate research verticals and does not have stores of advertising or consumer data, the subject of this book.

Finally, journalism is a human endeavor, and as in all human endeavors perfection is elusive. All mistakes are my responsibility.

INTRODUCTION

The Grindr Problem
and a Wine-Soaked Dinner

n 2019, a government contractor and technologist named Mike Yeagley began making the rounds in Washington with a blunt warning for anyone in the country's national security establishment who would listen: the U.S. government had a Grindr problem.

A popular dating and hookup app, Grindr had launched ten years prior and had become a sensation. It relied on the GPS capabilities of modern smartphones to connect potential partners through the app—bringing together users in the same city, neighborhood, or even building. The app can show how far away a potential partner is in real time, down to the foot.

The app quickly amassed millions of users and became an essential part of gay culture around the globe. As Tom Capon, a young gay man who came of age just as the app was coming on the scene, put it in a 2019 essay, "It's no longer necessary to head to a gay bar to try your luck."

But to Yeagley, the app was something else: one of the tens of thousands of carelessly designed mobile phone apps that leaked massive amounts of data into the opaque world of online advertisers. That data, Yeagley knew, was easily accessible by anyone with a little technical know-how. So Yeagley—a technology consultant in his late forties who had worked in and around government projects nearly his entire career—made a PowerPoint presentation and went on a road show around Washington to demonstrate precisely how that data was a serious national security risk.

As he would explain in a succession of bland government conference rooms, Yeagley was able to access the geolocation data on Grindr users through a hidden but ubiquitous entry point: the digital advertising exchanges that serve up the little digital banner ads along the top of not only Grindr but nearly every ad-supported mobile app and website. This was possible because a good chunk of the online ad space in the world was sold through near-instantaneous auctions in a process called real-time bidding and those auctions were rife with surveillance potential. You know that ad that seems to be following you around the internet? Well, it's tracking you in more ways than one. In some cases, it's making your precise location available in near–real time to both advertisers and people like Mike Yeagley, who specialized in obtaining unique data sets for government agencies.

Working with Grindr data, Yeagley began drawing what are called geofences around buildings belonging to government agencies that do national security work. He was looking for phones belonging to Grindr users who spent their daytime hours at government office buildings. If the device spent most workdays at the Pentagon, the FBI headquarters, or the National Geospatial-Intelligence Agency (NGA) building at Fort Belvoir, for example, there was a good chance its owner worked for one of those agencies. Then he started looking at the movement of those phones through the Grindr data. When they weren't at their offices, where did they go? A small number of them had lingered at highway rest stops in the D.C. area at the same time and in proximity to other Grindr users—sometimes during the workday and sometimes while in transit between government facilities. For other Grindr users, he could infer where they lived, see where they traveled, and even guess at whom they were dating.

Intelligence agencies have a long and unfortunate history of trying to root out LGBTQ Americans from their workforce, but this wasn't Yeagley's intent. He didn't want anyone to get in trouble. No disciplinary actions were taken against any employee of the federal government based on Yeagley's presentation. His aim was to show that buried in the seemingly innocuous technical data that comes off every cell phone in the world is a rich story—one that people might prefer to keep quiet. Or at the very least, not broadcast to the whole world. And that each of these intelligence and national security agencies had employees who were recklessly, if obliviously, broadcasting intimate details of their lives to anyone who knew where to look.

It wasn't only national security employees who could be compromised by this breach of privacy. Some Grindr users were not out to friends, family members, or their employers about their identity. As Yeagley showed, all that information was available for sale, for cheap. And it wasn't just Grindr, but rather any app that had access to a user's precise location—other dating apps, weather apps, games. Yeagley chose Grindr because it happened to generate a particularly rich set of data and its user base might be uniquely vulnerable. A Chinese company had obtained a majority stake in Grindr beginning in 2016—amping up fears in Washington that the data could be misused by a geopolitical foe. Until 1995, gay men and women were banned from having security clearances, owing in part to a belief among government counterintelligence agencies that their identities might make them vulnerable to being leveraged by an adversary—a belief that persists today.*

---

*   It remains gospel in the national security community that being gay could pose a national security risk, especially if the employee is not open about their sexual orientation. The author James Kirchick argues that in reality LGBTQ Americans were unlikely to be shamed into betraying their country to hide their sexual identity. His book *Secret City* about the history of gay Washington makes the point that fears about compromise or blackmail were frequently used to drum LGBTQ Americans,

Yeagley's point in these presentations was simple: data that most consumers didn't think twice about could be a resource for intelligence gathering and a threat to the privacy of citizens and the security of the United States. Either way, it needed to be guarded.*

Having spent a decade in Washington as a reporter first for *Politico* and later at *The Wall Street Journal* and the Allbritton Journalism Institute, I'm used to coaxing stories out of sources and receiving tips. But the most extraordinary tale I've encountered fell into my lap during a wine-soaked dinner in the winter of 2018. Thanks to my dining companions that evening, I was given a chance glimpse inside a hidden world that I hadn't even begun to contemplate. At the dinner, I was told of the existence of a government-linked effort to collect all the bits and bytes of advertising data that we were generating as consumers. It was being done through obscure contractors in the D.C. area, funded by the federal government. And because the U.S. government was buying this data from a commercial provider, it was sanctioned by the law. At the time, that data was being used abroad in the global war on terror. But as you will come to understand, things that start abroad rarely stay there, and it wouldn't be long until this surveillance program came to America's shores.

As a demonstration, I was told to pick up my iPhone and select

---

usually gay men, out of official positions. "The belief was that because this was so terrible . . . the homosexual would go to any lengths to keep his secret a secret, and if that meant betraying his country . . . he would do it," Kirchick said in an interview. Kirchick argues there is not a single example in the entire espionage literature of someone being leveraged to betray their country because of their sexuality, pointing to a Defense Department study of more than a hundred international cases of espionage.

*   Grindr has said in the years since Yeagley's demonstration it has drastically reduced the amount of data available to advertising exchanges and limited the number of data partnerships it has. It also doesn't sell ads in certain countries where being gay is a crime.

"Settings." From there, navigate to "Privacy," then "Advertising." There I found a toggle bar that asked if I wanted to "limit ad tracking." Below it, Apple explained that if I toggled on "Limit Ad Tracking," I would "opt out of receiving ads targeted to your interests."*

It was that simple, I was told. This seemingly mundane setting on billions of mobile phones was a tangible clue that spoke to an entirely new kind of surveillance program—one designed to track everyone. Everyone who possesses an iPhone or Android phone had all been given an "anonymized" advertising ID by Apple and Google, my companion explained. That number would be used to track our real-world movement, our internet browsing behavior, the apps we put on our phone, and much more. Billions of dollars had been poured into this system by America's largest corporations. And a repository of data that rich and that detailed had attracted serious attention from the world's governments, which were opening their wallets to buy up information on everyone, rather than hacking it or getting it from secret court orders.

What I was learning over dinner was different from what Edward Snowden had revealed in 2013: that the U.S. government was running a massive surveillance apparatus with the cooperation of the largest tech and telecom companies, overseen by a court that operates in secret. That surveillance effort was mostly focused on targets abroad, though some aspects of it touched on Americans and their data. Instead, what I was now learning about was a wholly separate effort. The government was buying its way into a commercial marketplace, one that few consumers even knew existed. The little "Limit Ad Tracking"

---

* Apple has made major changes in its settings since this time. As of this writing, "Limit Ad Tracking" is no longer buried deep in the iPhone settings. Instead, a very prominent box now asks users if they want to "allow apps to request to track." Disabling tracking is also prominently displayed in the privacy menu and has been relabeled "Tracking." As a result, there has been a drastic decrease in the number of iPhones being tracked in the years since Apple made these changes, because users have opted out. As such, some of the techniques described in this book have been degraded, at least on iPhones.

button was a way to limit some of the data that flowed into that marketplace. But no one can fully escape its clutches.

It would take more than five years after that dinner for me to fully understand the byzantine online ad ecosystem. Here's how it works. Imagine a woman named Marcela who lives in the Philadelphia suburbs. She has a Google Pixel phone with the Weather Channel app installed. As she heads out the door to go on a jog, she sees overcast skies. So Marcela opens the app to check if the forecast calls for rain. By clicking on the Weather Channel's bright blue icon, Marcela triggers a frenzy of digital activity all aimed at serving her a personalized ad. The Weather Channel has partnered with an entity called an advertising exchange to help pay for the app and deliver display ads to its millions of users. That exchange is basically a massive marketplace where billions of mobile devices and computers are telling a centralized server that they have an open ad space. And so in less than the blink of an eye after she opened the Weather Channel app, this machinery goes to work. To deliver her the most relevant advertising, Marcela's Google-assigned ad ID—called an AAID on Android phones—shared with the ad exchange so that it could serve her the most relevant possible ads based on what advertisers have inferred about her.

To the layperson, her AAID is a string of gibberish, something like bdca712j-fb3c-33ad-2324-0794d394m912. But to advertisers, it's a gold mine. They know that bdca712j-fb3c-33ad-2324-0794d394m912 owns a Google Pixel device with the Nike Run Club app. They know that bdca712j-fb3c-33ad-2324-0794d394m912 often frequents runnersworld.com. And they know that bdca712j-fb3c-33ad-2324-0794d394m912 was lusting after a pair of new Vaporfly racing shoes. They know this because Nike, runnersworld.com, and Google are all plugged into the same advertising ecosystem, all aimed at understanding what consumers are interested in.

Advertisers use that information as they shape and deploy their ads. Say both Nike and Brooks, another running shoe brand, are trying to reach female running aficionados in a certain income bracket.

Based on the huge amounts of data sloshing around, they might build an "audience"—essentially a huge list of ad IDs of customers known or suspected to be in the market for running shoes. And they tell a digital ad exchange how much they're willing to pay to reach those consumers every time they load an app or a web page.

When Marcela loads the Weather Channel app, she sends reams of data back to the ad exchange. That includes the IP address of the phone, the type of phone and the operating system it's running, the carrier, the app in use, and the precise GPS coordinates of the phone. The exchange gets an array of technical data about how the phone is configured: what languages the browser is using, what version of the operating system is running, even what the screen resolution is set to. And finally, advertisers also get that pseudonymized advertising ID number. Technically, we can reset this number, but few people bother to. Few people even know they have one.

Users do have some control over what they share. And the advertisers have access only to whatever data the consumer grants them. If consumers don't allow the app they're using to access GPS, the ad exchange can't pull the phone's GPS location, for example. (Or at least they aren't supposed to; not all the apps follow the rules, and Apple and Google don't always review the software in their app stores all that closely.)

Ad exchange bidding platforms do minimal due diligence on the hundreds or even thousands of entities that have a presence on their servers. So even the losing bidders still have access to all the consumer data that came off the phone during the bid request. An entire business model has been built on this: siphoning data off the real-time bidding networks, packaging it up, and reselling it to help businesses understand consumer behavior.

Geolocation is the single most valuable piece of commercial data to come off those devices. Understanding the movement of phones is now a multibillion-dollar industry. It can be used to deliver targeted advertising based on location for, say, a restaurant chain that wants to deliver targeted ads to people nearby. It can be used to measure consumer behavior and the effectiveness of advertising. How many people saw an ad and later visited a store? And the analytics can be used for planning and investment decisions. Where is the best location to put a new store? Will there be enough foot traffic to sustain such a business? Is the number of people visiting a certain retailer going up or down this month, and what does that mean for the retailer's stock price?

But this kind of data is good for something else. It has remarkable surveillance potential. Why? Because what we do in the world with our devices cannot truly be anonymized. The fact that advertisers know Marcela as bdca712j-fb3c-33ad-2324-0794d394m912 as they're watching her move around the online and offline worlds offers her almost no privacy protection. Her habits and routines are unique to her. Our real-world movement is highly specific and personal to all of us. For many years, I lived in a small thirteen-unit walk-up in Washington, D.C. I was the only person waking up every morning at that address and going to the *Journal*'s offices. Even if I was just an anonymized number, my behavior was as unique as a fingerprint even in a sea of hundreds of millions of others. There was no way to anonymize my identity in a data set like geolocation. Where a phone spends most of its evenings is a good proxy for where its owner lives. Advertisers know this. Governments know this too. The only people it hasn't been explained to in a clear and resonant way is the general public.

Marcela—and the rest of us—were being tracked through a strange unholy alliance of big government and big business. Her data was being bought, sold, and traded in a marketplace that she didn't even know existed. The buyers were the largest advertisers and the biggest intelligence agencies.

This was the tantalizing and harrowing story laid out for me over that long-ago dinner. With growing horror as I swilled my wine and listened, I toggled the "Limit Ad Tracking" switch to on. And I did the only thing I knew how to do. I started reporting.

———

Writing this book took five years of my life, a lawsuit against the U.S. government under the Freedom of Information Act, and hundreds of interviews with skittish and reluctant sources. What I have come to understand is this: the technology embedded in our phones, our computers, our cars, and our homes is part of a vast ecosystem of data collection and analysis primarily aimed at understanding and in some cases manipulating our consumer behavior. Digital advertising is only one piece of it. Our public spaces are blanketed by networked cameras and other surveillance systems put up in the name of public safety or personal security. And pretty much everything that emits a wireless signal of any kind—and today that list has grown to include routers, security cameras, televisions, home entertainment systems, Bluetooth keyboards, wireless headphones, and every single tire of every car manufactured since the mid-2000s, to name a few—can be and often is being covertly monitored. And the internet itself is built upon the backbone of a Cold War–era Defense Department computer network—with the routers, switches, packets, domain name lookups, and web addresses all subject to monitoring and manipulation in various ways.

Governments around the world—chief among them, the United States and its geopolitical rivals such as China and Russia—have accordingly come to view the internet not as a tool for self-expression, education, or commerce but as a mechanism for turning every single piece of consumer hardware and software on earth into a tool for intelligence gathering, "situational awareness," and in some cases social control. This is made possible not by hacking and breaking in—though governments do a lot of that too on their hardest and most valuable targets—nor by using expensive military hardware like overhead drones, spy planes, or satellites. In most cases, there's no need to go to such lengths because the consumer technology we use every day generates an unimaginable amount of data. And much of that data is for sale in opaque marketplaces and digital bazaars where the personal information of billions of consumers is bought, sold, and traded by the petabyte. Each piece of data on its own is not particularly valuable—

a cell phone GPS ping here, the tire pressure reading on a car there. But woven together by government entities that operate in the shadows with multibillion-dollar budgets and powerful computer systems unavailable to the general public, the end result has been to blanket the globe in sensors, microphones, cameras, and scanners that are impossible to escape.

The modern digital ecosystem would not exist without surveillance—what the author and Harvard professor Shoshana Zuboff termed "surveillance capitalism" in her landmark 2019 book, *The Age of Surveillance Capitalism.* Consumers, for better or worse, have begrudgingly come to accept that basic bargain. While we are not clear on the details, most of us have come to a rough understanding that our attention, behavior, and personal lives are being mined for behavioral insight by companies in exchange for free or discounted services. Zuboff recognized the government surveillance potential of the stores of data collected by the nation's largest corporations—data that she said was "raw material" for the system of surveillance capitalism she described. This book aims to fill in the details and bring into vivid relief just how deep the relationship between government intelligence agencies and our data goes.

This torrent of information is transforming government's relationship to its citizens. In some cases, it's for the better. Public health, city planning, transportation, medicine, and energy efficiency are being altered by insights unleashed using big data. But this revolution is also challenging every aspect of intelligence, law enforcement, and military operations—with profound consequences for the privacy, liberty, and dignity of citizens. Even in democratic countries, these activities are being done with scant public debate and little oversight from legislatures that barely understand the issues or the technology. And consumers and citizens have been kept in the dark—first by corporations, which do not want public scrutiny of the amount of data collection that occurs, and then by governments, which do not want to lose the specialized warrantless tracking capabilities that they have come to rely on.

Government lawyers have invoked the fact that this data is available publicly as the legal justification for its bulk acquisition and use. How much do we really care about our privacy if we've given this information away freely to the world's largest corporations? their argument goes. We all have consented to sharing intimate details of our lives for convenience and free services, and the government's counterterrorism and national security mission is much more important than selling patio furniture.

This is the paradox at the heart of this story. Corporations are loath to talk about the scale and scope of data collection because consumers find it distasteful and there is money to be made. And governments have withheld critical details from us about how that data is being used in an expanding system of mass global surveillance while claiming that we have consented to its collection. The truth is that no consumer or citizen can know what data is being collected about them or how it's used, let alone consent. To say that anyone has consented to live in this world is a lie, because there is no way for the average consumer to even begin to understand the flow of data from their consumer technologies to corporate America and then to the security services of nearly every powerful nation on earth.

All of this has also been accomplished with almost no public discussion of what kind of world we're building in the twenty-first century.

This book is a chronicle of how different kinds of data became available for purchase by the U.S. government after 9/11 and the consequences for our privacy. I've spent years trying to unravel this world—a fun house of mirrors draped in nondisclosure agreements, corporate trade secrets, needlessly classified contracts, misleading denials, and in some cases outright lies. This story is in rough chronological order, but because it sprawls across half a dozen government agencies over a two-decade time frame, that's not always possible and the story is not always perfectly linear.

Over years of thinking and reporting on this topic, I came to classify the data brokers in this story as belonging to one of four overlapping generations. First, there are *consumer data brokers* like Acxiom, Thomson Reuters, LexisNexis, and TransUnion that collect information like names, address histories, and consumer preferences. Second, there are *social data providers* that emerged to monitor the conversation on social media. Third, there are *advertising and location data brokers* that sprang up to understand the movement of phones and the behavioral preferences of their owners. Finally, there are what might be called *gray data providers* that specialize in the most niche data sets.

My classification system is a vast oversimplification; the industry is in constant flux and large brokers like Thomson Reuters amass huge numbers of disparate data sets under one roof now. But these four types are a good way to think about the evolution of the industry. And as the market evolved, the government at each turn moved to take advantage of the possibilities offered by each new iteration of the data industry.

The four parts of this book roughly correspond to these four generations of data providers and the corresponding government efforts to capitalize on them. Part I traces the origins of consumer data brokers and the discovery that after 9/11 they might have something to contribute to the counterterrorism mission. Part II documents the rise of social media and the government's early attempts to responsibly monitor it. Part III is about advertising data and smartphones and the new vectors they offered to understand geographic behavior. And part IV is about the increasingly weird world of esoteric data that, without even knowing it, we're all generating, with vast consequences for our ability to move around the world without being subjected to persistent surveillance.

While this story focuses primarily on the activities of the U.S. government, the privacy issues raised in this book are global in scope. Every government on earth is eager to acquire data in any way possible to help it better understand the world.

There was never a grand overarching plan or conspiracy behind any of what I've described here. Rather, it's a story of different people at different periods in time working for different government agencies or contractors coming to the same realization: that data is available for sale and that it can be used for whatever mission is important at the time. This is a story about how a series of tiny, experimental programs, data vendors, and obscure contractors have brought us to the precipice of a digital panopticon—one built by corporate America and blessed by government lawyers.

"We are backing ourselves into a surveillance state," one former senior national security official told me one day in 2020. This was a man who had worked at the highest levels of American government and who had been intimately involved in the government's secret surveillance efforts after 9/11. But the growing aggregation of unclassified data gnawed at him far more than any secret surveillance program.

Information is power, he said. In the context of state power, data collection tilts the power toward the government and away from its citizens. What was being done today was arguably lawful but not thoughtful, he said—a myopic conversation among insiders that has excluded the general public and failed to recognize a legal problem that was becoming a threat to the civil liberties and constitutional rights of Americans.

"Nobody should want this," he said.

PART I

SIGNATURES

CHAPTER 1

The Bad Guys Database

ACXIOM, ARKANSAS
AND WASHINGTON, D.C., 2001

I t was a crisp New England morning when Acxiom consumer
No. 254-04907-10006 cleared the security checkpoint at Boston's
Logan Airport. Consumer No. 254-04907-10006 was a twenty-
two-year-old Saudi national named Waleed al-Shehri. He was of
slight stature and pale complexion and had been in the United States
for only about five months on a tourist visa. But he had generated
enough of a paper trail to be captured and indexed by Acxiom, which
at the time was the world's largest consumer data repository, holding
billions of records on consumers drawn from corporate America as
well as public records like court filings, voter registrations, and property deeds.

In his twenty weeks in America, al-Shehri had been busy. He had
obtained two copies of the same Florida driver's license (A426-893-
78-460-0) with slightly mismatching addresses, giving him a duplicate that he could pass to an associate. He opened a bank account at
SunTrust Bank in Florida (account number 0385008119775 linked to

Visa debit card 4011 8060 7079 6163) and bought, insured, and then sold a 1993 Dodge Colt. He had bounced around motels and apartment complexes for weeks, generating even more records. The Bimini Motel and Apartments in Hollywood, Florida. Lago Mar Motel in Lake Worth. The Homing Inn in Boynton Beach. Lisa Motel and Apartment in Lake Worth. The DoubleTree in Lake Buena Vista. He'd availed himself of a number of services: a membership to the Body Perfect Fitness Center in Lake Worth and later the World Gym in Lantana. A Mail Boxes Etc. rental. He traveled extensively: to Freeport in the Bahamas, to Boston, to San Francisco, to Las Vegas. He made reservations at the Bahamas Princess Resort. Finally, he flew to the Boston area, where he checked in to the 144-room Park Inn in Newton, Massachusetts, a leafy upscale suburb just outside the city. Six days later, he and the two men he'd been sharing a room with—his older brother Wail al-Shehri and a Saudi law school dropout named Satam al-Suqami—checked out of the motel. The trio headed for Boston Logan International Airport.

Corporate data banks were not the only computer systems to take note of al-Shehri. Somewhere in a database called the Computer-Assisted Passenger Prescreening System, or CAPPS, al-Shehri was flagged for additional screening as he made his way to his gate because something about his travel pattern had set off the system.* However, under the security procedures in place at the time, additional screening applied only to checked luggage—not carry-on. Because al-Shehri had no checked bags, he cleared the security checkpoint without issue. The metal detectors at the time were calibrated to detect the metal content of a .22-caliber handgun, not blades like what the men were carrying. (Knives and other blades under four inches were permitted

---

* The criteria that led to being chosen for additional screening by CAPPS have never been fully explained even in the years after the system was retired and replaced; however, things like buying tickets in cash or at the last minute reportedly triggered an alert.

under the theory that they could not pose any serious danger if wielded as a weapon.)

Tucked away in yet another federal computer system run by the U.S. Immigration and Naturalization Service were other unusual records: U.S. government travel and visa files that showed al-Shehri shouldn't even be in the country. He and al-Suqami had tried to visit the Bahamas a few weeks after al-Shehri arrived in America. They flew out of Miami, handing in their U.S.-government-issued travel authorizations. But once in Freeport, Bahamian authorities turned them away over their lack of visas, and they were forced to board the next flight back to the United States. Under U.S. law, they had never left America because they had never legally entered the Bahamas. But their reentry into the United States was never logged by the immigration computer systems. Their aborted trip to the Bahamas was shown as an exit. As far as the U.S. government was aware, neither of the two men strolling through Logan's Terminal B were in the country at all.

At Logan Airport, the al-Shehri brothers and al-Suqami took their seats in business class of American Airlines Flight 11, offering nonstop service from Boston to Los Angeles. They were joined on that flight by two other associates: Mohamed Atta and Abdul Aziz al-Omari, both of whom had flown in from Portland, Maine, earlier that morning. About fifteen minutes into the flight, the five men sprang into action—stabbing two flight attendants, slashing the throat of a passenger in first class, and spraying a chemical irritant at the front of the plane to force the passengers and crew to the rear. By the time the plane passed near Albany, New York, the five hijackers had firmly established control. With Atta at the controls, they turned the Boeing 767 south toward New York City. Perhaps unfamiliar with the in-flight address system and intending to address the passengers and crew of Flight 11, Atta barked from the cockpit, "We have some planes. Just stay quiet, and you'll be okay. We are returning to the airport. . . . Nobody move. Everything will be okay. If you try to make any moves, you'll endanger yourself and the airplane. Just stay quiet."

But he transmitted it not over the intercom in the cabin but out over the plane's external radio to other pilots and air traffic controllers—a chilling warning to the rest of the world that something was not right in the skies that September morning.

Why had none of the systems in place stopped them? It was a failure to connect the dots. The government had plenty of information, but it had failed to adequately capitalize on the disparate intelligence leads and anomalies in the data that already existed. The FBI knew, in the summer of 2001, that two of the hijackers, Khalid al-Mihdhar and Nawaf al-Hazmi, were al-Qaeda operatives who had entered the United States in January 2000. The bureau was actively hunting for al-Mihdhar in the days before al-Shehri and his associates destroyed the North Tower of the World Trade Center and left a gaping hole in the side of the Pentagon—scouring the country to see if al-Mihdhar was still there and to determine what his intentions were.

In fact, all summer long U.S. intelligence had been picking up vague and unspecific terrorist "chatter" warning of an unspecified threat to the homeland. President George W. Bush's August 6, 2001, daily intelligence briefing contained an item titled "Bin Ladin Determined to Strike in US." That was the thirty-sixth time bin Laden or his al-Qaeda terrorist group had been mentioned in a presidential briefing in 2001. There was a memo from the Phoenix FBI field office, where an agent named Kenneth Williams warned in July that he believed the terrorist leader Osama bin Laden was trying to dispatch students to flight training in the United States. There was an FAA warning that same month of "reports of possible near-term terrorist operations" and ongoing threats against civil aviation, including the threat of hijacking. As the CIA director, George Tenet, later told the 9/11 Commission assembled to investigate the attacks about the increasingly dire intelligence warnings piled up on the desks of national security officials in the summer of 2001, "The system was blinking red."

September 11 taught us something else, too: namely that data valuable in understanding the attacks wasn't just hidden in government databases. In corporate America's vast and growing collection of consumer data, there were patterns of bizarre behavior, unusual rentals, confounding address histories, and duplicate licenses. These were all potential signals to law enforcement or the intelligence community that something was potentially amiss—if only law enforcement had bothered to look. In the wake of the attack, the FBI put together a detailed chronology with 3,441 total entries chronicling the steps the hijackers had taken in their planning—bank transactions, travel records, hotel stays, gym check-ins, visa applications, and credit and debit card transactions that told the story of the attacks, from the date of the eldest hijacker Mohamed Atta's birth in September 1968 to a handwritten letter the FBI found in a mailbox rented by some of the Florida-based hijackers, dated September 10, 2001, with a message to one of the hijackers: "Hammza, whatever you do, do not tell anyone what you are about to do tomorrow. Okay?" It was a chillingly detailed look at the years of planning that went into carrying out the attacks, much of it drawn from records maintained by corporate America.

And as the government soon found out, corporate America was eager to help.

At the heart of this story is a kind of company that few Americans give much thought to: data brokers. Beginning in the 1960s, these data warehousers sprang up to help America's largest corporations advertise more efficiently. At first, these brokers were collecting fairly basic information: address history and some simple demographics. But as computers grew more powerful and digital storage grew cheaper, so did the capacity to collect and collate huge volumes of information and derive increasingly personalized insights from that data. Data brokers emerged to cater to advertisers' demands for more and more detailed information on all of us.

Acxiom was part of the original generation of data brokers, with a history dating back to the 1960s. Within days of the attack, Acxiom's leadership came to the realization that the data it had amassed on hundreds of millions of people inside the United States for the purposes of doing targeted advertising could also be deployed on the vexing problems of airline security and identity verification exposed by the 9/11 attacks. This was a new development for government. It already had access to the best and most in-depth information on the population: the census, tax records, draft records, Social Security numbers, and so on. But government records could tell only a partial story of who people are. The emergence of corporate data brokers and their wares presented a new vector for understanding the world.

Acxiom traces its roots back to the small city of Conway, Arkansas, located about thirty miles outside Little Rock. The local school bus magnate Charles Ward happened to have access to an IBM mainframe, a rarity in the late 1960s, and had the idea of splitting off the bus company's data-processing department and running it as a separate services company. In 1969, Demographics Inc. was born as a small firm that could do billing and other basic computerized tasks on a clunky mainframe computer programmed by punch card.

Ward was also a Democratic Party activist. He had a notion that data processing could help build mailing lists to send individualized pieces of mail to voters—bringing a new kind of precision to political campaigns and boosting the Democratic Party's political fortunes. The company began scanning phone books to compile direct mailing lists.

After founding the company, Ward turned day-to-day management of the firm and eventually full ownership control over to a young IBM systems engineer and gadget geek named Charles Morgan, and it was Morgan who took the company from school bus spin-off to billion-dollar behemoth in his thirty-six years at the helm of the company. Demographics Inc. was renamed Conway Communications Exchange, or CCX, in 1979 to avoid brand confusion with another data business. It went public under that name in 1982 and later rebranded as Acxiom—a permutation of the word "axiom," meaning a self-evident statement or proposition, with a nod to its heritage as CCX tossed into the mix.

Over the years, under Morgan's stewardship, Acxiom turned to more corporate work. It was not a credit bureau, though it processed some of that data through partnerships with TransUnion and many of the largest banks, whom it counted as customers. Instead, Acxiom was sitting on marketing data: names, addresses, household demographics, and assumptions about consumer likes and dislikes. Acxiom could process the data that the big credit bureaus and credit card companies collected, combine it with other data such as census records, and derive "business intelligence" from it. It could help banks figure out how to tailor their marketing of various financial products and give detailed demographic and interest-based lists to companies that wanted to do targeted advertising.

Acxiom's breakthrough, and what set it apart from other companies in the nascent field of cultivating consumer data, was that it figured out how to pull disparate records and tie them together into a single consumer profile. People gave different variations of their names in different circumstances: Thomas John might be known to his friends as T.J., for example. Victoria might go by Vikki in almost all situations other than on her birth certificate and her passport. Marriages and maiden names posed their own challenges. And then there is the fact that any large-scale data set is beset by human error or intentional deceit: typos, failure to update addresses, and consumers intentionally providing inaccurate or outdated information to dodge spam. But to deal with this problem, Acxiom had invented a system called AbiliTec—a way of joining together disparate fragments of data such as addresses and maiden names and linking them to a specific individual. AbiliTec aimed to assign each individual in the United States a single, stable unique identifier and then organize all of the consumer information about that person under that identifier. It was thanks to AbiliTec that Acxiom could say with some confidence that Waleed Alshehri, Shehri W. Al, W. Al Shehri, and Waleed al-Shehri were the same person and give him the stable identifier 254-04907-10006.

Acxiom's journey from corporate marketing tool to national security database started after 9/11 as the nation was reeling from the shock and horror of the terrorist attacks. In a meeting in a conference room in its Little Rock offices on Friday, September 14, Morgan and the company's chief lawyer Jerry Jones considered the possibilities: Acxiom had vast stores of names and address history taken from both public and private sources. It could link those attributes together better than anyone else. Isn't that exactly the kind of service government might need to understand who is asking for a visa or trying to board an airplane?

Toward the end of the meeting, a privacy and compliance specialist named Jonathan Askins suggested that the company go beyond just brainstorming about a security product and actually run the list of nineteen terrorist hijackers through Acxiom's data banks. The FBI that day had posted the list online naming the suspects, Askins told his superiors. If we want to show the world the value of our data, we should see what we have first, he said.

That afternoon, Askins drove up to the data center in Conway, about thirty minutes away from the Little Rock offices. There, he corralled some data analysts in a room and began running queries on the stores of data that Acxiom had in its databases on these nineteen names. He found eleven of them. Then one of Acxiom's analysts had an idea: What if they looked for other people who had shared addresses with the known hijackers more than once? Acxiom had a vast database of where people lived and when. Acxiom could do something called a "rooftop" search: meaning it could see that people lived in the same building but not the same unit. So it could find everyone who lived at 123 Main Street at the same time, even if one person lived in apartment 1C and the other person lived in 4D. If a known terrorist had shared an address with someone more than once, that might be something the government would want to know. It could just be statistical noise—two unrelated people bouncing around the same metropolitan area and ending up in large apartment buildings more than once. Or it could be a sign that they were possible associates or at the very least acquaintances. Askins gave the analyst permission to conduct the search.

It was dinnertime, so he stepped out to get Chinese takeout for the team working on the data queries. When he returned, the analyst looked ashen. She found hundreds of names when running the search—more than three hundred people who had shared an address twice with the hijackers.

Morgan decided to double down. The company's new secret project, hatched a few days after 9/11, would continue for months. Possible patterns began to emerge. For example, they found one man who lived in Mohamed Atta's apartment building and worked at a 7-Eleven but had amassed a huge amount of credit card debt: $150,000 across fourteen cards. The 9/11 hijackers also appeared to run up large credit card bills and then abruptly stopped paying even the minimum balance in the weeks before the attack. Was this a possible template to identify other would-be terrorists? No use worrying about your credit score if you are going to commit a suicide attack, after all.

The things the team was finding were too tantalizing to keep to themselves. Askins called Jerry Jones to relay what they had found. Could these be terrorist sleeper cells? Part of a second wave of attacks yet to be unleashed? Because Bill Clinton had come up through Arkansas politics in his rise to national prominence, Jones had some connections to the former president's administration. He placed calls to the former White House chief of staff Mark McLarty and the former secretary of transportation Rodney Slater, both of whom encouraged the company to alert the government of their findings. Jones also called a former law partner who was now with the Arkansas State Police. He helped connect them to federal prosecutors in Little Rock and the local FBI field office. *Is this data in a format where you can share it?* the government lawyers and agents asked Acxiom on a late-evening conference call. Askins offered to put it into Excel spreadsheets and then burn it onto a CD-ROM. They would make the exchange in person.

It was close to midnight when Askins met an FBI agent at a gas station at a midway point between the bureau's downtown Little Rock offices and Acxiom's Conway data center. The FBI agent flashed his lights, showed his badge, and took the disk from Askins before driving off into the Arkansas night.

For Acxiom, this was the beginning of a whirlwind experiment in becoming a government contractor. In the weeks, months, and years after the parking lot meeting, the company's executives and sales reps would be ushered into rooms all over Washington. The biggest coup was a summer 2002 meeting with Vice President Dick Cheney. After the meeting, Cheney scribbled a note to an aide asking if the White House was providing any assistance to the company. "Looks promising," Cheney wrote. In the weeks after 9/11, Askins shifted full-time to Acxiom's government efforts—with the hopes that the company could eventually sell a product to the U.S. government. The Justice Department arranged to formally subpoena Acxiom for the company's data, turning it into a witness in the sprawling 9/11 investigation. Acxiom in turn arranged with its data partners to get deeper access to information like credit bureau data. Half a dozen FBI counterterrorism agents took up residence in the company's Conway data center.

As part of its Washington rollout, the company would produce a thirteen-page memo titled "Data Integration in Government Agencies." The first paragraph states, "The September 11 terrorists looked and acted like many others in America. They used our educational systems, our financial markets, our transportation systems, and our societal freedom to attack us like we have never been attacked before. This is certainly frightening, but it is also encouraging. Because our society, for the most part, is an electronic society. Every credit card transaction is captured; every airline ticket recorded; every financial transaction stored." Would it be possible, the memo asked, to use this data to ID potential terrorists before they carried out their plans?

Morgan's solution: a "Bad Guys Database."

His 2015 self-published memoir, *Matters of Life and Data*, is light on the details of what exactly the database is, saying only that he had thirty Acxiom employees working on it. But its task was essentially racial profiling. Running the kind of data-intensive queries that the FBI wanted on the hundreds of millions of people whom Acxiom had data on required substantial amounts of time and computer power. It would help if you could focus those queries on the people most likely to be suspicious. The company was building what in the marketing world was called a look-alike campaign—basically looking for people who shared characteristics with the 9/11 hijackers. In this case, however, it was essentially building a list of young Arab Muslims in the United States. And Acxiom wasn't alone.

On the evening of September 13, 2001, Hank Asher was in his sprawling home in Boca Raton, Florida. Asher—the CEO of one of Acxiom's chief rivals, Seisint, which stood for Seismic Intelligence—was a garrulous, flamboyant man on the cusp of his fifties. Prior to becoming a computer programmer and entrepreneur, Asher had a brief stint as a drug smuggler when living in the Bahamas in the 1980s. As a result, his federal data contracts were constantly in jeopardy—whenever a potential client did due diligence on the company's founder—and he had been dogged by controversy at the helm of the companies he founded and ran.

Like the rest of the country, Asher was reeling from the shock of the attacks. He and a friend were standing around his kitchen. And Asher was drinking. It was around 8:00 p.m. when he had the same sudden realization that Jonathan Askins would have a day later in Arkansas. Finishing the last of his oversized martini, he said suddenly, as if struck by a lightning bolt, "I know how to find these guys."

Despite having a guest over, he retreated to his bedroom and stayed there all night coding. Asher's goal: devise a system that could identify potential terrorists. Asher ran all 450 million people in Seisint's vast databases—names drawn from government records like property deeds, driver's licenses, and consumer records, like banking, for example—through his new algorithm. He also made some assumptions about what a terrorist profile might look like. It took him sixteen hours to come up with a list of people he believed were worth scrutinizing. About 120,000 people had elevated risk scores under Asher's algorithm, and 419 names would have extremely high risk scores. Of the 80 people with the highest scores, 5 were terrorist hijackers that participated in the 9/11 attacks, and 15 more were already known to the FBI and the targets of investigations. Thirty more people became FBI targets later, Seisint claimed in materials it prepared for the government.

Asher's system was just like Morgan's Bad Guys Database. The algorithms that he had programmed would ultimately end up mainly screening for Muslims. The idea was to look for people whose address history and financial transactions were suspicious. That tended to flag recent immigrants from predominantly Arab or Muslim countries with a lengthy address trail, but it also might flag people with suspicious patterns of behavior or data trails such as multiple IDs. Asher refined the system after the initial version to use information like age, gender, driver's license and pilot license data, credit history, and Social Security number anomalies to generate a score. Like the search Askins authorized of people who shared addresses with known hijackers, Asher gave people an elevated score for living in proximity to a "dirty" address belonging to a terrorist. And in a presentation he gave months later in January 2003 to Vice President Cheney, he would acknowledge that "ethnicity" was a key characteristic in giving elevated risk scores.

After Asher coded the initial version, he told a friend in Florida law enforcement about what he had built and suggested it could be a tool for fighting terrorism. Days later, the FBI descended on his home just as they would at Acxiom. The onetime drug smuggler would be invited into closed-door meetings all over Washington over the coming months and years, and he would try to build out the demonstration into a bona fide law enforcement and counterterrorism tool that would be called MATRIX. One senior Defense Department official recalled meeting Asher shortly after 9/11 and being blown away by the amount of data Seisint had as well as the amount of detail that his algorithm had captured. Asher came to the meeting with specific warnings of a possible insider threat: his computer system had red-flagged what looked like a U.S. service member with a high risk score living on an air force base.

The Pentagon official left the meeting with Asher feeling both impressed by the technology and alarmed by the large number of people across the country with high risk scores. A short time later, he mentioned Asher and his data analysis tool to a Defense Department colleague in Hawaii, where there were ongoing fears of an attack on U.S. military facilities.

A few days later, a Defense Department lawyer knocked on the official's door to ask if he had been talking up a commercial data-mining tool for base and facility security purposes. He acknowledged he had.

"This is the DOD. We don't do that shit," the lawyer said, warning him to knock it off.

That legal advice would, in the years to come, go largely unheeded.

CHAPTER 2

The Supersnoop's Dream

DARPA, WASHINGTON, D.C., 2002–2003

John Poindexter had a dream.

Poindexter, the retired navy vice admiral who had played a central role in the Iran-contra scandal while serving on President Ronald Reagan's White House staff, had spent more than a decade in exile from the halls of power. In that time, he had fought a successful legal battle to vacate his five felony convictions on charges of lying to Congress. He had kept busy teaching himself various computer programming languages, and he earned a living by doing some consulting work for defense contractors.

The 9/11 attacks had changed everything for him. Beginning in early 2002, he was put in charge of a major research program at the Pentagon's in-house research and development office, the Defense Advanced Research Projects Agency, or DARPA. This effort was called Total Information Awareness.

What had brought Poindexter back into government was a bold idea: that terrorists, like the Soviet nuclear submarines he had once hunted, leave faint *signatures* that could be detected and offer a potential warning sign of impending attacks. To carry out their plans, terrorists need to communicate, plan, train, and travel. As a result, their communication patterns, their purchases, and their travel histories could provide signature templates for intelligence analysts to scan for. And if that data could be captured, stored, and organized properly, it could be a powerful detection system that could be turned loose on counterterrorism.

The signature of a terrorist should look different from that of an ordinary person, Poindexter hypothesized. Indeed the digital breadcrumbs that the 9/11 hijacker Waleed al-Shehri left behind during his few weeks in America looked nothing like the average American's. What Total Information Awareness, usually abbreviated as TIA, proposed building was a suite of specialized tools that could be trained on large-scale data to try to distinguish terrorists from law-abiding citizens by looking at their transaction records, travel history, communication patterns, and more. To do that kind of scanning would involve ingesting an unimaginable amount of data that the government had never before tapped and would require enormous amounts of computing power. And much of the data that Poindexter was interested in weaving together was in the hands of corporate America's data brokers or in the data banks of travel agencies, rental car companies, and airlines.

Though it was the most infamous, TIA was just one of many government efforts all dedicated to this question of whether the vast amalgamation of electronic information about the global population could be harnessed and scanned for insights. Central to those experiments was the kind of data that Acxiom, Seisint, and their competitors had by the terabyte. The question was, could all this data be weaved together and scanned? Could computers reveal dangerous patterns or secret plots if given enough information?

America would spend the next two decades trying to find out.

TIA was born out of the personal friendship and professional collaboration between two former U.S. Navy men: Poindexter and another former navy officer turned defense contractor named Brian Sharkey. TIA was the fusion of two things: first, a secure computer network to enable information sharing and, second, a suite of experimental tools and algorithms to assist law enforcement, intelligence analysts, and military operators. The network provided a secure computer environment where various government agencies could collaborate on problems related to counterterrorism. In a bid to get territorial federal agencies to better cooperate, DARPA encouraged them to bring their own data sets and share them with other users on the experimental network. Prior to the TIA program, it would often take years to get any sort of software algorithm approved for Defense Department use because of security and vulnerability concerns. TIA aimed to create a place where tools could be built, tested, and evaluated quickly.

Some of the tools that the Information Awareness Office was working on were uncontroversial: digital language translation and speech-to-text capabilities, for example, or algorithms to detect potential misinformation in public sources. Other research was highly technical, such as how does one bring various disparate databases together and have them interact? And still others were included from the get-go to mollify critics and civil libertarians and head off possible controversy. DARPA had funded an entire area of research into privacy-preserving technology that could be built into TIA.

Some of the research would showcase just how powerful computers were becoming, especially as applied to intelligence and national security. One area of research was focused on "connecting the dots"— using computers to identify rare, unusual, or anomalous behavior in huge data sets, much like Charles Morgan's Bad Guys Database and Hank Asher's MATRIX.

DARPA had assembled a "red team" of experts whose sole job was to plot fictitious terrorist attacks—meticulously documenting what steps they would need to take to carry out their scheme. Then the TIA team would see if they could detect those attacks in the data they wanted to scan. It would then examine what kinds of transactions were needed to carry out an attack: Rent a car? Buy an airline ticket? Take flying lessons? Gather material? Communicate? The hope was that the team could preprogram technological systems to scan for certain templates of activity and to distinguish the signature of, say, a family going on vacation from a terrorist plotting a bombing.

As part of their research, DARPA had begun having discussions with data brokers like Acxiom about their capabilities. "The US may need huge databases of commercial transactions that cover the world," one member of the TIA team wrote after a meeting with the company. "Acxiom could build this mega-scale database." And indeed, the grand vision Poindexter was pursuing—a technological system that could look for signatures of outliers—was not all that different from what Acxiom's CEO, Charles Morgan, and Seisint's CEO, Hank Asher, were doing in the days after the 9/11 attacks with the Bad Guys Database and MATRIX. But the TIA team thought they could do it better—with the budget and imprimatur of the federal government behind their efforts. They could bring far more data to bear on these problems than Asher or Morgan. Poindexter's dream was to combine the government's classified stores of intelligence with the corporate world's data and build a perfect surveillance tool.

Both Poindexter and his boss, DARPA's director, Anthony Tether, wondered at times whether TIA should be classified. But they'd ultimately decided that attracting top-flight technical talent was made more difficult in a classified program. In addition, there was nothing inherently secret about what they were working on. It was essentially big data algorithms and secure computing, neither of which was a technology unknown to the public. Finally, there was another consideration: they knew that what they were proposing would ultimately require public acceptance and a public debate about the contours of government authority in the age of terrorism.

But by the fall of 2002, their decision not to hide the program behind the intelligence community's curtains began to feel like a mistake. Poindexter had publicly announced the program a few months earlier in August 2002 to little fanfare at a defense technology conference in California. It got a few write-ups in the trade press, but nobody else paid much attention. By the fall, however, things were different. National media outlets had begun to dig into the details of the research under way at the DARPA Information Awareness Office and were growing increasingly critical. In a widely read *New York Times* column published in November 2002, the conservative journalist William Safire blasted the program as an affront to civil liberties and a dangerous turn toward tyranny. In dire language, Safire warned that such a system would start to ingest every purchase, prescription, magazine subscription, bank deposit—even students' grades. Safire dubbed it "the supersnoop's dream"—an "Orwellian scenario" playing out in real time.

Within days of the Safire column, the TIA program was the talk of Washington. "How is this not domestic spying?" one reporter asked senior Pentagon officials at a contentious press conference. "You have these vast databases that you're looking for patterns in. Ordinary Americans, who aren't of Middle East origin, are just typical, ordinary Americans, their transactions are going to be perused?"—a comment that reflected the prevailing point of view, namely that Muslims living in America were the ones who should be singled out for suspicion, not the population at large.

The mounting pressure in the press forced DARPA into a sudden and unexpected defensive crouch. It was just doing research into the art of the possible, Poindexter's team insisted. They weren't proposing any kind of data collection that wasn't already permitted by law. And while some experiments were being run with classified data obtained by the U.S. intelligence community, the program never got to the step of actually ingesting data of the sort Safire was concerned about. In most cases, it was fed synthetic data designed to mimic real-world databases and real-world conditions to test a hypothesis and run experiments about whether computers could detect terrorist signatures. They were just doing research at this stage.

Poindexter and his team's protests didn't matter. In Washington, the press swims around big controversies such as TIA like hungry sharks. And there was definitely chum in the water. The fight over the future of the program was on.

January 16, 2003, was a cold, gloomy midwinter morning in Washington, D.C., when Senator Ron Wyden strode into the room at the center of the U.S. Capitol known as the Crypt. Adorned with statues of important Americans and forty arched sandstone columns that supported the weight of the massive Capitol dome, the Crypt had a subterranean feel despite being on the ground floor. It was a fitting place for what Wyden had in mind that morning. The Oregon Democrat had called the press to the Crypt that day not to praise TIA but to bury it.

Wyden was accompanied by two fellow senators, Russ Feingold of Wisconsin and Jon Corzine of New Jersey. He had also put together a coalition of strange bedfellows: civil society groups from across the political spectrum. Representatives from three staunchly conservative groups—the Free Congress Foundation, Americans for Tax Reform, and the Eagle Forum—had joined the trio of Democratic senators and left-leaning civil libertarians from groups like the American Civil Liberties Union and the Electronic Privacy Information Center.

"Our country must fight terrorists, but America should not unleash virtual bloodhounds to sniff into the financial, educational, travel and medical records of millions of Americans," Wyden told the reporters assembled in the Capitol's Crypt.

Wyden was giving voice to the growing number of Americans on both the left and the right who had become concerned about government overreach after 9/11. Soon, Wyden told reporters, the Senate would vote on a provision he had authored that he intended to attach to a must-pass spending bill that would force the Defense Department to explain itself in a report to Congress and put a pause to funding for the Total Information Awareness program, all with the aim of giving the public time to understand what exactly the Pentagon was up to.

Typically, a member of the minority Democrats would not have much sway over what happened on a major spending bill; it was the majority Republicans who would control the floor debate and whose support would be needed to pass his amendment. But Wyden expressed confidence.

One week later, Wyden's amendment came up for a vote as promised. His hunch was right: it sailed through the Senate on a voice vote—a procedure typically reserved for the most uncontroversial measures—and was successfully incorporated into a bill that was headed to the president's desk. On February 20, 2003, George W. Bush signed it into law.

Congress had fired a warning shot at a national security program for the first time since 9/11. The future of the Total Information Awareness program was suddenly in doubt.

Wyden had come to intelligence issues almost by accident. He had been elected to the Senate in 1996 after fifteen years in the U.S. House. The Oregon Democrat had wanted to join the Finance Committee since he'd been elected to the chamber and was angling for a seat on the panel in the new Congress that assembled in January 2001. But there was only one open Democratic seat on the panel that year, and party leaders wanted to ensure there was at least one woman on the Finance Committee. Wyden would have to wait for another open seat in a future Congress.* As a consolation prize, the Democratic leader, Tom Daschle, offered him a seat on the secretive Senate Intelligence Committee.

---

*   Wyden would eventually get his slot on the Finance Committee. He'd rise to be the chair in 2014–15 and again take the gavel in 2021.

Wyden had joined the Senate Select Committee on Intelligence a few months before 9/11. The learning curve was steep. Intelligence issues are highly technical. After the 9/11 attacks, Wyden and his fellow senators were asked to vote for expanded surveillance and law enforcement powers in the USA Patriot Act. Ninety-eight of them, including Wyden, had voted for it. Feingold had been the only no vote.

But from his perch on the Intelligence Committee, Wyden had started to wonder if the public wasn't always being told the truth about the scale and scope of U.S. surveillance programs and began to believe that perhaps the country was going too far. "In those post–Patriot Act months, I saw more and more evidence that what was being said in public didn't square with what I knew behind closed doors," Wyden recalled.

By early 2003, the political winds were shifting, and there was a growing unease about privacy and civil liberties in a legislature that in the previous sixteen months had been giving the Bush administration carte blanche on national security. What Wyden was pointing out about government overreach struck a nerve—both with the public and with lawmakers of both parties. There were certainly optics issues: the name Total Information Awareness exuded totalitarian vibes. (In the following weeks, as the controversy mounted, TIA would be hastily renamed the Terrorism Information Awareness program.) Nor did the logo of the program's sponsor, DARPA's Information Awareness Office, inspire much confidence. It depicted the all-seeing eye of Providence—the triangular oculus floating above a pyramid that's on the back of U.S. currency—staring over the entire globe.

But there were also more substantive concerns. The idea of disparate pieces of people's lives being fed into a government tool and mined by powerful computers for evidence of suspicious activity was a bridge further than what even a jittery public suddenly fearful of terrorism was willing to accept. The public had by and large lined up in support of new screening measures at airports, new spending on expensive overseas operations, and new authorities for law enforcement and intelligence agencies. But a massive data-mining operation turned against them? That raised alarm bells.

Historically, the U.S. Congress had sought to strike a compromise between national security, public safety, and personal privacy. Congress put sharp limits on government use of telephone wiretaps in the 1930s. In the 1960s and 1970s, Congress regulated information collected by the growing credit card industry. In 1974, after the abuses of the Nixon administration, the legislature passed a strong privacy law restricting what kinds of information government could collect about citizens and how that information had to be handled. In 1978, Congress created a new court to oversee national security wiretaps. It protected the personal information of cable television subscribers from certain disclosures with the Cable Communications Policy Act of 1984. In 1988, a journalist obtained and then published the video rental history of the Supreme Court nominee Robert Bork from a local Washington, D.C., video store. Congress responded by protecting what VHS tapes Americans rented in the Video Privacy Protection Act of 1988. Other laws protecting telecommunications records, medical records, driver's license information, children's online privacy, and credit information followed in the 1990s.

In enacting these laws, Congress foresaw that people had some privacy interests in information collected by private companies and sharply limited how much of that information government agents could access. In some cases, they restricted what private entities could do with certain kinds of data—telling companies that they could not wantonly share private health data, financial data, video rentals, or cable subscriber information with just anyone.

Congress wasn't alone in grappling with the question of Americans' right to privacy. For more than two hundred years, lawyers and judges have consistently struggled with how the march of technological progress affected the balance between public safety and limited government. The questions of how telegraphs, telephones, and eventually satellites, GPS, cellular phones, computers, and the Internet of Things fit into the contours of a constitution written mostly in the late eighteenth century are not easy ones. Time and time again, it would be technology that would test the boundaries of law.

What the courts never fully settled is whether Americans had a *right* to privacy and what it might look like for Americans to meaningfully exercise such a right. The U.S. Constitution makes no explicit mention of a privacy right; however, some jurists have seen something resembling it while squinting hard enough at parts of the document. The Supreme Court justice Louis Brandeis wrote that the Constitution conferred "the right to be let alone—the most comprehensive of rights and the right most valued by civilized men." Brandeis had long been mulling these issues. Before joining the court, he co-authored a seminal law review article called "The Right to Privacy"—an essay that single-handedly influenced generations of legal thinking on the topic. By the 1960s, the Supreme Court saw "penumbras" of the right to privacy in the Bill of Rights and decided that a Connecticut state law banning the use of contraceptives by married couples intruded on a "zone of privacy" that citizens were generally entitled to. The high court relied on similar logic in cases affirming the right to an abortion, to same-sex intimate relations, and to the possession of pornography.

But whatever right or zone of privacy Americans are entitled to has never been something that we can walk into court and cite. And the Supreme Court has grown more conservative in recent years and less inclined to see vague, unenumerated rights lurking in the shadows of the Constitution. As a result, Americans are now generally at the mercy of Congress and a handful of regulatory agencies such as the Federal Trade Commission to determine how much privacy they are entitled to under the law.

In the twenty-first century, just as data was becoming big business, Congress basically stopped legislating on the issue of privacy. After 9/11, it wanted to encourage government access to information, passing new law enforcement and intelligence authorities. And as the internet grew in importance, Congress did not want to stifle innovation with onerous regulation. When the TIA controversy erupted, it was clear that Congress was at a crossroads: deeply uncomfortable with

the implications of Poindexter's proposal yet unable to muster the political courage or will to deal with the situation head-on.

After Wyden's amendment in January 2003, the program was in
something of a limbo. The amendment paused any domestic-facing
deployment of a TIA system and demanded a report within ninety
days. The Defense Department obliged, delivering to Congress on
May 20, 2003, a 102-page document that explained in extensive detail
what DARPA was working on. It laid out in detail all the lines of research that the TIA program was pursuing and made the case for their
utility in the fight against terrorism. But that did not mollify Wyden
and the growing bipartisan chorus of critics of the program. Action
then shifted to the annual appropriations process, where the critics of
TIA hoped to defund the entire program.

After months of debate, House and Senate negotiators came to a
compromise. Officially, on paper, the program would end. Congress
would be able to say to its constituents that Poindexter and his program were finished. But in secret, large swaths of the research would
continue at a different research organization, the Advanced Research
and Development Activity. ARDA was a research and development
organization just like DARPA, but it focused exclusively on intelligence work and was run by the National Security Agency out of
the public's view. The details of what programs were being transferred
were spelled out in a classified annex to the spending bill—essentially
a secret law—that even two decades later remains under wraps.

Sharkey—who helped birth the program with Poindexter—had
been working as an outside contractor on the program at a firm called
Hicks and Associates that had a $19 million contract to build compo-
nents of TIA. Congress's funding decision "caused a significant
amount of uncertainty for all of us about the future of our work," he
wrote in an email to TIA subcontractors. "Fortunately, a new sponsor
has come forward that will enable us to continue much of our previous

work." That sponsor was the Advanced Research and Development Activity, an even more secretive version of DARPA run by the intelligence community.

The public, however, would be told a different story. Marc Swedenburg, another Hicks and Associates official, reminded everyone: "TIA has been terminated and should be referenced in that fashion."

To this day, the full story of TIA and its legacy has never been told. What I've been able to piece together—from people who remain relatively reluctant to talk about it on the record even two decades later—is that the research on Total Information Awareness would never really stop. The only definitive decision Congress came to was that a lightning rod like John Poindexter could not be allowed to run a research program with an Orwellian name in public. It did not address the substantive concerns of the civil libertarian critics like Ron Wyden, nor did it write rules of the road going forward about government access to private data. It did not pass new laws balancing public safety and personal privacy. Congress simply moved the entire line of inquiry behind the veil of the intelligence community's secret budget and walked away.

Total Information Awareness—under a new code name, Basketball—would run for a total of seven years at ARDA. References to Basketball would sometimes surface in budget documents, where it was called the Research Development Experimental Collaboration. The secure, experimental network would thrive behind the curtain of the intelligence community's classified budget. More than six hundred tools, algorithms, and other experimental digital techniques would ultimately be tested on the network. It never became the kind of full-fledged surveillance system that ingested huge amounts of commercial data that Poindexter had envisioned, but key elements or experiments informed or directly inspired operational intelligence programs, particularly at the National Security Agency. And that agency's tentacles would be nearly inescapable, collecting huge stores of data and enlisting the agency's computer systems to do exactly what Poindexter had envisioned: map the relationship between people, entities, and events and develop early warning systems that could prevent attacks.

The one feature of TIA that didn't survive? The privacy technology that would have cloaked the personal details of Americans from intelligence analysts scanning for terrorist templates. As Poindexter pointed out, those measures were integral to winning public support.

The most significant victory that Wyden and other congressional critics won was a prohibition on using Basketball technologies on Americans. Whatever came of the research could not be deployed domestically. That never solved the broader legal issue, however. In the years to come, there would be all manner of surveillance programs that would involve the data of Americans. Other agencies—namely, the FBI, the Defense Department, and the Department of Homeland Security—would create data-mining and pattern-matching programs that would do what Poindexter envisioned. But none of them drew the attention of the public in the way that TIA did.

Today, nearly every capability or technology in the Information Awareness Office's 2002 research portfolio has become an ordinary part of the government's tool kit: computerized language translation, biometrics and facial recognition technology, machine learning to detect anomalies and patterns, information fusion to bring together disparate data sources, and social network analysis to understand how people are connected to one another. It didn't all come out of research at DARPA or ARDA, but somewhere in the sea of national laboratories, government contractors, and research universities work continued on both the grand vision of total information awareness and the specific problems involved in weaving huge amounts of data together to understand connections between people, places, and things.

The lesson the intelligence community and the Defense Department took away from the fiasco was that bad branding, congressional politics, and a misguided attempt at transparency nearly doomed what was otherwise a useful program. They would wise up. Going forward, these projects would be incubated in the anonymous office parks of suburban Washington by faceless, nameless bureaucrats and low-profile contractors. They would be cloaked in nondisclosure agreements or hidden in classified contracts.

The dream of total information awareness would never die.

CHAPTER 3

The Gordian Knot

THE DEPARTMENT OF HOMELAND SECURITY, 2002–2009

n late 2002, Paul Rosenzweig was a fellow at the Heritage Foundation in Washington, D.C., a think tank dedicated to a brand of conservatism in the vein of Ronald Reagan—advocating a mix of free markets, social conservatism, and an activist U.S. foreign policy. He was frequently seen wearing a bow tie in his public appearances on television and before Capitol Hill committees, on the grounds that it was the "most polite way of standing out without actually proclaiming too loudly that you're an iconoclast."

Rosenzweig had taken a circuitous path to the think tank. As a young man, he'd been enthralled by earth science, studied chemistry as an undergraduate, and earned a master's degree in chemical oceanography. But he found the process of actually doing science involved too much paperwork and not enough debate and, as such, wasn't very much fun. So he went to law school at the University of Chicago. He then came to Washington to do stints at the Justice Department and on a GOP congressional committee. He also worked on the Whitewater investigation into Bill Clinton.

After the November 2002 William Safire column in *The New York Times* taking on the Pentagon's Total Information Awareness program landed like a hand grenade, Rosenzweig began following the controversy. To Rosenzweig, Poindexter's program raised interesting questions: First, could technology provide a solution to the problem of terrorism? And second, how far should society go in sacrificing privacy in the name of security? Rosenzweig asked for a briefing from DARPA on the controversial program, hoping to learn more.

The TIA staff agreed to bring him in. Led by its deputy director, Bob Popp, the TIA team was on something of a low-profile charm offensive in Washington, trying to generate favorable publicity from any prominent journalists, lawmakers, or public intellectuals who they thought might have an open mind. It wasn't going well.

Rosenzweig did go in with an open mind. After sitting through numerous briefings, he was impressed by the vision and completely dismayed by the ineptitude with which it was introduced and launched. He was not indifferent to the concerns of civil libertarians like Senator Ron Wyden. But to Rosenzweig, these concerns were not insurmountable, let alone a reason to shut down the entire program. They could be mitigated with policies, procedures, or technological safeguards to ensure there would be no abuse or misuse. Where Wyden saw Big Brother, Rosenzweig saw a smart way to use technology to solve a new problem.

In Rosenzweig's view, the balance between civil liberties and national security was a pendulum. It swung in response to historical developments such as wars, terrorist attacks, and other crises. And then swung back the other way in times of peace, prosperity, and calm. Sometimes America had made grave mistakes when the pendulum swung too far—such as internment of the Japanese during World War II or enactment of the Alien and Sedition Acts to crack down on criticism of President John Adams during a period of tension with France. But the system usually self-corrected. President Jefferson pardoned everyone convicted under the Alien and Sedition Acts and Japanese Americans had gotten an official government apology and reparations decades later, Rosenzweig argued.

Further, Rosenzweig saw the post-9/11 response as quite moderate and sensible—nothing like what the United States had done a century earlier—and he wasn't shy about making this point in public. He gave lectures around this time titled "John Ashcroft Is Not Darth Vader: The Patriot Act: Myth and Reality," referring to the then-serving attorney general. Rosenzweig was brave enough once to deliver the Darth Vader lecture at the lefty bastion UC Berkeley, only to have a student stand up and explain that Ashcroft was worse than the Dark Lord of the Sith. "Even Darth Vader redeemed himself in the end," the student said. In Rosenzweig's view, yes, the executive branch was claiming new powers in the counterterrorism arena and, yes, citizens might have to deal with more inconveniences at airports and at border crossings. But the sky was not falling, and the United States was not sliding dangerously toward authoritarianism by creating a data-mining program like TIA.

Having been convinced as to the utility of their research, Rosenzweig pledged to help Poindexter and his team from the outside. From his perch at Heritage, he would write numerous briefings and op-eds defending the research effort. He'd make the rounds on Capitol Hill to talk up the program to lawmakers in private meetings. He'd appear in the media, calling it "premature" to wind down an experimental program that wasn't even close to being deployed. He'd testify publicly on behalf of saving it in major public hearings before Congress, arguing that data-mining programs like TIA could work—with the proper safeguards.

TIA or TIA-like data-mining systems should be used only for their intended purpose, terrorism, Rosenzweig said in one appearance before Congress. These programs "should not be used to fight the improperly named 'war on drugs,' combat violent crime, or address other sundry problems," he told lawmakers.

However, Congress was ultimately unswayed—spooked by the growing public controversy and wanting to rid themselves of the problem. They swept TIA under the rug and moved on.

But this wouldn't be the last time Rosenzweig would find himself in the fray around data mining.

The debate over when personal privacy must give way in the face of a government demand can boil down to a deceptively simple question: What is a search? At the heart of that question is a fifty-four-word amendment to the Constitution written in 1789: "The right of the people to be secure in their persons, houses, papers, and effects, against unreasonable searches and seizures, shall not be violated; and no Warrants shall issue but upon probable cause, supported by Oath or affirmation, and particularly describing the place to be searched, and the persons or things to be seized."

Since this provision, the Fourth Amendment, came into effect, American courts have spent more than two centuries grappling over its meaning. What is an "unreasonable" search? Who exactly are "the people"? Is the warrant requirement absolute or are there exceptions?

By the early twenty-first century, the prevailing view of the Supreme Court was that a search was conducted when the government intruded upon a person's reasonable expectation of privacy. Things that people sought to conceal or keep private were generally afforded strong legal protections. A letter in a sealed envelope. Documents in a desk drawer. Items placed in the trunk of a car. To conduct a search in those circumstances, government agents are required to have probable cause of a crime, and in many situations, especially involving a search of a person's home, they would need to get a search warrant signed by a judge. On the other hand, anything that could be observed in plain sight was afforded less protection. Drug paraphernalia sitting on the passenger seat of a car. The comings and goings of people in public places. Words spoken in a shared space in earshot of others. The court's standard was flexible: the "reasonable" standard could change as social norms changed.

But a series of decisions in the 1960s and 1970s also held that if citizens voluntarily shared information with a third party, they lost the expectation of privacy that was core to their Fourth Amendment rights. In one 1979 case titled *Smith v. Maryland,* the court held that the use of a device called a pen register did not violate the Fourth Amendment. A pen register records all of the numbers dialed from a particular telephone line, but it does not reveal any of the audio content of the call. "We doubt that people in general entertain any actual expectation of privacy in the numbers they dial," a majority of the court concluded in *Smith.* "All telephone users realize that they must 'convey' phone numbers to the telephone company, since it is through telephone company switching equipment that their calls are completed." In other words, because telephone subscribers must by the nature of the technology share the number they wish to dial with the telephone company in order to complete a call, they have no expectation that such information would remain private. Why, they see an itemized list of their long-distance calls on their monthly bill, the court pointed out.

Smith v. Maryland inadvertently created a new distinction in American law between what would come to be called metadata and content. Metadata is information about information, or data about data. Consider the act of mailing a letter. The text of the letter itself is the *content,* a form of pre-internet data. The outside of the envelope is *metadata.* In the telephone context, metadata is the who, what, where, and when of a call—the stuff that appears on your phone bill. This distinction came about because you generally have to tell a third party—the telephone company or the postal service, for instance— whom you'd like to contact. And because you've shared that information with a third party, you lose your expectation of privacy.

In other words, the government could not listen to your telephone calls without probable cause to believe you were involved in criminal activity, but it could review your entire call history without meeting such a burden. This is why today the government needs a warrant to open an envelope. But the outside of every single envelope can be scanned and saved by the U.S. Postal Service. The address and return address on an envelope are metadata and are not protected by the Fourth Amendment. Only the letter inside is private content, which therefore means it receives the strongest possible protections under American law.

A 2016 Stanford study that collected the phone metadata of volunteers willing to be surveilled in the name of science gave examples of what inferences one could draw from the telephone records of participants. Participant B, for example, "received a long phone call from the cardiology group at a regional medical center, talked briefly with a medical laboratory, answered several short calls from a local drugstore, and made brief calls to a self-reporting hotline for a cardiac arrhythmia monitoring device." Participant D "placed calls to a hardware outlet, locksmiths, a hydroponics store, and a head shop in under 3 weeks." And participant E "made a lengthy phone call to her sister early one morning. Then, 2 days later, she called a nearby Planned Parenthood clinic several times. Two weeks later, she placed brief additional calls to Planned Parenthood, and she placed another short call 1 month after." It's safe to assume that participant B recently had a heart attack, that participant D was preparing to grow marijuana, and that participant E was seeking an abortion. All of that could be inferred without ever tapping their telephone lines and listening to the content of their calls. Metadata can tell you a lot. The former director of both the CIA and the NSA, Michael Hayden, put it even more bluntly in 2014: "We kill people based on metadata."

When Rosenzweig and others were considering these issues after 9/11, everything in modern life was becoming digitized. More and more metadata on intensely personal matters was being collected—"conveyed to third parties," in the language of the Supreme Court. Commercial information of all kinds was being vacuumed up in bulk—by Acxiom, LexisNexis, and Seisint. These companies had no real consumer relationship with the average American. But in the eyes of the law, Americans had waived their reasonable expectation of privacy because a third party—a telephone company, a search engine, an email service provider, and a data broker—had a window into their lives. And as time went on, that window became larger and larger. In the 1970s, it was bank records and telephone calls. Then it was credit card transactions. Internet web pages that Americans loaded would trigger dozens of trackers. Apps downloaded convey data to hundreds of parties that are trying to serve digital advertising to them. And so on.

At the heart of U.S. privacy law is an unresolved tension: that corporate data conveyed voluntarily does not "count" as surveillance. Under nearly fifty years of Supreme Court precedent, the government can buy data. After all, all of that information had been conveyed to third parties at some point, before being repackaged and sold by Acxiom, LexisNexis, and Seisint.

And at no time was the government's desire for data more acute than in the days after the 9/11 attacks.

After 9/11, no task was more urgent for the U.S. government than securing the nation's transportation system. And no solution was consistently more alluring—or more controversial—than tapping the huge reserves of data sitting in consumer data banks to screen travelers and visa applicants. As the nation considered how to rebuild its air travel and immigration screening systems, researchers inside and outside government were grappling with the same questions that John Poindexter and Brian Sharkey were asking at DARPA and that teams at Acxiom and Seisint were working with the FBI to answer. Instead of just screening known threats like the names of terrorists, could computers be programmed to look for unknown threats, possible terrorists, and lone wolves?

This wasn't the first attempt at a computerized passenger screening system. In fact, CAPPS—the one in place at the time—had successfully flagged 6 of the 19 hijackers on September 11. But it also flagged 92,000 non-hijackers out of 1.8 million passengers who flew in the twenty-four hours leading up to the hijackings. In some cases, all it did was trigger some additional baggage checks. After 9/11, the government wanted to build a successor to CAPPS—a beefed-up system that would collect the names of travelers, check their identities against criminal watch lists, and then use computer algorithms to tap commercially available data from LexisNexis and Acxiom to generate an overall risk profile. It also collected many of the agencies that had been responsible for domestic security and immigration and put them under the umbrella of a new cabinet department, the Department of Homeland Security.

Given the civil liberties concerns inherent in creating a domestic security agency, Congress had mandated that DHS employ a privacy officer. A former lawyer at the pioneering online ad firm DoubleClick, Nuala O'Connor was one of the few lawyers in the country with extensive experience in the emerging field of privacy law when she took the job. To better assist the department in navigating these controversies, O'Connor created the Data Privacy and Integrity Advisory Committee, or DPIAC, an advisory panel composed of academics and industry and other outside experts. Rosenzweig would be the chair. Lisa Sotto, a partner at a New York law firm and a Democrat, was elected vice-chair.

At the panel's inaugural meeting, Rosenzweig acknowledged the challenges the department was facing in trying to sell an increasingly skeptical public on greater security measures. The proposal had generated furious pushback from civil libertarians who did not like the idea of black-box corporate algorithms deciding who got on airplanes. Still, Rosenzweig wanted the panel to "advance the ball." Sotto had a personal connection to the 9/11 tragedy. Her brother-in-law was on the 106th floor of one of the Twin Towers and perished when it collapsed. She too believed that a compromise could be achieved on some of the new security programs the department was considering. "We can have security without surrendering our privacy," Sotto said at the meeting.

But first, they had to build a consensus—a tricky proposition on a panel full of people who did not always see eye to eye. The group had some genuine privacy hawks who were deeply suspicious of large-scale data mining. In particular, a fellow think tanker named Jim Harper would be the leading skeptical voice—often taking the position that government intrusions on civil liberties should be shown to be effective before being implemented. One of his fellow panelists would call him "the conscience of the committee." On the surface, Harper had a résumé similar to Rosenzweig's. He too belonged to the conservative Federalist Society and was a former Capitol Hill lawyer for a Republican congressional committee. He worked for the Cato Institute, a conservative Washington think tank, one with a much more libertarian bent than Heritage.

Harper would never really come around to most kinds of data mining. To Harper, such a system would generate too many false positives. There were far too few examples of real-world terrorist attacks to begin to draw up patterns as Poindexter wanted to do. Building consumer profiles for marketing purposes, by contrast, was easy: tens or hundreds of thousands of consumers could be used to build out templates for new products or services. And the consequence of being wrong in the consumer context was pretty low: someone might get a piece of junk mail for a product they're not interested in. Counterterrorism was not quite so low stakes. Someone identified as "anomalous" by a computer system could see the full resources of the richest and most powerful state on earth be thrown against them.

But the committee, under Rosenzweig and Sotto's leadership, would eventually reach some rough consensus for the issues that were at the top of their agenda: Namely, what kind of data should the United States collect either directly from the population or indirectly, through purchases from data brokers, in order to vet the people getting on airplanes?

Three reports drafted by the committee under Rosenzweig and Sotto would deal with the question. Harper signed on. After the CAPPS II outcry, the government had scaled back the program, cut out Acxiom and LexisNexis, and renamed it Secure Flight. The committee's first report, released in 2005, would be about Secure Flight. The second was about the use of commercial databases to reduce false positives in airline programs. And the third was something of a broad meditation on under what conditions and rules the government should be allowed to use commercial data from companies like Acxiom and other data brokers. The government wasn't obligated to abide by the committee's recommendations. But together, they represented one of the first times that anyone in an official capacity had tried to advise the federal government on how to grapple with being an electronic society.

The committee's findings cited concern for "the potential for harm to the individual," concluding that "the use of commercial data by the government requires advance scrutiny."

The committee's contention was that it was one thing for a company to use consumer data to sell people things. But the use of the same by the government for counterterrorism or law enforcement deserved a higher level of scrutiny.

One day in the mid-2000s, Rosenzweig found himself speaking on a panel with Stewart Baker, a veteran Washington lawyer who had done a stint in the 1990s as the general counsel of the National Security Agency. They had known each other a bit, both being lawyers in the capital, and they found themselves sharing a train back to Washington after the event, where they struck up a long conversation about privacy and national security debates.

In 2005, Baker was nominated to be the first-ever assistant secretary for policy for the U.S. Department of Homeland Security. The job would be to help make policy for a brand-new department charged with an ambitious mission. Baker called up Rosenzweig and offered him a job. "Either come and help me fix it or stop writing about it," Rosenzweig recalled Baker's pitch years later.

Rosenzweig did, coming on board as the deputy assistant secretary for policy—a position he'd stay in until the very last day of the Bush administration in 2009. The job took Rosenzweig all over the world and put a dizzying array of issues in front of him.

But most important, it was during this period that Rosenzweig and others inside DHS came to help settle some of the controversies that were roiling the country over air travel and privacy. Like the DPIAC and its reports, it was a compromise; nobody got all of what they wanted. But it did help move the country beyond the fights over airline security and border security.

As part of navigating the United States out of the airline privacy mess, the government expanded what were called trusted traveler programs. A program that allowed expedited entry between the United States and Mexico called SENTRI had been in place since the mid-1990s, and a second program that allowed transit between the United States and Canada called NEXUS began in 2000. Both required applicants to go through a background check, pay a fee, and be deemed low risk in exchange for speedier crossings. But new programs were created late in the Bush administration: first with Global Entry, which allowed a speedy trip through U.S. customs, and second with TSA PreCheck, which allowed quicker transit through domestic airports.

Rosenzweig spent a significant amount of time working on the policies for those new programs—to the point where he was among the first ten people to ever enroll in Global Entry.

The flying public now had a choice: they could submit themselves to additional vetting, including providing extensive background information, proof of identity, and biometrics. If they were deemed low risk, they could breeze through an easier screening process. And the government did not waste its resources and time screening them. If they had objections to that kind of data sharing with Uncle Sam, fine. As Rosenzweig put it, "One of the best answers is choice. You want to get physically screened because you don't want to give up access to your criminal data? Fine. You go to this line. If you're willing to make the trade, you go in this line."

Global Entry and PreCheck were particularly American ways to cut the Gordian knot of privacy and security: *choice*.

Ultimately, Rosenzweig and his colleagues at DHS were grappling with just a tiny part of a larger problem. In this same period, Mark

Zuckerberg had launched Facebook in his Harvard dorm room. The first tweets were already being sent on a new social network called Twitter. Instagram wasn't far off, and Apple was working on a smartphone prototype that it would introduce to the world in 2007. The problems raised by being an electronic society where all manner of data could be captured were not going away; if anything, they were about to grow exponentially.

CHAPTER 4

Electronic Footprints

THE FEDERAL BUREAU OF INVESTIGATION, 2001 ONWARD

It was about 7:30 p.m. on July 10, 2003, when three federal law enforcement agents knocked on the door to apartment 201 in an aging apartment building at 2 Copley Road in Upper Darby, Pennsylvania, about six miles west of downtown Philadelphia. "Police!" one of them called out.

Authorities were urgently searching for a man named Agha Ali Abbas Qazalbash, a Pakistani cabdriver and convenience store clerk who for a few days that summer would be one of the most wanted men in America. At the peak of the operation, more than fifty federal agents were involved in the manhunt to find Qazalbash, who they believed had ties to a Pakistani militant group.

The Qazalbash manhunt had been set off after the FBI received information that he might have ties to terrorism. He had come to the United States in 2000, with authorization to stay until April 2001. He first worked at the deep-fry station at a Crown Chicken before getting a job at a Sunoco gas station and later his cab license to ferry passengers around Philadelphia. He applied for permanent residency after he had married an American woman whom he never cohabitated with—a love match that didn't work out, the woman would tell investigators.

But by the summer of 2003, probably as part of the process of scrutinizing his visa application, the government had come to believe that Qazalbash was a member of an outlawed Pakistani group called Sipah-e-Mohammed Pakistan. The SMP was a Shia Islamic group active in the Punjab region of Pakistan. It had never been known to target the United States and at times seemed to aspire to be more of a political party than a terrorist group. Qazalbash would tell family members it was formed to protect the Shia population in the region against sectarian violence. Qazalbash himself had been involved in street protests back home in Pakistan and had once been shot in the leg during a demonstration.

The FBI's pursuit had led them to the apartment in Upper Darby. It was there that they hoped to find him and arrest him on a federal immigration warrant. Instead, a twenty-six-year-old Pakistani woman named Humaira Jawed came to the door holding her infant son. She was greeted by the immigration agent Walter Beddow and the FBI agents Donald Bain and A. J. Pelczar. Jawed allowed the agents inside the small one-bedroom apartment, where they performed a search. They saw men's clothes and shoes in the apartment but no Qazalbash.

Seeing that their target was not present, the agents lied about their purpose for visiting. They showed Jawed a picture of a complete stranger—a man they claimed to be looking for. She had never seen the man before in her life, she told the agents. This kind of ruse was standard operating procedure at the time: immigration agents sometimes don't want to tip off family members that they're looking for a suspect in case it causes them to flee. So the trio of federal agents began chatting with Jawed—casually asking about her children and her visa status. Agent Pelczar, looking around the apartment, saw there were some photographs in the living room of Jawed and Qazal-

bash together. The agent pointed to the photo and asked Jawed if that
was her husband. She said yes, but that he had been living in Pakistan
for the last two years.

In fact, Qazalbash had recently obtained a Muslim divorce with a
simple declaration that he wanted to dissolve the marriage with Jawed,
who was also the mother of his two young children. The two were still
close; in fact, federal agents had been told by neighbors they were still
living together despite the divorce. Their youngest son had been conceived after the split. The agents pressed her about her immigration
status. Jawed acknowledged she had come on a student visa but was
not currently in school as was required by the terms of her immigration status. She had received permission from the Community College of Philadelphia to delay her enrollment because she had been
expecting her second child, she said. They thanked her for her time
and left.

Investigators turned to their next lead: Qazalbash's cab. There were
no licensed taxi drivers with that name, so from the Philadelphia
taxicab regulator the FBI pulled the entire database of licensed drivers and began combing through it. They found a match: a photograph
from Qazalbash's immigration file matched the driver of Olde City
cab P-1017. Except, according to the commission, that man was
named Hussain Ali.

Authorities found the taxi three days later, on July 13—but once
again, no Qazalbash. Instead, the cab was being driven by his friend,
Hamid Sheikh. Sheikh also knew Qazalbash as Ali. He said he would
help federal agents locate him. He tried to place calls to Qazalbash's
cell phone number but got no answer. He took them to Qazalbash's
home—the same Upper Darby apartment they had visited a few days
earlier. With agents watching, Sheikh parked outside the apartment,
honked his horn repeatedly, and shouted, "Ali!" Qazalbash was not
home.

In the days and weeks after federal agents first interviewed Sheikh
and Jawed, it became clear to them that both had lied. Scrutinizing
call records, they could see Jawed had called Qazalbash more than a

dozen times in the hours after agents left her home—deeply shaken by the visit and not fooled by the trio of agents pretending to be interested in some stranger. Qazalbash had been driving his cab in downtown Philadelphia when she called. He had immediately begun to make plans to flee. Sheikh had then driven his friend from Philadelphia to a travel agency in Brooklyn one day before agents caught up to him driving Qazalbash's cab. Despite being a wanted man, Qazalbash had managed to depart the United States on Pakistan International Airlines Flight PK-712 to Lahore on July 12, 2003, using a slight variation of his name on the ticket. Though he was wanted for deportation anyway, his escape deprived the FBI of a chance to interrogate him and collect intelligence on what it believed were his ties to an outlawed Pakistani group.

Qazalbash was one of thousands of people who were caught up in a post-9/11 data-driven dragnet. The dragnet had two aims: to stop known or suspected terrorists from entering the United States and to identify any individuals already in the country with ties to terrorism. This chapter in our nation's history has largely faded from our collective memory, but at its height it involved detaining more than a thousand non-Americans in the aftermath of 9/11 and deporting many of them under the government's immigration authorities. The FBI was transformed overnight from a law enforcement organization that was best known for nabbing bank robbers and fighting organized crime to one tasked with preventing the next terrorist attack. That meant the bureau would need to start gathering intelligence, developing sources, and scrutinizing people all over the world. Together with the new Department of Homeland Security, much of their attention turned toward immigrants from Muslim-majority countries. Rarely were the people caught up in this manhunt prosecuted as terrorists. Because these cases often involved foreigners on visas or present in the country unlawfully, immigration enforcement was the tool that the government most often turned to. This had the secondary effect of shielding the sources and methods that were used to identify possible terrorists from public scrutiny—because the government had to prove not something like terrorism but merely that someone ought to be deported for an immigration violation.

With Qazalbash's having evaded them, the federal government turned to punish the two people who helped him escape. Both Sheikh and Jawed were arrested and charged with lying to federal investigators. They both pleaded guilty, and both got sentenced to sixteen months in prison, a stiff sentence for first-time offenders. Both also were deported back to Pakistan after serving their sentences, losing their lives in the United States.

In the words of Kathy Lambert, a longtime FBI counterterrorism agent who worked on their case: "When we identify someone who is engaged in some terrorist activity, we will use any means available to us."

Qazalbash would probably never have been ensnared in a fifty-agent multistate dragnet if the government hadn't learned to combine its classified intelligence with the stores of data in the possession of corporate America.

After 9/11, the U.S. government went on a data binge. The FBI got at least an entire year of passenger travel records from Northwest, data that was burned on six thousand CD-ROMs. It would get similarly large data dumps from other airlines in the wake of the attacks. United Airlines made thousands of pages of records available to the bureau—setting up facilities in Chicago, near the airline's headquarters, where FBI agents could review passenger records. It was the largest aviation-related information request that the industry had ever received—aimed at allowing the bureau to examine whether any other airline passengers fit the archetypal pattern of the 9/11 hijacker. This was the kind of pattern recognition and signature detection that the TIA team was researching.

That was only the beginning of the data that the FBI would start to ingest in bulk. Sometimes they would ask nicely for business owners to turn it over. And sometimes they would come bearing legal demands. In the spring of 2002, agents started showing up at scuba shops all over the country demanding lists of everyone who had taken diving lessons since the late 1990s—presumably because such skills might be a danger to the United States or be at issue in a terrorist plot. Some shop owners complied; others refused. Eventually the Professional Association of Diving Instructors turned over its entire list of more than two million Americans who had learned to scuba dive since 1999, complete with their names and addresses. Other commercial entities would have similar experiences. "In the year and a half since Sept. 11, 2001, supermarket chains, home improvement stores and others have voluntarily handed over large databases of customer records to federal law enforcement agencies—almost always in violation of their stated privacy policies," a trade publication would report in 2003.

To acquire much of this data, the FBI began to lean heavily on a little-known legal tool called a national security letter to compel the disclosure of all kinds of new information in total secrecy. A national security letter is similar to a search warrant, but it doesn't require the signature of a judge and is targeted at business records like customer information. It also contains a gag order that forbids the recipient to disclose that they received the letter. Though national security letters existed prior to 9/11 and were typically used to obtain banking records for terrorism or espionage suspects, Congress now granted the government authority to use them in a much wider array of circumstances on a much broader array of information. With that new authority, the FBI's use of national security letters soared—from about eighty-five hundred national security letters in 2000 to more than fifty-six thousand in 2004. Most of the recipients were telephone companies, internet service providers, credit bureaus, and banks.

A lot of that data was fed into a low-profile unit of the FBI called the Foreign Terrorist Tracking Task Force (FTTTF, or F-Tri-F when it is pronounced out loud). Created just weeks after 9/11, the FTTTF identified people it believed could have links to terrorism and then scoured government and commercial databases for any evidence that those people, their families, or their associates were inside the United States. It would also scrutinize people applying for visas or residency—people like Qazalbash—for any links to terrorism in their backgrounds. Four data brokers would end up being contractors to the program: Acxiom, Seisint, and their competitors LexisNexis and ChoicePoint. Their data would be combined with the government's own proprietary travel records. Armed with both corporate and internal databases, the government could do things like map out people's social networks. Who shared an apartment with someone with ties to terrorism? Who traveled with them on international flights? Who lived next door and might be willing to be interviewed about their neighbors if a federal agent dropped by for a chat?

The FTTTF's job was to "monitor the electronic footprints of terrorists and their supporters, identify their behaviors and provide 'actionable intelligence,'" according to one FBI document. When the government needed to quickly process the data it received from the Philadelphia taxicab commission in the Qazalbash case, it turned to the FTTTF and its advanced data-processing capabilities. When the intelligence community got a tip that helicopters might be used in a terrorist attack, FTTTF managed to pull all the data from the Federal Aviation Administration's active pilots database and identified 165 pilots from "countries of interest," including at least 6 with "derogatory information" that might indicate a terrorist threat or connections to terrorist groups. It vetted 504 candidates for flight schools on behalf of the Transportation Security Administration, flagging 51. And the FTTTF played a major role in the case of Russell Defreitas, a U.S. citizen who pleaded guilty in 2007 to being part of a foiled plot to destroy buildings, fuel tanks, and fuel pipelines at JFK Airport. Defreitas had been a cargo handler employed at the airport, and the FTTTF was pivotal in identifying his links to an overseas terrorist group called the Jamaat Al Muslimeen. This kind of data-intensive investigative work was typical of what the FTTTF did, though much of it remains shrouded in secrecy even years later.

As fears of terrorism receded in the years after 9/11, FTTTF would be folded into a larger organization within the FBI called the National Security Analysis Center, or NSAC, where it would be part of an expanded mission that would eventually include forays into white-collar crime, tracking U.S. domestic extremists, and trying to counter Chinese espionage. It still exists to this very day, within the bowels of the FBI, dedicated to capturing and analyzing large amounts of data in service of the national security mission of the U.S. government.

Over the years, the FTTTF had to fight off comparisons to the ill-fated Total Information Awareness program from lawmakers. In June 2007, a group of lawmakers wrote to the FBI, "The expanded and sweeping scope of the NSAC bears striking resemblance to the Defense Advanced Research Project Agency's Total Information Awareness program which Congress terminated funding for in 2003 because of privacy and other concerns." Instead, the lawmakers argued, it seemed to be doing the kind of data mining and pattern matching that Congress had expressed discomfort with back in 2003.

"There is no relationship between the NSAC and the TIA program," the FBI wrote in response.

Maybe not on paper. The two organizations were born separately; one was a creature of the FBI, the other of the Pentagon's research arm. But the two programs had similar aims. While Poindexter had flown much too close to the sun and been burned, the FTTTF and its successor, the NSAC, by contrast, burrowed deep into the national security bureaucracy, keeping a low profile for the better part of two decades. The FBI described FTTTF's physical office in one document as "not classified but sensitive."

That ethos applied to the task force as a whole.

And it wasn't just the federal government that would need this kind of information. For the United States to be successful in deterring terrorism, it would need to enlist the help of people without security clearances.

The 9/11 hijackers had a number of run-ins with local law enforcement in the months and weeks leading up to the attacks. The hijacker Mohamed Atta was stopped twice by police while living in Florida, for example. And days before 9/11, Maryland police pulled over the hijacker Ziad Jarrah for driving ninety miles an hour in a sixty-five-mile-per-hour zone. Police ran Jarrah for warrants and came back empty. However, there is evidence that Jarrah might have been on the CIA's radar prior to 9/11 as having potential ties to terrorism—a fact unknown to the Maryland police.* Jarrah was given a $270 ticket and allowed to proceed.

In the aftermath of 9/11, there was a sense within the government that the plot could have been foiled if Atta and Jarrah had been picked up by local police. The result was a major movement to push terrorism intelligence information all the way down to local police. That didn't mean that local police would get every scrap of foreign intelligence or be privy to everything the government was doing with data, but it did mean that the intelligence community sometimes needed to put its information in a form that could be shared with people without clearances. In 2004, President Bush signed Executive Order 13356, which among other things called for "the interchange of terrorism information between agencies and appropriate authorities of States and local governments." Within the intelligence community, that meant creating an entirely new information architecture that could identify persons of interest with suspected ties to terrorism.

To accomplish this, agencies had to do what was being called iden-

---

* What the CIA actually knew about Jarrah remains a matter of some dispute. Sources in the United Arab Emirates told CNN in 2002 that they stopped Jarrah while he transited through Dubai at the request of the agency, seeking to question him about why he was in Afghanistan. The CIA denied that Jarrah was on their radar. A congressional inquiry concluded in 2002 that Jarrah was unknown to the CIA prior to 9/11. *The 9/11 Commission Report* is silent on the matter. But an FBI article from 2007 flatly states Jarrah "was on a CIA watch list" when he was stopped by Maryland state troopers.

tity resolution. If Waleed al-Shehri was a suspected terrorist, they needed to ensure they were also capturing entries for Shehri W. Al. If Qazalbash had the alias Hussain Ali, that was something that investigators needed to know as well. These aliases and idiosyncrasies needed to be tied together to create a single stable profile around every individual so that the government could merge everything from corporate data to police records to intelligence information.

At the center of some of these government-wide efforts to resolve these information-sharing issues was Acxiom. The company's AbiliTec product could do just that—correct for name changes and address changes and make a probabilistic guess as to whether Shehri W. Al was Waleed al-Shehri and whether Qazalbash was also going by Ali. The company started working on an experimental project inside the intelligence community called Janus—a prototype to help the government understand how to build its own version of AbiliTec.

Acxiom's rivals LexisNexis, ChoicePoint, and Seisint would also become government contractors. If the government identified someone as a possible terrorist, these companies had extensive records that could indicate whether the suspect had a presence inside the United States. It was very hard for any individual to stay out of corporate America's data collection abilities. Property records, marriage certificates, boat licenses, credit bureau data, address history collected by magazines or credit cards—all of these would be at the heart of the "electronic footprints" that President Bush had ordered the FBI and its intelligence agency partners to start searching for.

To what extent were there really terrorist sleeper cells in the United States? The question remains cloaked in ambiguity even decades later. Was Qazalbash actually a threat to the nation? Or merely an activist in the violent rough-and-tumble of sectarian politics in his native Pakistan who wanted a fresh start in America? It's very difficult to say. But either way, his presence in the United States was unauthorized, and with the country in a fearful mood the bureau was not going to take chances in letting an officer in a banned militant group drive a cab in Philadelphia.

The officials forced to respond after 9/11 did not have the luxury of knowing what we know now: that there would be no more large-scale terrorist attacks in the years afterward and that the U.S. attempts to degrade al-Qaeda would be a success, with many arguing that the U.S. government's stepped-up intelligence efforts played a major role. They also could not know whether there were sleeper cells or other plots in the works. The September 11 attacks were a tremendous trauma for the country, and government agencies at all levels were under pressure to respond with all tools available.

That pressure also led the United States to launch two invasions in which the country's military would invade, occupy, and reconstruct Afghanistan and later Iraq. Both of those conflicts would feature at times the large-scale deployment of conventional military forces: big, traditional army and marine combat divisions, as well as the heavy use of airpower by both the navy and the air force. But by and large, the brunt of the nation's counterterrorism missions in the wake of 9/11 have been undertaken by small, secretive elite special operations units operating clandestinely.

Vice President Dick Cheney summed up the kind of conflict that the United States was planning to wage just days after 9/11 in an appearance on NBC's *Meet the Press,* and in the years since the United States has hewed remarkably close to the vision he laid out in that appearance, even across four separate presidential administrations. "We also have to work through sort of the dark side, if you will. We've got to spend time in the shadows in the intelligence world. A lot of what needs to be done here will have to be done quietly, without any discussion, using sources and methods that are available to our intelligence agencies, if we're going to be successful," Cheney said.

This is a book about the rise of open-source, unclassified intelligence and commercially available data, neither of which figured prominently in the early stages of military operations in Iraq and Af-

ghanistan. But to fully understand this topic, it's important to understand the central role that U.S. special operations have come to play in
the U.S.-led war on terror. More specifically, it's the key to understanding the role that data came to play in U.S. special forces operations during this period. In the same way that new digital technology
was beginning to transform the rest of society, it would revolutionize
U.S. special operations as well.

CHAPTER 5

The Dots Guys

THE DEPARTMENT OF DEFENSE, 2001–2009

It was exactly 6:12 p.m. on June 7, 2006, when a five-hundred-pound bomb crashed through a boxy two-story home about fifty-five miles north of Baghdad. As it struck its target, it exploded with a flash. Overhead, American F-16s circled, and one was already coming around for another pass. The plane unleashed a second munition, striking the same target again, this time sending a plume of smoke into the evening sky and all but leveling the house. And then the F-16 vanished out of sight.

Within minutes of the attack, Iraqi police were on the scene, accompanied by an ambulance. Amid the rubble, they found five bodies: two men, two women, and a young girl—all dead. The police placed the lone survivor of the attack—a thirty-nine-year-old Jordanian dressed head to toe in black—on a gurney. He had a messy dark beard and a tall forehead. His left cheek was smeared with blood, and his breathing was ragged. He was alive but only barely.

Several policemen were struggling to get him into the back of the ambulance when they were interrupted by the sound of two U.S. military helicopters landing about four hundred yards away. Out of the two choppers poured a team of U.S. special operators who demanded the Iraqi police step away from the survivor and place their hands above their heads. After disarming the Iraqi police, an American medic tried to save the life of the man that U.S. forces had just tried to assassinate via fighter jet. As the medic worked to save the Jordanian's life, the rest of the U.S. special operators combed through the rubble for anything that might have intelligence value.

At 7:04 p.m., less than an hour after the first bomb, the medic pronounced Abu Musab al-Zarqawi dead. The end of his life also marked the end of one of the most resource-intensive manhunts of the three-year-old Iraq War. After Osama bin Laden, Zarqawi was probably the second most wanted man in the world and was public enemy number one in the newly liberated Iraq. The Americans had placed a $25 million bounty on his head and had spent the better part of three years trying to dismantle the Iraqi affiliate of al-Qaeda that he oversaw.

What had led to this moment was the fact that American special operators under the authority of a secretive arm of the U.S. military called the Joint Special Operations Command, or JSOC, had spent three years kicking in doors in one dangerous night raid after another, taking prisoners and stripping terrorist safe houses and hideouts of every last scrap of usable intelligence at a breakneck pace. The aim was to keep the entire Iraqi branch of al-Qaeda so off balance that it would be impossible for them to operate.

Zarqawi and his network had become the top priority of General Stanley McChrystal when he took command of the Joint Special Operations Command in 2003, giving him leadership of the top-tier special forces units operating in the Middle East. When McChrystal took over JSOC, he inherited an organization that excelled at knocking down doors and putting bullets in foreheads. What it lacked was a coherent strategy to dismantle al-Qaeda in Iraq.

McChrystal and his top advisers quickly came to realize that they were fighting a *network*. Unlike the Iraqi leader Saddam Hussein's conventional forces, which had been routed fairly quickly, there would never be a coup de grâce against al-Qaeda in Iraq. There would never be a moment where its leadership could be persuaded to surrender and its fighters would lay down their arms and go back to their families. Even killing Zarqawi himself would not end the threat; he would simply be replaced by another charismatic terrorist leader, and the attacks would continue. Indeed the future self-proclaimed Islamic State would emerge from Zarqawi's al-Qaeda in Iraq.

The philosophy of special operations in the global war on terror is best summed up by a slide that McChrystal was shown by a subordinate while being briefed one day in late 2004: "Find—Fix—Finish—Exploit—Analyze." What this meant was that a target needed to be identified (*found*), put under surveillance (*fixed*), then killed or captured (*finished*). But that wasn't the end of the task. The unit that conducted the raid also needed to collect any material that could be of intelligence value—including computers, hard drives, phones, and papers. If detainees were captured alive, they should be interrogated. This material should then be *exploited* for intelligence leads, and the intelligence it yielded should be *analyzed* to better inform whom to target next in service of destabilizing the entire network. And then the whole cycle would begin anew with the selection of another target. Lather. Rinse. Repeat. Eventually, *disseminate* would be added to the cycle, meaning to share the information broadly within government, giving the entire process the ridiculous acronym F3EAD.

The F3EAD strategy had an immediate impact. In August 2004, McChrystal's special operations task force was able to execute only eighteen raids in Iraq. Two years later, in August 2006, they executed three hundred raids.

What changed? Prior to 9/11, the national security apparatus of the U.S. government was aimed at countering the Soviet Union. Traditionally, intelligence had been about trying to understand the military posture and political intentions of foreign states. Only paranoid authoritarian regimes needed to turn the full weight of their security apparatus on their own population.* Now, however, the task of fighting terrorism meant mining the personal lives of ordinary people to try to separate out law-abiding citizens from terrorists.

The hunt for Zarqawi was perhaps the most emblematic of the man-hunting missions that U.S. special operators undertook after 9/11, but it was by no means the only one. Thousands of such raids have been conducted, often with little fanfare, against a plethora of terrorist groups all around the world. The defining rhythm of the war on terror was the intelligence-driven data cycle that McChrystal's men had invented. The men and women who undertook those raids were the most visible manifestation of American power, and they represented the *finish* part of the intelligence cycle developed by JSOC. But behind every single night raid or precision air strike was a multi-agency team of intelligence analysts and military planners who were responsible for the rest: the *find, fix, exploit, analyze,* and *disseminate* parts of the endeavor. Those elements were just as important to JSOC's successes and failures across the Middle East.

New organizations across the federal government would be created to support the expanding man-hunting mission of the United States. One was called the SKOPE Cell. Organized by the National Geospatial-Intelligence Agency to support JSOC, it was essentially a technology incubator designed to bring computers and data to bear on some of the hardest problems in national security. One person involved described it as an effort to "match predictive analytics and people with clearances to solve hard problems." Tapping the expertise of data scientists and coders is standard practice today in organizations of all kinds and sizes, but in the mid-2000s the idea that nerdy computer programmers writing Python scripts might have something to offer military operators wasn't obvious. SKOPE was turned loose on hard problems: hunting for top terrorist and insurgent targets and

---

* Though, of course, numerous investigations in the 1970s did reveal that the U.S. intelligence community had arguably violated the civil liberties of some Americans through surveillance efforts aimed at civil rights protesters and antiwar activists.

trying to understand the human geography of places like Iraq and Afghanistan. In addition, SKOPE eventually gained access to a lot of the top-secret NSA communications data, allowing them to look for patterns, anomalies, and outliers. This could be used in service of JSOC's man-hunting mission. With this kind of data, SKOPE could map out the social networks of people of interest. Who called whom? And whom did those people call? In an era before the widespread adoption of text messaging and social media, these call records were a powerful tool to look at the social web of an individual or a community. In many respects, this was the same kind of data mining and social network analysis that the TIA team and the FTTTF team were working on.

SKOPE's offices in the Washington, D.C., area were located at Building 213 at First and M Streets SE. The building had long housed agencies that interpret secret photographs from spy planes and satellites, so its windows were blacked out all over the building. But SKOPE created an office designed to transport you away from Washington.

"The cell sat somewhere on the third floor in a dark room," recalled Robert Cardillo, who was a senior intelligence official when SKOPE launched and would eventually rise to become the director of the NGA. He described SKOPE's offices as having "a theater-like kind of intensity and atmosphere—like a war theater."

A group of NGA analysts serving in Iraq and Afghanistan were learning the same lessons as the SKOPE Cell. Early on, the NGA had decided that it wanted to put its civilian analysts into war zones alongside the uniformed troops serving overseas. Part of this was practical; it often took a long time to transmit information back to Washington, and having analysts sitting at forward operating bases around the world helped speed up the intelligence cycle. But another part of it was to remind analysts that the country was at war and that they were a part of that war—a bid to create an esprit de corps among the civilian analysts and to remind them that they were important to the war effort.

Embedded in the military hierarchy in Afghanistan and Iraq, NGA analysts started collaborating with their uniformed peers as well as other intelligence agencies that were also sending their personnel into war zones. They would combine aerial footage from drones—a new technology coming onto the battlefield—with all sorts of other data at their disposal—their secret intercepts and well-placed human sources, nascent open-source intelligence such as internet message boards and local news reports, historical military data on ambushes and more, demographic data on the local population—and then map it. Taken together, these analysts had a whole new way of looking at military problems.

What they were looking for were patterns or outliers—evidence of unusual activity in large quantities of data. This kind of intelligence analysis—sometimes called activity-based intelligence—owed an intellectual debt to a law enforcement method called crime mapping. In the 1990s, enterprising New York City police commanders had created a crime-mapping tool called CompStat to track crime statistics. What intelligence officers were doing in Iraq was effectively the same. The military borrowed this basic data-mapping philosophy from law enforcement and applied it to a whole new problem. Measuring where an insurgency set off improvised explosive devices, IEDs, wasn't all that different from mapping patterns of homicides and rapes. It was taking large volumes of data and looking for patterns. Did homicides spike on weekends? Were they more common in the summer or the winter? You could do the same kind of pattern analysis with IEDs.

Some military commanders would start referring to these NGA analysts as "the dots guys"—for their ability to display information across an easily digestible map. Commanders would come to rely on them. The analysts trained in these techniques would rotate in and out—sometimes replaced by new analysts ignorant of how to do this kind of data fusion and mapping. And military commanders would feel their loss. As one intelligence officer recalled, "They'd say, 'Where's my dots guy? Where'd he go? I want another dots guy out here.'"

One technique that intelligence analysts in Iraq and Afghanistan were perfecting was called pattern of life analysis, which involved mining large data sets for clues about activity. A concept similar to activity-based intelligence, pattern of life analysis was more about understanding the habits and routines of a target.

To give an example: If you could acquire all my movement data—say, by hacking into my cell phone—you'd realize that most days, I would leave my home in southeast Washington, D.C., in the mornings and ride my bike to my office downtown. Some nights I go to the gym while other nights, I'll go to a happy hour with colleagues or go out to dinner with a friend. That is my geographic pattern of life, and it can change over time. During the pandemic, for example, you could see that I mostly worked from home for almost two years but gradually started going back to the office a few days a week beginning in 2022.

You can perform pattern of life analysis off other kinds of data. If you had access to my communications records, you could see that I spend a lot of my workday on the phone—working sources and trying to get information. But after 6:00 or 7:00 p.m., I rarely make calls unless there's urgent breaking news; I usually message my friends on a messenger app about where to meet up or what's going on around town. Or you could do pattern of life analysis around a geographic spot on the earth rather than a person. Say you had a camera fixed on *The Wall Street Journal*'s bureau in Washington. You could see that some reporters arrive as early as 8:00 a.m. while others straggle in closer to noon. Some correspondents who cover Congress come into the office only on Fridays, when the legislature is out of session, and those who cover the presidency are constantly walking the few blocks between the bureau and the White House whenever the president has an event or a press conference.

Pattern of life analysis is exactly what McChrystal's forces were doing the day they killed Zarqawi. That day, they had actually been stalking another target, Abu Abdul al-Rahman. After fifty-one interrogation sessions, a lower-level Iraqi prisoner swept up in one of JSOC's raids had provided the Americans with the name and address of Rahman, whom he identified as a spiritual adviser and top lieutenant to Zarqawi. The two men would meet fairly regularly—as often as every seven to ten days.

After this tip, American special operators began watching Rahman around the clock for weeks, tracking his every move with three separate aircraft and studying his habits, patterns, and routines.

That day—the last day of Zarqawi's life—Rahman had been extra careful and deviated from the usual routine that the team had observed. He'd left his Baghdad home driving a silver sedan in the mid-morning, making his way out of the city on the six-lane Sabbah Nissan through thick traffic. Rahman ditched the car in the mid-afternoon, jumping out in busy highway traffic, walking a few yards, and quickly getting into a blue Bongo truck. This was the behavior of a man concerned about surveillance, and indeed in two separate U.S. military operations centers special operators, intelligence analysts, and military planners were watching a live feed of his every move. A few hours later, Rahman had arrived in Baqubah, about thirty miles to the northeast of Baghdad. There again he'd swapped the Bongo for a white pickup and driven off, again headed north to its final destination— a two-story house in an isolated area between the villages of Hibhib and Khalis. It was there that watching a feed from the aerial surveillance, Americans had seen a man in black enter the home with Rahman. It was Zarqawi. Rahman had led JSOC right to the man they had spent the better part of three years hunting.

Tracking Rahman was done using the tried-and-true intelligence techniques that were common during this period of the war: largely surveillance drones and cell phone intercept technology. But over time, another lesson became clear: *classified does not mean better.* The analysts trained in doing pattern of life analysis realized that as social norms about sharing online changed and as more and more data became digitized and obtainable in unclassified channels, the same kind of analysis could be done with other data sets.

SKOPE would be succeeded by a program called Voltron, run by the intelligence contractor Booz Allen Hamilton. Many of SKOPE's analytical tools were built at the top-secret level. Voltron brought them down to the secret level—making them easier to share with a wider circle of people inside the U.S. government as well as foreign partners. But why stop there? Couldn't the same thing be done with unclassified data? It didn't matter whether you identified the target through secret intelligence obtained by human sources or through clues in a jihadi web forum; the end result was the same. That was a revelation that would take a long time to sink in in military circles.

In twenty years at war, U.S. special operators and intelligence analysts had become adept at targeting using classified data. But over time there was a shift in the cultural norms. Those shifts were subtle as people bought digital cameras in the late 1990s and early 2000s, then adopted services like Facebook beginning in the mid-2000s, and then started buying smartphones a few years later. With these changes, all sorts of information became available digitally. Special operators would start hauling computers and hard drives out of insurgent safe houses and taking mobile phones off suspected terrorists, sucking up all the data on those devices and mining them for clues. They would grow adept at lurking on obscure web forums or nascent social media sites where jihadis exchanged ideas. They would become experts at picking out faces or geographic clues in digital photographs. And eventually they would become fluent in the techniques of marketing, persuasion, and influence wielded by America's largest corporations.

Ultimately, these kinds of special operations man-hunting missions would be revolutionized by one of the greatest cultural shifts of the twenty-first century: a sudden impulse to share everything about your life online.

PART II

A NEW NERVOUS SYSTEM

CHAPTER 6

The Firehose

SILICON VALLEY AND WASHINGTON, D.C.,
MID-2000s ONWARD

On the night of March 11, 2011, a powerful earthquake struck forty-five miles east of the Tohoku region on the east coast of Japan. It was one of the most powerful quakes in recorded history, and the ensuing tsunami swept through Japanese cities and towns along the coast, killing nearly twenty thousand people and displacing hundreds of thousands more. Even as the waters receded, the crisis was far from over. The tsunami had badly damaged the Fukushima Daiichi nuclear power plant, crippling the plant's backup emergency generators and causing a triple nuclear meltdown. As the world watched, engineers raced to avert a catastrophic release of radioactive material into the water and contain the damage to the facility. In total, the earthquake, tsunami, and their aftermath would be the costliest natural disaster in history.

Thousands of miles away in Washington, D.C., a twenty-six-year-old intelligence analyst named Katie Zezima was at her desk when the first reports of the earthquake began to come in. Zezima was a novice geospatial analyst at the National Geospatial-Intelligence Agency, the agency within the U.S. government charged with collecting and interpreting geospatial intelligence like imagery from satellites. A self-described hippie who was interested in humanitarian crisis response, Zezima was assigned to a section of the NGA that focused on disaster relief. She had worked on a number of other previous relief efforts and had been impressed by the power of the internet to provide new forms of social organizing.

A year earlier, when an earthquake had ripped through Haiti, a PhD candidate in Boston named Patrick Meier had been inspired by a report on CNN to set up a crowdsourced effort on an interactive mapping platform called Ushahidi. Ushahidi basically allowed various forms of data to be displayed geographically. Meier and a group of other volunteers had fed reports from Twitter, YouTube, and Facebook into the platform to create a map of the unfolding crisis—allowing them to see the scope of the damage and to survey the humanitarian needs of the Haitian people. The project mushroomed almost overnight. More than three hundred students at Tufts University in Boston would volunteer their time to keep the Haiti Ushahidi site up and running. Over the coming weeks, they would enlist a thousand volunteers fluent in Haitian Creole and the Haitian dialect of French to help translate pleas collected by text message and social media and connect Haitians in need of assistance with international volunteers.

Watching the reports out of Japan a year later, Zezima saw a similar pattern. Already, a spontaneous crowdsourcing effort was unfolding online: someone had started a Google document that was collecting thousands of people's requests for help that was being updated and translated live by thousands of volunteers. The hashtag #prayforjapan was trending worldwide on Twitter. The internet was playing a major role in how people communicated and sought help in disasters.

Watching all this unfold in real time online, Zezima wondered to herself: Could she rerun Meier's crowdsourced Haiti playbook but this time from inside government? Relying entirely on social media, could she get insight about the needs of the Japanese people? Twitter at the time was popular in Japan, and the social network was built on openness—with most of the platform's activity being entirely public. Twitter also had fairly permissive rules about accessing bulk data on its millions of users. What if they could feed geocoded Twitter data onto a map to evaluate the scale and scope of the disaster? Could they extract any meaningful data or insight from this?

After securing the approval of her section chief, Zezima placed a call to a small mapping start-up and NGA outside contractor called GeoIQ and explained her idea. She wanted to build a heat map of people using the phrase "help needed" in Japanese who also had GPS location coordinates attached to their tweets. They would overlay the geographic location of those Twitter users and measure the distance to the nearest hospitals—showing the relationship between people who needed help from where they knew hospitals to be. She and the GeoIQ team would need to collect the data, translate it, and map it on the fly. Over the course of a few days, Zezima helped create one of the first social media intelligence products in NGA history and one of the earliest in the intelligence community.* Her product was a proof of concept that there was actual value in social media information.

Zezima knew her map wasn't the whole picture; after all, the user base of Twitter was not representative of the population as a whole. Twitter users at the time, whether American or Japanese, skewed younger and more tech savvy than the average citizen. Still, the effort was a start, and it posed a question with provocative implications: What other insights could the intelligence community glean from social media—for disaster response, for counterterrorism, and for better understanding, or some might say surveilling, the world at large?

---

* The first social media product in intelligence community history won't be known for decades, if ever. Sources have described JSOC rooting around web forums and nascent Facebook posts during the 2000s for tactical information. And the CIA had invested resources in being able to look at social media feeds prior to 2010. But in general, social media had not been widely discussed in government as a possible intelligence source by the time of this product.

The CEO of GeoIQ, the contractor who helped Zezima put the Japan earthquake intelligence report together, was a geography nerd named Sean Gorman. Gorman had an unusually keen understanding of the debate between openness and secrecy that was playing out in the post-9/11 era. When the attacks happened, he was just weeks into a PhD program at George Mason University in the suburbs of Washington, D.C., researching the physical nature of the internet. Consumers don't think about it, but all those fiber-optic cables connecting homes, businesses, and cell towers have to run somewhere. Gorman had long been lurking around highly specialized web forums, collecting maps of the major U.S. telecommunications systems. Over the course of years, he had undertaken a quixotic project to map the architecture of the internet—where different network carriers physically exchanged data, for example, and how fiber-optic cables ran across the Rocky Mountains.

In the post-9/11 era, questions about physical infrastructure had become important. When he saw a George Mason University law school advertisement for grant funding to study critical infrastructure vulnerabilities, Gorman sent in a proposal to see if he could get money for his research on the vulnerabilities in the physical fiber-optic network and other physical infrastructure. He heard nothing back for months—until the new head of the critical infrastructure program at George Mason called him out of the blue.

"Is this real data in your proposal or synthetic?" asked the voice on the other end of the line.

"It's real," Gorman replied.

"Come down and show us."

Before 9/11, a professor had once called Gorman's dissertation topic "tedious and unimportant." But suddenly everyone in Washington was interested. Gorman's demonstration so unnerved the critical infrastructure program's head that he placed numerous phone calls to the university's contacts inside the U.S. government.

The student ended up on an impromptu speaking tour of top national security and homeland security officials in Washington. He briefed the White House critical infrastructure board, the Federal Reserve Bank, the President's National Security Telecommunications Advisory Committee, the National Security Agency, the newly created Department of Homeland Security, and so on.

Everyone wanted to know how a graduate student without a clearance had acquired the precise technical specifications of the nation's critical infrastructure and compiled them into a dissertation that he was preparing to submit for a grade and eventually publish. Here's the message Gorman got over and over again: This should be classified. It should not be something a civilian can just collect and publish. But this was also the United States—a free and open society. It wasn't easy to hide information about infrastructure running on public land. And the U.S. government has no authority to prevent the publication under existing Supreme Court precedent.

Gorman would become a minor media sensation after a *Washington Post* reporter got wind of his work. The result was a story titled "Dissertation Could Be Security Threat" that published on what Gorman would recall later was a "slow news day" in July 2003. In it, the former U.S. counterterrorism official Richard Clarke was quoted suggesting that Gorman burn his dissertation after he got his grade. Cable news picked up the story, and Gorman ended up doing a number of TV interviews in the weeks that followed. The tenor of the coverage was this: grad student helping terrorists by unearthing vulnerabilities and making them public. "Made for a good headline, but was not particularly accurate," Gorman said with a chuckle years later.

From this whirlwind experience, GeoIQ was born. Gorman had always been obsessed with maps. Now he had the chance to turn that passion into a consulting business that could answer pressing questions about vulnerabilities in the real world. Oak Ridge National Laboratory in Tennessee gave him and his fledgling company a contract, allowing them to expand on Gorman's work as a graduate student into mapping and discovering vulnerabilities in overlapping networks like fiber optic, power, and energy distribution. They also pitched their services as consultants to the private sector. For example, a bank might want to know if an attack or natural disaster that destroyed a bridge or a tunnel could affect its ability to facilitate trades or communicate with customers. But over the years, as the acute horror of 9/11 faded into the background and the public concern over terrorism became less important, GeoIQ found that kind of consulting wasn't a growth area.

So Gorman got increasingly interested in what was then being called user-generated data, especially data with a geospatial component attached to it. The photo-sharing site Flickr was big then and had geotags, or geographic information, embedded in many digital pictures. Yelp was a growing social media site offering reviews of businesses both small and large. All were interesting to map nerds like Gorman and his small staff at GeoIQ. They began creating what Gorman called "mash-ups"—data sets overlaid on top of early versions of Google Maps. They would post the results of their mash-up on the company's blog for all to see, and occasionally one of their posts would get picked up by a big web aggregator like Digg and bring in a flurry of traffic and attention. Eventually, GeoIQ would develop a mapping product, building a way to map data with a geospatial component and do analysis. After the pivot, they landed an investment from the CIA-backed venture capital firm, In-Q-Tel.

This was early in the era of what was being called Web 2.0—an era that gave rise to websites and services that encouraged sharing, collaboration, openness, and self-publication. Wikipedia, Flickr, Facebook, Twitter, and blogs were all Web 2.0 phenomena, where user-generated content from millions or even billions of people was made available in bulk for curation, analysis, and debate.

Nothing, however, was more alluring to geospatial nerds like Gorman than Twitter. Launched in 2006, early iterations of the site were popular mostly among San Francisco Bay Area early adopters and techies. Twitter was then offering 140-character bursts of information; it would expand to 280 characters only in 2017. What drew Gorman and others to Twitter was the public nature of the conversations that could occur on the platform and the very real-time, constantly up-dated nature of the site. It would quickly catch on with journalists and financial analysts—anyone who needed to know *now* what was hap-pening in the world. Twitter also developed something of a bottom-up culture, with users first creating features that the platform would later formally build into the technology. For example, the retweet function that makes it so easy for things to go viral on the platform was origi-nally something the platform's users invented. To share a tweet they enjoyed, they would repost the entire tweet but add "RT" in front—signifying that it was a retweet. Twitter would later formally build that mechanism into the platform itself. Likewise, it was Twitter users who invented the idea of the hashtag, or placing the # symbol before a key-word to make it easier to monitor and search tweets by certain topics.

Similarly, a man named Dave Troy—tweeting under @davetroy—essentially invented the location function on the platform in 2007, giving a once-text-based platform a new geographic dimension. He encouraged users to share their location by appending "L:" to the tweet. So under Troy's convention, if I wanted to share that I had eaten a delicious sandwich at Bub and Pop's in downtown Washing-ton, I could tweet, "The Hebrew Hammer sandwich @ Bub and Pop's owns. L: 1815 M Street NW, Washington D.C. 20036." Or alterna-tively, I could tweet the GPS coordinates instead of the address, ap-pending "L:38°54'20.6"N 77°02'32.6"W" to show my appreciation of the deli's unique twist on a classic Reuben. Troy's convention caught on, and Twitter began letting users embed their precise GPS into tweets as part of a feature that the company built.

"At that time there was a lot of belief in being transparent and let-ting data be data. That was a good thing. It was the Wild West," Troy recalled years later.

This was a bonanza for data nerds like Gorman. Now real-time, live, instantaneous geographically tagged tweets could be vacuumed up in bulk, displayed on maps, or analyzed geographically. Twitter gave GeoIQ access to an early demo of its GPS capabilities, and the team increasingly started using Twitter data for the kinds of things that Zezima wanted to do: overlaying Twitter data onto maps for better insights about the world. And instead of stamping out this kind of data mining, Twitter called the full feed of every public tweet "the firehose" and began licensing its data to companies that could then resell it. At first, it gave large search engines the full feed so that they could index the content. It would later authorize several social media monitoring start-ups as official "resellers" of Twitter's firehose data. (Gorman sourced his Twitter data from one of these: Gnip, a Boulder-based start-up that one writer dubbed "Grand Central Station for the social web.")

That firehose would grow to contain previously unimaginable amounts of content by 2011. The nascent social network saw about 5,000 tweets a day in 2007. By 2008, it was up to 300,000. By the time of the earthquake and tsunami that tore through Japan, Twitter was seeing a daily volume that was approaching 200 million tweets a day—a milestone it would officially cross a few months later.

Private direct messages between users were not part of the firehose. Nor were "locked" profiles that were visible only to certain approved followers. But everything else was. Twitter's terms of service at this time explicitly warned users that the social network encouraged broad access to the data posted on its platform. "What you say on Twitter may be viewed all around the world instantly. You are what you Tweet!" the platform reminded its users.

Over the course of Gorman's short career, he had seen the winds of change shift. After 9/11, his thesis was deemed a security threat. Ten years later, openness and transparency were cardinal virtues. President Barack Obama had raised huge sums of money online in 2008, powered by a groundswell of social media enthusiasm for the young Illinois senator and his outsider campaign. He'd swept into office promising to run the most transparent administration in history and set up new portals such as USAspending.gov, Recovery.gov, and ForeignAssistance.gov to give Americans new ways of understanding what their government was doing. He ordered federal agencies to make data more available and insisted that each draft a plan about how they were going to increase transparency and accessibility in government. In a 2010 speech, Secretary of State Hillary Clinton called the emerging social web "a new nervous system for our planet." She said, "When something happens in Haiti or Hunan, the rest of us learn about it in real time—from real people."

Beginning in 2008 with Obama's rise, social media promised to be a new technology that could radically transform government and civics for the better. Obama's reelection campaign would ultimately use data culled from Facebook to map the social networks of more than a million Americans, thanks to supporters who consented to share their friends lists. The public and press reaction to Obama's massive social network mapping effort was on balance positive, treating it as a major innovation in political campaigning.*

The same year as the earthquake slammed into Japan, a series of antigovernment protests exploded across the Middle East as a newly mobilized generation of young people took to the streets against government corruption and malfeasance, organized in part online. The precise role that social media played in sparking or fueling the Arab Spring remains a topic of intense disagreement among scholars, policy makers, and activists. But what's undoubtedly true is that the prevailing sentiment, at least among those in Washington watching what was unfolding in the Middle East, was that these tools and technologies unleashed by American technology companies could be forces for good, bringing needed transparency, openness, and voice to people all

---

* When a political data vendor named Cambridge Analytica associated with Donald Trump would try to do something similar in 2016—albeit through more underhanded means of collecting the data and mapping out people's social networks—it would be treated as a data breach and a violation of trust on Facebook's platform.

over the world, especially those living under authoritarian governments.

What was also clear was that both the intelligence community and civil society groups that study the Middle East were caught off guard as widespread protest rippled from the Western Sahara to Iraq. While intelligence community analysts had been warning for years about the potential for civil unrest, as well as the instability and corruption of governments in North Africa and the Middle East, few had forecast a once-in-a-generation event that would sweep across nearly every country in the region in some form or another, toppling numerous governments and sparking multiple civil wars. "We had become too accustomed to stealing secrets and were not paying enough attention to important information that was streaming on Twitter for the world to see," the deputy CIA director Michael Morell conceded in his memoir after his retirement from government service.

While it's easy in hindsight to see Zezima's Japan earthquake product as a harbinger of things to come, she was at the time wading into completely uncharted territory. Legally, there were scant Defense Department or intelligence community guidelines that addressed what she wanted to do. The intelligence community had not grappled much with this kind of material before. Her initial Japanese earthquake analysis was distributed as a finished intelligence product inside the NGA, where it ran promptly into the buzz saw of the NGA's lawyers who didn't know what to make of the idea of getting actionable information from Twitter and were uncertain if Zezima was legally allowed to keep doing similar work. They raised lots of questions that lacked clear answers: What if these Twitter accounts belong to Americans—would NGA be violating the intelligence community rules that require it to minimize collecting their information? Can we make any kind of decision off social media information if it doesn't represent a sample of the population?

Beyond the legal concerns, there were other kinds of resistance. Zezima had impressed the top leaders at NGA. She received support and encouragement from the then director of the agency, Letitia "Tish" Long, as well as other leaders who liked her forward thinking. She was invited to give a number of briefings all over Washington about her work on the Japanese earthquake. She and Gorman got write-ups in the NGA's internal magazine *Pathfinder*. She eventually got legal to sign off on the limited use of social media for disaster response and continued to develop her methodology for how social media might inform disaster response. But elsewhere in the NGA, there was much more skepticism. A lot of mid-level and senior analysts were more wedded to the traditional way of doing intelligence and skeptical that social media was anything but a passing fad. They viewed Zezima as young and inexperienced.

And things inside government often moved at a glacial pace. In 2012, Zezima found herself assigned to what the intelligence community called a Tiger Team organized by the Office of the Director of National Intelligence, the agency responsible for coordinating policy across the different intelligence agencies of the U.S. government. The aim was to hash out some of the issues raised by social media and to discuss how it could best be integrated into the intelligence community's work. There she found a similar group of misfit toys: young intelligence officers and analysts from other agencies who had a sense of the growing importance of social media to national security but who couldn't get senior leaders at their agencies to take them seriously, devote resources to it, or develop policies around it. She left NGA for a job elsewhere in government in 2013 before the Tiger Team finished its work. She would not be involved in writing the rules for social media. But as the military and the intelligence community would see over and over again, the social web just could not be ignored.

Something needed to be done.

The same year that Zezima and Gorman coded the Japanese earthquake prototype, another event displayed the importance of social media to understanding the world.

Around 1:00 a.m. on May 2, a Pakistani information technology consultant named Sohaib Athar, who had relocated to the small city of Abbottabad in northern Pakistan from Lahore, was awake working on some coding projects when he heard the sound of helicopters hovering nearby.

Under the handle @ReallyVirtual, Athar fired off a series of tweets describing in near–real time the unusual course of events that was unfolding in the small mountain city. "Helicopter hovering above Abbottabad at 1AM (is a rare event)." Annoyed by the commotion, he followed that tweet up with "Go away helicopter—before I take out my giant swatter:-/" Finally, he added, "A huge window shaking bang here in Abbottabad Cantt. I hope its not the start of something nasty :-S"

There was indeed something nasty going on. A few miles away, seventy-nine U.S. special operators and one dog had stormed the nearby compound where the terrorist leader Osama bin Laden was in hiding. They killed him on Barack Obama's order, ending a decade-long manhunt for the perpetrator of the 9/11 attacks and stepping on some toes in the process. The United States had entered without advanced notice to Pakistan, an ostensible ally, throwing the country's civil and military leaders into confusion over what was occurring in their own territory.

In certain quarters of Washington, Athar's tweets were a wake-up call. Here was a night owl who, armed only with an internet connection, exposed what was perhaps one of the most important U.S. military operations in history in real time. That Athar didn't understand what was happening and that his tweets weren't more widely noticed until after the raid was only a matter of luck. What if the Pakistani military had been alerted through social media of strange happenings and managed to scramble a response while U.S. forces were still on the ground? What if the Taliban had become aware that U.S. forces were nearby? What if word had spread quickly through the local Abbottabad online community and the operation drew a curious crowd while it was still ongoing? What if that crowd grew violent?

One person working in a secretive government program recalled proposing and drawing up a prototype of a social media monitoring effort shortly after the bin Laden raid. It would feature a global feed—including the data of Americans. Like Zezima, he ran into bureaucratic inertia and legal uncertainty. His supervisor was aghast. "You're going to jail," the supervisor warned.

But this was a shortsighted answer.

The U.S. government could not afford to ignore the online world. It was where revolutions were being fomented; where millions of people were connecting and speaking; where terrorists were recruiting and propagandizing; where criminals were communicating in plain sight; and where foreign nations were running influence operations. It was clear that the intelligence community, the military, and law enforcement would need rules of the road.

CHAPTER 7

The Ugly Stepchild

THE INTELLIGENCE COMMUNITY, 1940s–2010s

N orman Schwarzkopf had a plan. It was the run-up to the 1991 Gulf War, sparked by Iraq's invasion of neighboring Kuwait, and the American general wanted to give the impression that the United States was planning an amphibious landing in Kuwait City from ships massed in the Persian Gulf. In reality, Schwarzkopf had ordered U.S. ground forces massed in Saudi Arabia directly into Iraq on a 150-mile "left hook" maneuver.

The problem was that U.S. military planners needed to know a key detail: Could the U.S. Army's tanks move quickly through the desert soil in that part of Iraq? Would the army need specialized bridging equipment to cross the expanse? Or was the ground solid enough for the rapid crossing that Schwarzkopf's plan called for? The Defense Intelligence Agency didn't have that kind of information on hand. The military considered drastic measures like dropping U.S. special operators deep into Iraq to collect soil samples in advance of the invasion. Then somewhere in the intelligence bureaucracy, someone asked an obvious question: Did anyone check the Library of Congress?

Sure enough, they found their answer there. In the early twentieth century, an American archaeological expedition had passed through the exact same region. Back then, they were on camels, not in M1 Abrams tanks. But nevertheless the expedition had taken detailed notes, including on whether the soil could support transporting large objects like artifacts. And so without risking any lives on a dangerous reconnaissance mission, the military got its answer by taking advantage of information buried in materials the U.S. government already had gathering dust in a library.

When Operation Desert Storm was launched, U.S. tanks swept through the undefended desert. Caught off guard and risking being encircled and trapped in Kuwait without supplies, Iraqi forces retreated. All told, it took about a hundred hours for U.S. and coalition forces to evict the Iraqi army from Kuwait once the attack began.

What these intelligence officers were practicing is called open-source intelligence, or OSINT, which is as old as the printing press, or perhaps even the parchment scroll or the cuneiform tablet. As long as there has been written material, governments have read it to better understand their adversaries and allies alike.

As a formal intelligence discipline practiced by the U.S. government, OSINT emerged during World War II. But in the twenty-first century as new forms of information blossomed on the web, it would see a remarkable renaissance. Once called the "ugly stepchild" of intelligence, it would be transformed by the rise of the web and the growing quantities of unclassified data available there for the taking.

In 1941, President Franklin D. Roosevelt directed the Federal Communications Commission's National Defense Activities directorate to start transcribing and translating foreign broadcasts for policy makers and military decision makers. Thus the Foreign Broadcast Monitoring Service, the first federal agency charged with OSINT, was born. Its first-ever analytic intelligence report was produced one day before the Japanese attack on Pearl Harbor. It described Japanese radio broadcasts as taking a "defiant, hostile tone" and full of "bitter" commentary on the United States. After the war, the organization was renamed the Foreign Broadcast Information Service, or FBIS, and would become part of the Central Intelligence Agency.

For decades, it was a well-regarded operation but rarely seen as core to the agency's mission. During his confirmation as CIA director in 1997, George Tenet summed up the views of many in the agency when he said of OSINT and the FBIS, "I don't want to be in the position where we lead people to believe that we are going to be the open source repository for the entire government, or pay to develop that kind of a capability, because quite frankly I don't think we have the money to do it, and I don't think it's our mission." A few years later, Tenet would be even more blunt, stating that "we only pay for secrets"—a neat summation of the view of many in the intelligence community that there was little worth learning in the unclassified sphere.

And yet beginning in the 1990s, the intelligence community came under increasing pressure from the outside to look at better developing its OSINT capabilities as a cheaper, more cost-effective alternative to pricier forms of intelligence gathering. Those calls grew even louder after 9/11. The 9/11 Commission floated the idea of the creation of a stand-alone open-source intelligence agency, a recommendation echoed several years later by the Commission on the Intelligence Capabilities of the United States Regarding Weapons of Mass Destruction. In addition, a new generation of leaders began challenging the notion that secret was always better, observing that changing social norms and the wider availability of digital information meant that more information than ever was available openly. A widely read paper co-authored by a military officer named Michael Flynn, who would later have a short stint as Donald Trump's national security adviser before becoming a conspiracy theorist, asserted in 2010, "The Cold War notion that open-source information is 'second class' is a dangerous, outmoded cliché."

OSINT was appealing in the post-9/11 period for a number of reasons. Before the attacks, the intelligence community and military were geared toward understanding and counteracting other nation-states. A counterterrorism mission, however, would involve a new cast of characters, including people like airline executives and local police officers. Not all of those people would have security clearances. OSINT made it easy to share information with people who were involved in counterterrorism but could not be given secret intelligence. Beyond that, the war on terrorism was also being fought largely outside the United States and sometimes involving countries that the United States did not have long-standing intelligence-sharing agreements with. Just as OSINT could be easily shared with police and local first responders, it could much more easily be shared with foreign partners as well. Finally, secret sources and methods were often vulnerable. Using them too freely risked compromising them; a human agent could be arrested, for example, or an adversary could develop a countermeasure to a technical capability. Open-source information carried fewer risks.

OSINT's profile grew after Congress passed legislation to reorganize the federal government's intelligence community, creating the Office of the Director of National Intelligence and naming a senior official who was responsible for OSINT. In 2005, the DNI also created the Open Source Center. The center trained thousands of intelligence officers both civilian and military as well as law enforcement analysts. It would send open-source specialists into every military command and build out a central repository called opensource.gov, where it would post unclassified open-source products for others in the U.S. government. It also helped procure data, software, and other computerized capabilities for the intelligence community. Under the leadership of the DNI, it would host two open-source conferences in 2007 and 2008. These were the first two conferences ever open to the general public in the history of the intelligence community.

But by far the most important innovation would be an early focus on tapping nascent social media networks. Even prior to the Arab Spring and the Japanese earthquake, a group called the Emerging Media Center inside the DNI Open Source Center had begun to study ways to collect information from social networks that were growing in importance and scale. When the social web began to take off in earnest and many inside government were caught off guard, the Emerging Media Center team was ready to take advantage of these platforms.

As U.S. special operations raids increased in Iraq, Afghanistan, and elsewhere in the Middle East under the new "find-fix-finish" battle rhythm set by the Joint Special Operations Command, operators were bringing back items like cell phones and hard drives full of pictures and documents. This wasn't exactly public information, but there wasn't any sort of secret technique used to pull data off a cell phone or a hard drive either. Often, analysts just had to power up the device or connect the hard drive to a computer. Eventually, commercial technologies would spring up to extract all of the data from a phone or a computer with ease.

And embedded in digital photos that were recovered off such devices were often clues that analysts could work with. One analyst who worked on special operations programs said that they could do things like determine where a photograph was taken from tiny clues in the background. "You might have a picture with mountains or something like that—some sort of reference point," he said.

With those clues, the United States could then tap into its specialized capabilities to get confirmation. Could it fly a drone somewhere to obtain imagery on whether a certain building matched a digital photograph gathered in a raid? Could it use its human sources to identify individuals or locations seen in those pictures? OSINT became a way to start an investigation—the tool of first resort to look for little clues that might turn a hunch into actionable intelligence.

But the real revolution would come when people began shifting their digital habits. With the dawning of the social media era, it became increasingly common for people to post about themselves in digital forums. First it was Friendster and Myspace, then Facebook,

YouTube, and Twitter, then Instagram and Snapchat, and today TikTok, Discord, BeReal, and whatever comes next. The platforms have changed, but the impulse to curate a digital persona has not— even among terrorists and insurgents.

The rise of this kind of social sharing raised profound new legal questions that had not been addressed in previous generations of OSINT.

When Katie Zezima wanted to use Twitter data to better understand the damage wrought by the Japanese earthquake, she had waded into an emerging legal debate. The intelligence community operated under decades of carefully constructed guidelines. But the explosion of new technologies, data sources, and capabilities that were blooming across the web was testing those limits.

Contrary to the impression that many Americans have about the spy agencies, they operate with a staggering amount of rules and procedures that sharply limit what they can do, especially domestically. Law enforcement is different: the FBI, DHS, and other federal, state, and local police agencies have authorities that let them look at data about Americans for the purpose of public safety, crime solving, and situational awareness in some cases. In general, the intelligence community is exceedingly cautious about limiting its collection against Americans. U.S. intelligence agencies by law and by policy are not *supposed* to be operating domestically or turning collection capabilities against Americans, and certainly not in bulk. That's why bombshells like the 2005 *New York Times* story revealing that the Bush administration was running a warrantless wiretapping program generated so much controversy.

In the 1970s, in the aftermath of both Watergate and press reporting about intelligence community abuses, the Church Committee, led by the Idaho senator Frank Church, conducted a pioneering investigation into the activities of America's spy agencies. Over the course of a year, the congressional panel would expose one shocking truth after another about the clandestine activities of the CIA, FBI, and NSA.

Church's investigation would reveal that the CIA had attempted assassinations of foreign officials and stockpiled lethal poisons drawn from shellfish toxins and cobra venom in defiance of presidential orders to destroy them; that the FBI had engaged in a massive campaign of surveillance and harassment of peaceful antiwar demonstrators and civil rights activists; that the NSA vacuumed up massive quantities of telephone and telegraph traffic coming into and going out of the United States. The committee would reveal that the CIA and FBI had opened hundreds of letters, rifling through the mail of leading politicians like Richard Nixon, Ted Kennedy, and even Frank Church himself. Most infamously, Church's probe would reveal that the FBI had engaged in intense surveillance and harassment of the Reverend Martin Luther King, even once sending him a letter and a tape recording that the late civil rights leader believed was an attempt to drive him to suicide. All of this was done under a tenuous reading of the U.S. Constitution where spy agencies claimed vast powers to conduct illegal domestic surveillance for information- and intelligence-gathering purposes. Their argument was that so long as they weren't using the information in a criminal proceeding, they weren't bound by the U.S. Constitution's prohibitions on unlawful searches and seizures.

The Church Committee revelations spurred Congress into making major changes to the way intelligence was conducted. By the dawn of the 1980s, the United States had pledged not to engage in assassinations. It had established a new secret court to supervise national security wiretaps. It had two new congressional committees—the House and Senate Select Committees on Intelligence—whose mandate was to oversee all of the nation's intelligence and covert action programs. The entire intelligence community had been brought in line with the U.S. Constitution and ordered to respect the rights of Americans to be free from surveillance without due process.

Those basic principles and reforms were codified into a 1981 executive order by President Ronald Reagan, EO 12333. It's known within intelligence circles as twelve-triple-three—the Holy Bible of intelligence law. It sharply circumscribes intelligence community collection of information about Americans, U.S.-based companies, and lawful permanent residents wherever they are in the world. It's because of EO 12333 that intelligence community lawyers were concerned about Zezima's use of Twitter and why another's boss warned him he was going to be arrested if he built his social media tool.

However, maybe those lawyers were being too reflexively cautious. Executive Order 12333 contains a provision that would appear to let the U.S. government's agencies look at social media sites as long as it was part of their lawful mission. Section 2.3 explicitly allowed the intelligence community to collect information that is "publicly available or collected with the consent of the person concerned." There were still restrictions: the government must not be targeting anyone specifically because of their First Amendment protected speech, for example. But in general, no firm prohibition existed against looking at Twitter or Facebook.

Hence, after an initial bout of squeamishness, government lawyers would come to rely on this term "publicly available information" as the legal basis for looking at the wide array of new online data sources. Data that seemed to be related to Americans still needed to be minimized whenever possible. But by and large, lawyers eventually cleared the use of social media monitoring tools like what Zezima wanted to use. By 2016, the term "open-source intelligence" had fallen out of favor, and publicly available information, or PAI, was what most intelligence officers in the Defense Department took to calling social media.

In part, the rebranding of OSINT as PAI was a clever legal maneuver to get more information into the hands of not just intelligence analysts but also operational units. In reality, OSINT and PAI are slightly differing concepts. *Intelligence* was something that only trained collectors and analysts operating under strict legal supervision were supposed to be doing. But increasingly, units operating in hostile environments wanted to be able to look at social media as part of their missions too. They wanted to know things like has their presence on the ground been detected? What is happening nearby? Who are the important local leaders in the place they're going, and what are they saying?

Collecting this kind of ambient situational information fell short of doing *intelligence* but was nevertheless important to many missions across the Defense Department. As a result, new definitions, guidelines, and terms were needed. The Defense Department would therefore refer to the raw social media information as publicly available information. Service members who were not intelligence officers could access such information as part of their authorized missions to understand the environment they were operating in. Once social media or other unclassified information became used in an intelligence report, however, it became *open-source intelligence.*

The Defense Department would also draft up a bevy of new policies and rules around access to such information. But it has never bothered to explain them to the public. For a long time, these guidelines were considered classified because some of this government activity violates the rules that social media companies have around inauthentic behavior on their platforms by governments. Facebook, Twitter, Instagram, and others have rules that ban governments from creating fake accounts and disseminating propaganda through those fake accounts, though such campaigns are notoriously hard to police.

The Pentagon would categorize the accessibility of publicly available information into different levels. Level 0 PAI was browsing "safe" websites such as those with a .gov or .mil domain. Level 1 was passive observation of foreign or domestic online content that could include logging in to a service that requires creating an account. Reading FoxNews.com, for example, would be Level 1 PAI. Level 2 collection involved mostly passive collection of information in closed spaces. Logging in to a Facebook account to passively browse content or "friend" a target is an example of Level 2 PAI. Some limited interactions designed to maintain a cover persona was allowed, such as requesting access to a message board or a closed Telegram channel pretending to be a jihadi or a hacker. But in general, Level 2 PAI involved passively lurking in private online spaces. And finally, Level 3 collection involved the creation of false personas doing full interactions with other people online. Level 3 PAI activity was tightly controlled—usually done only by three-letter U.S. intelligence agencies and treated like any other covert operation. The creation of a "fake" social media account that interacts with terrorists on Twitter in order to get information from or conduct psychological operations against them is an example of Level 3 collection. No matter which level, all of these online activities required weighing risk. Even Level 1 PAI often required the creation of a "cover plan" designed to mitigate the risk and ensure that whatever the Defense Department was doing online was in line with its authorities.

In other words, a lot of paperwork was required just to get online. But the military had joined the twenty-first century. At first, this took the form of monitoring what was ostensibly already public—the ever-increasing social chatter that was coming to define the Web 2.0. But in time, the amount of data available for the taking would expand dramatically.

CHAPTER 8

The Berber Hunter

SUNET AND U.S. SPECIAL FORCES, 2006 ONWARD

O ver hundreds of years, both North and South Americans have connected communities across their two vast continents by highway, creating a continuous system of public roadways stretching from Prudhoe Bay, Alaska, above the Arctic Circle, to Tierra del Fuego at the southern tip of South America. The only significant break in that otherwise unbroken network is the Darién Gap—a sixty-six-mile no-man's-land where road builders gave up trying to cut through the thick jungle over environmental, logistical, and cost concerns.

But in recent years, this remote region, straddling the border between Panama and Colombia, has become a popular migrant route. After arriving in Ecuador or Brazil, people from as far away as Africa, Asia, and the Middle East will often take the dirt roads into the swampy jungles as far as they can and then walk the rest of the way through punishing terrain—braving bugs, snakes, heat, and a near-total lack of resources and logistics all for a chance to try to reach the

United States. On its border with Colombia, Panama processes many of these migrants coming out of the jungles, taking their biographical and biometric information, and then allows them passage into Costa Rica.

In 2017, half a dozen or so Somali migrants crossed the Darién Gap, where they were processed by the Panamanians as per the usual procedure—their names collected, their faces photographed, and their fingerprints and retinas scanned. And then they were sent on their way, allowed to continue their journey north.

Just as some of the Somalis had reached the Golfito camp in Costa Rica, an urgent call came in from the American government. Was a man named Ibrahim Qoordheen in the camp? U.S. officials wanted to know. The Costa Ricans confirmed he was.

Qoordheen, one of the Somalis who had crossed into Panama via the Darién Gap, had triggered alerts up and down Central America because the United States had reason to believe he had ties to terrorism. He was quickly arrested by Costa Rican officials and interrogated by U.S. immigration authorities, who subsequently asked the Costa Ricans to deport him.

Qoordheen had been ensnared in a low-profile but far-reaching U.S. information-sharing system designed to enlist Central American countries' help vetting migrants as they traveled the long route from the jungles of Central America to the U.S. border. But that vetting involved significant challenges, including the logistical hassles of collecting biometrics in a rugged, isolated place such as the edge of the Darién Gap, getting them into the hands of U.S. authorities, and eliciting the cooperation of half a dozen countries between the Colombian frontier and the U.S. southern border.

After Qoordheen's biometrics were taken in the jungle by Panamanian authorities, they were sent to U.S. agencies. Because of the remoteness of the Darién Gap, this process can take a few days, though in recent years the U.S. government has funded the installation of better communications technology in the jungle to help speed up information processing. After receiving the data from the Panamanians, U.S. authorities got a hit on Qoordheen's fingerprints in one of their terrorism databases, indicating he was a potential danger.

Underlying this giant information-sharing partnership is a little-known U.S. government-funded international computer system called SUNet, or the Secure Unclassified Network. Panama and Costa Rica sit on the network to facilitate information sharing with U.S. immigration and border authorities.

Since its creation, SUNet had become one of the largest repositories of publicly available information, mostly for U.S. special forces. The contractor that managed SUNet, ECS Federal, served as the gatekeeper, deciding which vendors marketing open-source intelligence tools and data sets got access to U.S. Special Operations Command's huge counterterrorism budgets and which ones didn't and doling out millions in funds. That suite of open-source tools was appealing for the U.S. government to use because increasingly it had to enlist allies in the global war on terrorism. Some of those allies were trustworthy longtime U.S. security partners, but many more were not. Highly classified technical intelligence such as information obtained by hacking, secret spy satellites, or classified signals intelligence equipment was hard to share without compromising sources and methods. But *unclassified* social media data and other open-source information? That could be shared government to government with countries that the United States did not necessarily trust.

SUNet's origins lie in the aftermath of the Total Information Awareness debacle.

After Congress moved the program behind the secret black intelligence budget, Brian Sharkey remained deeply involved. He helped transition most of the research from DARPA to the National Security Agency's Advanced Research and Development Activity under its new Basketball code name and continued to manage the project as the prime contractor.

Though John Poindexter had been the public face associated with TIA, Sharkey had been its co-creator. TIA had been born from a long-running conversation between the two men that stretched back years about the problems in intelligence and the promise of new technologies. Both Sharkey and Poindexter nursed a keen interest in technology and national security. But their interests and temperaments were different, and they did not always see eye to eye on the priorities of the TIA program. To many who knew him at this time, Poindexter seemed embittered from his treatment by Congress during the Iran-contra affair more than a decade earlier. To Sharkey, he sometimes seemed too eager for a fight with anyone who doubted his vision. Shortly after DARPA tapped him to go back into government to run the Total Information Awareness program, Poindexter told Sharkey, "I'm going to break some eggs," Sharkey recalled years later.

Poindexter had a lofty vision for the technological capabilities of the program. He was convinced that technology could solve the problem of counterterrorism. And he was equally convinced that the privacy problems inherent in the bulk collection of huge amounts of data could also be solved with technology: names could be stripped from data; huge data sets could be siloed from each other and only cross-correlated under very specific conditions.

Sharkey was much more interested in the technical challenges: how to get computers, sensors, and algorithms to work together in a network that was secure against outside snooping, hacking, or tampering. In addition, Sharkey wanted to examine questions like how could they get analysts in very different parts of government to share data, to be able to use tools, and to collaborate? And how could the government get better at deploying new technologies quickly? Such questions were more interesting, and certainly more pressing, to Sharkey than Poindexter's expansive dreams for an all-seeing computer system.

When the dust settled after Congress cut off funding for TIA and the program became Basketball, it would look a lot more like Sharkey's vision than Poindexter's. Because Senator Ron Wyden and other congressional critics had barred Basketball from using any U.S. data, the grand vision of sweeping up huge amounts of commercial records never came to pass. Instead, Basketball's research was more about the technical problems of secure computing, collaborating, and deploying algorithms.

But after a few years of working on Basketball, Sharkey was growing restive. His kids were out of college, relieving him of a major financial strain. By now he had spent a long career in national security with stints as a naval officer, a civilian government employee, and an outside contractor. One day in 2005 over beers with a colleague named Doyle Weishar on a work trip to San Diego, Sharkey blurted out his frustrations. He was tired of working for a giant defense contractor's bottom line and had begun thinking about maybe starting his own company. "Let's do it," Weishar replied.

And so, Information Systems Worldwide was born in 2006. Known as i_SW, it would become a small but well-regarded Beltway contractor specializing in technology and engineering research. Sharkey would be the president and Weishar the executive vice president. The two men made their move at an opportune time. They were key managers on the continuation of the TIA program, and that contract was up for renewal. Given the timing, i_SW could have put together a proposal and tried to steal the contract renewal away from their former employer, SAIC. Fearing losing out of the business to two senior figures who had been involved in the program since it was TIA, SAIC cut a deal with them: don't compete with us for the Basketball contract, and we'll bring your new company, i_SW, on as a subcontractor. Sharkey and Weishar agreed, giving their new venture a foundation to build on.

A few years later, they got a chance to try again on a TIA-like project. The company had managed to secure a $20 million grant from an organization called the Combating Terrorism Technical Support Office. The CTTSO was yet another research and development arm of the Pentagon, much like DARPA and ARDA. They would go out and look at the new technologies that were coming out of private industry and evaluate whether they might be able to help the U.S. military—in this case U.S. special forces, who were often being given some of the most difficult and complex missions in this time period. The employee who had drafted the proposal had called it Lochan, the Scottish Gaelic word for small lakes or ponds.

After a few years of being a prototype, it was rebranded the Secure Unclassified Network, or SUNet. SUNet was simply a secure network that lived outside the Department of Defense computer systems. The original aim was to allow the U.S. government to bring in foreign partners and share data. But over time, it would evolve into a major tool for the collection and analysis of the ever-growing assemblage of data about people, places, and things that was available to be downloaded, purchased, queried, or accessed on the web. It would become one of the foremost publicly available information repositories inside the U.S. military.

SUNet rose to meet a growing need. During the late 2000s and early 2010s, Department of Homeland Security officials had been struggling with how to securely share leads on potential drug smugglers with law enforcement partners in Africa. The United States had just started offering direct flights to Lagos, Nigeria, and they wanted to share intelligence on known smugglers with partners in Nigeria in order to intercept them before they boarded flights to the United States. But Nigerian law enforcement officers did not have government-provided email accounts; they were using commercial email providers like Yahoo, which were not secure. International phone calls were not secure either. Even though the information the United States was transmitting was not classified, the names of potential drug smugglers still deserved some privacy protection. It dawned on U.S. officials that there might be a need for a computer system that allowed secure information sharing at an unclassified level.

U.S. and Nigerian partners soon developed a way to share data between the two countries about potential drug smugglers, but that was only the start for SUNet. The system hosted some work in Central

America about gangs in El Salvador and Honduras and was used during the 2013–16 Ebola crisis to facilitate quick and responsive information sharing. And then of course there was the border security and human-smuggling work in Central America that had tripped alarm bells when Ibrahim Qoordheen crossed the Darién Gap.

But the network's big break came when SUNet managers got some time in front of General Joseph Votel, the commander of all U.S. Special Operations Command. He met with the team of contractors and subcontractors developing SUNet at a meeting at West Point in 2015 and was impressed. Votel suggested offering their services to the Joint Special Operations Command. If anyone could make use of this tool, it was JSOC.

Around this time, Sharkey and Weishar sold their business to another defense contractor, ECS Federal. It was a difficult time in Sharkey's life; his wife had recently died, and he'd lost his appetite for running the business. The result was something of a culture change: i_SW had always been a relatively small contractor with a workforce numbering in the hundreds that did highly specialized work, whereas ECS was a sizable entity—a midsized federal contractor with thousands of employees. But at the end of the day, i_SW's work on the SUNet contract would end up transforming ECS as the government poured millions into publicly available information.

The dramatic influx in new spending came thanks to SUNet. By 2015, the government had aspirations to start using the network for more than information sharing. It started developing what it called the Conflict Zone Tool Kit, a suite of data and visualization tools initially designed to help analysts and planners. But over time, the tool kit would become more and more focused on the proliferation of publicly available information—social media, in particular.

This would be SUNet's "killer app"—a Silicon Valley term for a software program that's so necessary and important it guarantees the success of the technology platform. What would make SUNet indispensable to numerous military intelligence agencies and organizations such as SOCOM, JSOC, the U.S. Air Force, and the Defense Intelligence Agency was a suite of tools designed to help the government monitor and analyze the growing amalgamation of interesting information on the unclassified web. The name would change from the Conflict Zone Tool Kit to the Berber Hunter Tool Kit. Why a Berber Hunter? Nobody I interviewed seems to know. The best guess I heard is that it was named after a statue by the German sculptor Arthur Waagen depicting a North African hunter on horseback, holding up the severed head of a prey animal as his dogs tear away at a carcass.

By 2016, the military was shoveling money at SUNet. It had grown from a small effort worth a few million dollars a year to a hundred-million-dollar behemoth. The U.S. Army, in one of the contracts that provided a major expansion for SUNet, explained its view of the new information environment: "The explosion of social media and interactive internet services has revolutionized the Information Environment (IE), and fundamentally created a sensor system comprised of billions of citizens observing and reporting activities across the globe." In other words, the Defense Department had come to view the social web as a sensor. And SUNet would be its window on the world—particularly the social web and the growing collection of photographs, text, and video that the global population was sharing.

There were limits, of course. ECS Federal would also manage the training courses for the thousands of analysts who needed access to the open-source intelligence tools it was selling. ECS did not mess around when it came to the privacy and civil liberties questions that were raised by PAI. One vendor got sideways with the company for doing a demonstration about how, when they were conducting a social media search, analysts needed to take into account slang and nonstandard usages. They gave a humorous example of how their product could identify that some social media users were calling Donald Trump the "Cheeto-in-chief" due to his predilection for tanning. This demo triggered what one person described as a "four-alarm fire" inside ECS. The vendor had broken a cardinal rule of the military and the intelligence community: you do not point intelligence tools, even ones that rely on social media, toward targets inside the United States.

Of course that was only because ECS was operating under military rules and authorities. The same vendors whose data made up ECS's tool kit were also separately doing business with local, state, and federal law enforcement who were using these tools against U.S. citizens for public safety, situational awareness, and crime solving.

By 2021, SUNet and the Berber Hunter Tool Kit had become a major part of intelligence analysis inside and outside the U.S. special operations community. More than 320 people at SOCOM had SUNet accounts, and Special Operations Command planned to host as many as 400 accounts in the future. Thousands more at other government agencies or military branches—DHS, the Defense Intelligence Agency, the U.S. Air Force, and many others—would have accounts. Even the Department of Health and Human Services at the height of the COVID-19 pandemic would buy Berber Hunter licenses.

Built into SUNet was also a clever system of what the government called "managed attribution"—a way to conceal the identity of whoever was doing the open-source searches. After all, it would not be wise for U.S. government intelligence analysts to be exposing their targets to the web; it could tip off adversaries as to their plans and intentions. In fact, there were certain countries, one analyst told me, where even googling the name of the country on a government computer system was an operational security lapse. What the government built was a system of unattributable browsing and concealment that could help analysts conduct online research without the security risk. Every Berber Hunter user got a gibberish email address at the benign-sounding domain 761link.net, meant to conceal their personal identity and their status as U.S. government employees from the web.

ECS would load that network up with all sorts of commercial tools from tiny obscure vendors that had sprung up to cater to this market. There was OpeniO, a sort of digital man-hunting and backgrounding tool that could look at social data to evaluate threats in real time. There was Scraawl, Zignal, and Echosec, which specialized in social media analytics. Another vendor called Flashpoint focused on dark web material.

And then there was Babel Street—a company founded by some veterans of Acxiom that for a time would be the largest and most visible company in the Berber Hunter Tool Kit. It would take advantage of the increasing hunger for social media content within government, landing millions in federal contracts. And Babel would show the promise—and the peril—of an industry built on trying to monitor the digital space.

CHAPTER 9

Decipher Your World

BABEL STREET, WASHINGTON, D.C.,
2009 ONWARD

There was one particularly memorable demo that Brendan Huff would do during his years as a senior vice president at Babel Street.

Huff, who was responsible for managing the company's relationship with the Defense Department, would use the company's Babel X open-source intelligence platform to drop a bubble around the Central Intelligence Agency's headquarters in Langley, Virginia, and vacuum up all the tweets that were coming from inside that perimeter. These were tweets where the user had chosen to share their GPS location on Twitter, and those GPS coordinates corresponded to the CIA's headquarters building.

This search would bring up one account in particular, a woman who appeared to be in her late twenties or early thirties tweeting under a silly pseudonymous handle. We'll call her @CrispCottonClouds. Based on her tweets that had been collated by Babel X, two things would quickly become clear: first, that @CrispCottonClouds was a security guard for a private company and seemed to be assigned to guard the CIA's parking lot; and second, that she was a walking counterintelligence risk. This was Huff's specialty. Prior to going to Babel, he was in army counterintelligence, focusing on whether U.S. government agencies, outposts, or personnel were at risk of being blackmailed, infiltrated, or exploited by foreign adversaries.

@CrispCottonClouds ran the gamut of social media oversharing: risqué tweets about her romantic life and her sexual needs and desires; posts about heavy drinking and drug use; highly personal comments about her boss or various other people in her social circle or her family; complaints about her job; and so on. That said, she had never revealed her last name or her workplace, and her account never had more than a few hundred followers. It's safe to assume that she didn't think her tweets would be noticed in the deluge of content sloshing around the internet or that anybody could infer too much about her because her full name was not attached to her Twitter handle. But because GPS locations were attached to some of her tweets, a lot could in fact be inferred about her: where she worked, where she lived, where she hung out. Other information could be inferred from her photos: she often posted duck-face selfies of herself on the job, wearing the uniform of a security guard. While she monitored the premises of an intelligence facility, intelligence contractors were watching her as living proof of the dangers of social media and the need to monitor it intensely.

Academics and journalists use the term "context collapse" to explain a phenomenon where a message intended for one audience finds its way to another and is read in a completely different light. A classic example of the genre documented by the journalist and internet social critic Charlie Warzel was a woman sitting in a pub who turned to Twitter to settle a low-stakes barroom debate about whether the 1979 sci-fi classic *Alien* was a horror film or not, only to attract the wrath of the internet masses, including prominent Hollywood celebrities, who joined the social media pile on over a random woman's "bad" film opinion. The security guard in Babel's demonstration is an example of context collapse. She believed she was speaking pseudonymously to a small handful of friends and acquaintances, while a longtime army counterintelligence guy pinpointed her real-world identity, seeing in her social media activities both a security threat and a way to make a point in a sales pitch. To spy agencies, employees or contractors carelessly tweeting about their bosses or their sexual exploits might be blackmailed or "leveraged" in some way for information or access to secret facilities.

This was part of the danger of Twitter. To early Twitter users, it often felt as if they were part of a small, intimate conversation among a few dozen or a few hundred friends or acquaintances. And unlike Facebook, where people were encouraged to use their real names and understood that their words were attributable to them, Twitter often attracted a large number of users tweeting under semi-anonymous pseudonyms. That gave them the illusion of privacy and anonymity. But those pseudonyms were not as private as people believed, and real insights into their identities and personalities were embedded in the data in their photos, the information in their tweets, the people or the topics that they followed, or just the sheer volume of tiny clues about their identity they left behind online. When the FBI director, James Comey, let slip once he was lurking on Twitter under a pseudonymous account, the Gizmodo writer Ashley Feinberg identified his supposedly private account after only four hours of digging. If the director of the FBI can't keep a low profile using a pseudonym, what hope is there for the rest of us?

But this was also the allure of Twitter in its heyday. It was so public that organizations couldn't resist trying to understand the nature of the social conversation that was occurring on the platform. It was also immediate. The entire network, as Hillary Clinton said, sometimes did seem like a new nervous system for the planet. News events were often breaking on Twitter before they hit the mainstream media. The night Osama bin Laden was killed, for example, a former aide to Secretary of Defense Donald Rumsfeld, Keith Urbahn, would take to Twitter with the news, preempting President Obama's announcement that U.S. special forces had killed the terrorist. The wrestler and actor

Dwayne "the Rock" Johnson would also somehow find out in advance and hint on Twitter that big news was coming. This was a pattern that would repeat over and over again: the earliest reports of natural disasters, mass shootings, terrorist attacks, celebrity deaths, and myriad other kinds of developments would first surface on Twitter.

As a result, specialized service companies sprang up to try to monitor the conversation happening on social media. Initially, they were developed to cater to corporations, helping them track metrics like brand sentiment. But they would quickly discover that this market was full of potential government customers who wanted the same window on the world.

Babel Street was one such company, but it was by no means the only one. For a while, it burned the brightest; it sold more licenses through SUNet and the Berber Hunter Tool Kit than all the other tools that the U.S. government evaluated. But it would also be buffeted by constant challenges as Twitter and other social networks debated how much privacy their users were entitled to and whether government had any business monitoring their platforms at all.

Babel Street was something of a spin-off of Acxiom, but it would end up brokering an entirely different kind of data.

Acxiom's post-9/11 foray into the government market, which included contracts with the FBI and intelligence community, was marked by a few major acquisitions, including the 2007 purchase of a company called Harbinger Technologies Group. Harbinger was founded by two former intelligence officers named Jeff Chapman and Ahmed Qureshi. Harbinger specialized in names—especially Islamic names. The name Mohamed, for example, could be transliterated into English dozens of different ways. Harbinger attempted to cut through the clutter of transliteration and translation using technology. One of its products was called Foxhound, which helped solve transliteration problems between Latin letters and other alphabets to make sure that names, places, or things could be extracted from documents accurately.

But the fit between the two companies was imperfect. Acxiom had come out of direct marketing, whereas Harbinger was founded by two former intelligence officers. And so Acxiom never really made full use of Harbinger's name technology and would begin a slow, long exit from the government market. A few years into its foray into government work, Acxiom's management had lost patience. Government contracting is arduous. The government operates in long acquisition cycles—often taking years to get from the testing and evaluation of a system or product to a fully operational program. On the way to getting a signed contract, contractors face a byzantine maze of regulations and procedures. For a commercial company like Acxiom used to doing business-to-business deals, working with the government was slow and painstaking. And worse, the profit margins were sometimes not even that great. On a balance sheet, having a government sales division often meant entire quarters or even years where there were no sales. Not only that, but the acute terrorism threat that everyone felt on 9/11 had begun to recede into memory just as the company's leadership decided that it wanted to focus most of its resources elsewhere. And so Acxiom's government sales division withered on the vine.

Chapman, the co-founder of Harbinger, drifted back into government after his short, ill-fated stint as an Acxiom executive, ending up in the Treasury Department at the tail end of the Bush administration. And crucially, he purchased back the intellectual property that he'd sold to Acxiom in the Harbinger acquisition. Those technologies would be incorporated into Babel Street.

In its marketing material, the tagline for Babel Street would be "Decipher Your World." Chapman, a Starkville, Mississippi, native who graduated from the U.S. Naval Academy, founded the company to solve two problems: First, it offered a way to search the ever-increasing amount of content on the web that had intelligence value, including blogs, internet forums, and social media. Second, a huge amount of that information was not in English, and Babel offered a way to search in multiple languages. If you typed "United States," Babel's systems would have a prebuilt taxonomy of terms in multiple languages: "Estados Unidos" in Spanish, "États-Unis" in French, and so on. It could then search across platforms for that term, giving analysts a multilingual search option. Babel would brag in marketing material that its capabilities allowed users to search basic terms across more than two hundred languages and do more advanced analytics in eighteen of the world's most popular languages.

The capability to search across many languages and a wide variety of digital sources helped distinguish Babel Street from the dozens of other start-ups that were flooding into the government market at the time. Most were focused around Twitter, though others also aspired to monitor all kinds of social media and social sentiment, including other big social networks like Instagram and Facebook.

Babel's ambitions were to be a one-stop shop for all of a government agency's publicly available information needs. It would offer access to social media, but it would go beyond that. At its height, it would allow users to search across dozens of sources: mainstream social media sites like Reddit, LinkedIn, Facebook, Instagram, and Twitter; international social media networks like Renren, VK, and Weibo; photo-sharing sites like Flickr; video-sharing sites like Periscope, Vine, Vidme, Vimeo, and YouTube; toxic web forums like 4chan, 8chan, and the white-supremacist-focused Stormfront; classified pages like Craigslist and the sex-focused Backpage; as well as the auction site eBay. It also contracted with other highly specialized open-source intelligence data vendors to allow access to their data within the Babel Street platform: its site allowed access to DarkOwl, a dark web aggregator, and cybersecurity companies like Intel 471 and REDLattice.

Babel really came into its own after the 2013 Boston Marathon bombing. In the immediate aftermath, Babel could collect social media posts that were geotagged in the vicinity of the blast. After Dzhokhar Tsarnaev was identified as a possible suspect, Babel's analysts were able to find his account on the Russian social media site VK and map out his entire social network off the data they could get from that site. From Tsarnaev's post history and his social networks, they were able to build a profile of the bombing suspect fairly quickly.

But whatever Babel's aspirations for branching out, Twitter remained the go-to data source for many of Babel's clients, even though it was the weirdest social media network. For one, Twitter users are completely unrepresentative of the population at large. And unlike other platforms, nearly all of its content played out in public. Many of its heaviest users were prominent people: politicians, journalists, celebrities, and comedians. And Twitter needed to maintain the trust of its users, especially its loyal cadre of power users, to deliver fully on its promise of being the twenty-first-century town square.

And Twitter was not so sure that having surveillance companies like Babel Street lurking around was good for business.

Early in its history, Twitter, which was launched in 2006 as a side project by a group of entrepreneurs working on a podcast service, embraced openness. There was robust demand for access to bulk Twitter data from marketers and advertisers, media outlets and government. As it focused on building out the platform, Twitter authorized four companies to access the "firehose" of every public tweet. These companies could then resell the raw Twitter data to other businesses, largely for the purpose of brand awareness and sentiment analysis.

One of these resellers that had acquired Twitter's data was Gnip. Sean Gorman, of GeoIQ, had used Gnip when he had helped build the Japanese earthquake analysis for Katie Zezima and the NGA. Later, realizing the power in social media data and analysis, Gorman would sell GeoIQ to a mapping company and go on to start a second company called Timbr.io that itself would make use of Twitter data in conducting social media analytics for government and private customers.

Numerous start-ups were pouring into the exact same space— obtaining data from resellers like Gnip to build their own products and services on top of them. And governments around the world were interested. Many of these firms got funding from the CIA-linked venture capital firm, In-Q-Tel, which makes strategic investments in companies that might benefit the U.S. national security community.

Companies with access to the firehose like Gnip were flooded with requests from governments or government contractors for access to data for all sorts of uses: real-time monitoring, disaster and public safety, and surveillance. These companies were forced to make difficult decisions, in conjunction with Twitter, about what was allowed and what was not. In the early days, Twitter did write generalized prohibitions into contracts against using its data for surveillance. But as the "firehose" data was bought and then relicensed, it became difficult for the platform to enforce rules about who got access. As demand increased, Twitter moved to take more control over the buying and selling of its users' data. In 2014, it bought Gnip outright and cut off other resellers, bringing its data sales business directly in-house. From then on, Twitter itself would decide who got access and who didn't.

Now it was Twitter that had to make the tough calls about how it wanted to deal with government requests for data. And the first signs that issue could cause a public relations problem for the company came in 2016. A few years earlier, a firm called Dataminr was one of the companies that In-Q-Tel quietly made an investment in. Dataminr was building a product that would use Twitter data to do real-time event detection—a way to detect terrorist attacks or natural disasters based off social media postings and send alerts quickly to subscribers.

From the start of their relationship, Twitter had written into its contract with Dataminr that it could not resell data to government agencies for surveillance purposes, *The Wall Street Journal* reported in 2016. But that year, the newspaper found that intelligence agencies had been using the service as part of a pilot through In-Q-Tel. Twitter insisted that the company was in violation of its agreement not to sell data for surveillance; Dataminr argued that In-Q-Tel was a nonprofit run legally separate from the CIA and that the company was not in breach of its contract. Adding to the awkwardness was that Twitter itself was also an investor in Dataminr. Twitter acted aggressively and cut the intelligence agencies off, prompting complaints that Twitter was depriving the government of a tool that private sector entities were buying without restriction.

That same year, the ACLU of Northern California revealed that Twitter, Instagram, and Facebook were indirectly providing social data to police departments around the country that were using it to monitor the racial justice protests and unrest that had begun in the summer of 2014 after the death of the black teenager Michael Brown by police in Ferguson, Missouri. They were doing so through Geofeedia, one of the dozens of start-ups all flooding into the same space as Jeff Chapman and Sean Gorman. Like Sean Gorman's GeoIQ, Geofeedia also received an In-Q-Tel investment. Geofeedia had distinguished itself by having five hundred law enforcement and public safety clients around the country, claiming to be able to provide access to extensive Facebook, Instagram, and Twitter data, according to the ACLU—at the time, the three largest and most important social networks. Notably, Geofeedia claimed it had a unique partnership with Instagram. In Baltimore in 2015, Geofeedia boasted that police officers were able to pull photos and run them through a facial recognition tool. That enabled them to find some people who had outstanding arrest warrants, Geofeedia's sales representatives said in an email obtained by the news media. Another company, Snaptrends, had bragged in marketing material about helping police departments increase their arrest rate by 400 percent.

In the wake of growing public concern about law enforcement access to a wide array of social media data, Facebook (which by this point had acquired Instagram) and Twitter both announced they were cutting Geofeedia and Snaptrends off from data feeds, citing general prohibitions against surveillance and law enforcement activity on the platforms. Neither Geofeedia nor Snaptrends would survive being blacklisted. Both went out of business quickly afterward.

Internally, Twitter decided that it needed more nuanced rules. The company's trust and safety team became responsible for oversight of acceptable uses of data. The service decided that it would allow certain kinds of government access to Twitter data but not others. It would issue a flat ban on using its social data feeds to track an individual Twitter user over time.* It would not allow its data to be used in counter-terrorism. It would not do business with countries with poor human rights records where access to Twitter data might be used against civil society or to crack down on protest organizing.

But some uses of Twitter data by what it deemed responsible, dem-ocratic governments were acceptable to the company. Twitter, for ex-ample, was willing to let the Defense Department do what's called force protection—essentially allowing it to look at tweets at a geo-graphic spot on the earth for the purpose of protecting troops on the ground or at military facilities.

Dataminr played ball. It agreed to abide by Twitter's rules and de-signed its product around them. In exchange, it was allowed to take certain government customers.

Babel Street, however, did not want to play by those rules.

Jeff Chapman became obsessed by what happened to Geofeedia. He would mention it constantly around the office and fretted that it might happen to Babel. He tried making a public case that the company was a responsible steward of social data. Chapman participated in a single *Washington Post* profile of the company where he talked up its com-mitment to privacy and responsible use of social media by the police, the military, and the intelligence community. But Chapman ended up unhappy with the story—convinced that a quotation he gave the paper ("There are billions of smartphones on the planet.... All you have to do is listen to them") had been presented out of context, im-

---

* Of course, Twitter was completely public in this time period. So the monitoring of an individual user's activity could still have been done by going to twitter.com /(username) and reading what's posting there.

plying that Babel was intercepting phone calls. (The *Post* hastily added a paragraph: "A spokesperson representing Babel Street contacted the *Washington Post* following the publication of this story to say the company does not literally listen to private phone calls. The company gathers information from public social media postings and websites.") That would be the last time Jeff Chapman would speak to the press, at least on the record.

Most in the defense and intelligence space believed that Geofeedia had been felled by its own hubris. "Them bragging to law enforcement that they had been monitoring the protests in Missouri—it was just such a flagrant, arrogant, and stupid thing to say," said one person who worked on national security programs.

They also believed the police themselves were far less disciplined than the intelligence community and that their usage of social media tools was imperiling what the intelligence community might have access to, even though the intelligence community rarely if ever was looking at Americans. A contractor who built one of the early specialized tools to help government analyze publicly available information like social media remembered once giving access to a police department as a trial—the first time his company had ever taken a law enforcement customer. A few days later, the chief of the department called him up and told him to turn it off; he had too many officers looking up their significant others and their ex-spouses. That was a lesson. "The po-po are a bunch of idiots. The police department cannot handle things like this. You have to have discipline," said the contractor. Under his watch, the company never sold to law enforcement again.

With the decline of Geofeedia and Snaptrends, Babel Street was one of the bigger players left standing and would win high-level contracts all over government and the private sector. It would also happily contract with federal, state, and local police and expand into the corporate security sector. Among its clients, it would count sports teams including the Carolina Panthers, as well as security personnel at companies and private sector organizations. But Babel's deepest ties were always to the Defense Department, given Chapman's background in the U.S. Navy and as an intelligence officer. The Pentagon was its first-ever client, and the many military units that purchased its software would remain one of its most important business lines. And much of what the Defense Department wanted to use Babel for was an explicit violation of the new rules Twitter had put into place.

For a while, Babel Street was a paying enterprise customer, buying data from Twitter just like any other party. But Babel Street would repeatedly cross the lines Twitter had established for players that wanted to license data. Twitter could see the kinds of searches that Babel's customers were running on Twitter data and could see that the data was being used for things that Twitter's rules banned. Eventually, Babel Street was cut off entirely.

Ironically, Twitter's own corporate security team was actually a Babel customer. After Twitter cut off Babel's firehose access, Chapman ordered that Twitter be cut off from Babel's tool. They got a call from Twitter's corporate security team shortly after, wondering what had happened to their Babel Street account access. Twitter itself was using Babel, not the company's internal tools, to monitor Twitter.

Cut off from buying data the aboveboard way, Babel tried a workaround, tasking employees with creating Twitter accounts to pull data from Twitter's limited public API. But in creating these dummy accounts, some employees used their Babel Street email addresses. For a company made up mostly of former intelligence analysts and military service members, this was something of a security lapse. Twitter realized what the company was doing and cut it off again.

"It was hard to sell Babel without Twitter," one employee acknowledged. Eventually, Babel found ways around the ban—buying the data from another source.

Huff would ultimately part ways with the company. He was butting heads with Chapman over the company's current and future business lines. One of his colleagues would say about Huff, "For a military guy, he sure didn't like to be told what to do."

Huff and two Babel Street colleagues named Jeffrey Heinz and Brendon Clark would set up their own company, Anomaly Six, in

2018. It would specialize in a new capability catching fire in government OSINT circles: tracking people through commercially available cell phone data, the kind that was described to me years earlier and that formed the basis of Mike Yeagley's Grindr demonstration. This would become the next iteration of publicly available information capabilities—a way to track the millions of mobile devices that were unknowingly leaching data into an advertising ecosystem their owners barely understood.

One of Clark's favorite demonstrations of Anomaly Six's capabilities? Drawing a geofence around the CIA's building and snooping on mobile phones that appeared there.

"I like making fun of our own people," Clark said with a chuckle in one demo.

CHAPTER 10

The Network of Death

U.S. SPECIAL FORCES, THE MIDDLE EAST,
2013 ONWARD

O pen up Twitter on a phone or a computer and a blank box stares back at you, beckoning you to compose a new tweet. "What's happening?" a prompt asks, an open-ended invitation to share something—anything—with the world.

Mark John Taylor was one of the hundreds of millions of people who wanted a voice, and he found it on Twitter under the handle @M_Taylor_Kiwi. Born in New Zealand's North Island, he served in the country's armed forces for a short time in the late 1990s before his life started to drift. A friend from the army once described him as "a lost little lamb" who was easily swayed by the people and environment around him. His first wife was a born-again Christian, so he too became a born-again Christian. That relationship didn't work out, so he eventually went to Indonesia, where he married another woman, converting to Islam along the way. He and his new wife quarreled over his habit of playing hours of video games. Taylor eventually departed, saying he was going to look for work in Turkey or Qatar.

He would resurface instead in Syria in 2014, fighting with the newly resurgent terrorist group that was known under various names in English: Islamic State, Daesh, ISIS, ISIL. Taylor posted a video on YouTube in April 2015 encouraging ISIS sympathizers in New Zealand to rise up on the country's annual remembrance day. "Now is the time to commence your operations, even if it means you have to stab a few police officers," he said. His social media feed was full of pictures of him posing with guns and knives and with other jihadi fighters.

Taylor's tweets would attract notice for another reason. Like the CIA security guard in Brendan Huff's demo, dozens of Taylor's Twitter posts while fighting for the Islamic State included GPS coordinates—some of them very precise. Analysts discovered, for example, that he was with ISIS forces fighting in Kafar Roma in October 2014, and they could pinpoint the specific house he was staying at in the Syrian city of Al Tabqah that December. After realizing he'd made a grave error, Taylor hurriedly deleted his tweets that included location information, and Twitter would later suspend his entire account as part of a wider crackdown on jihadi social media content. Media outlets would dub him the "bumbling Jihadist" and mock him for leaving a trail of digital breadcrumbs for intelligence analysts to follow.

Taylor was fortunate: none of his errors led to a visit by an American drone or Saudi warplane. He'd survive the war and eventually turn himself in to Kurdish authorities. Others would not be so lucky. Thousands of people like Mark John Taylor flooded into Syria and Iraq to take up arms on behalf of ISIS, the self-proclaimed Islamic State that dreamed of reestablishing a theocratic pan-Muslim state in the heart of the Middle East. Many of them were "dumb kids," in the words of one person who worked on targeting as part of the anti-ISIS campaign. Often they were such digital natives that they forgot to practice even the most basic digital security precautions. They were joining an international terrorist group that was being hunted by a multinational coalition made up of some of the most capable and sophisticated military powers on the planet. But they were so used to sharing their lives with strangers that it didn't occur to many that the GPS coordinates in their tweets, the mountains in the backgrounds of their photos, the faces of their fellow jihadis, and dozens of other digital breadcrumbs were all like homing beacons that the U.S.-led anti-ISIS coalition could use to target them. An untold many paid for those operational security errors with their lives.

The Brookings Institution in Washington conducted a study on about 20,000 Twitter accounts that ISIS used and found that 292 people had enabled precise location in at least one of their tweets, broadcasting their location in real time to every intelligence agency on the planet. And those 292 people were not lone wolves; they were living alongside dozens if not hundreds of other ISIS fighters and giving away their operational details. In December 2014, ISIS recognized this was a major problem and issued orders that its fighters not have mobile location services enabled on their phones, but Brookings found that few complied. A similar review a month later found essentially the same number of accounts with GPS locations in their tweets. And even those not broadcasting their location were often sharing a wealth of clues about the activities of ISIS on open channels. Buried in the steady stream of photos, tweets, Facebook posts, and videos were all sorts of breadcrumbs: technical data attached to photos, geographic clues in the landscapes behind posing militants, the faces of other ISIS fighters in the group's ranks, and much more.

All of this had real intelligence value, and governments all over the world had taken notice. The United States and its allies quietly created a secretive intelligence cell based at the King Abdullah II Air Base about seventy miles outside Amman, Jordan. Dubbed Gallant Phoenix and initially composed of a handful of American analysts under the leadership of the U.S. Joint Special Operations Command, it would eventually sprawl into a massive multinational effort to stem the foreign fighter flow onto the battlefield and apprehend those who tried to return to their home countries. The revolution, at least in Syria and Iraq, was being tweeted.

Barack Obama's annual vacations on Martha's Vineyard were usually laid-back affairs. When he wasn't with his family, the president spent much of his time golfing. But during the summer of 2014, the president's typically idle summer retreat was interrupted by global events. On August 19, a slickly produced video surfaced online that showed the brutal, violent murder of the photojournalist James Foley, who had been kidnapped in Syria in 2012. The video showed Foley, with his head shaved and clad in an orange jumpsuit, on his knees in the desert with a vast arid expanse behind him. Looming over him was a terrifying figure wearing black and carrying a dagger.

Foley's executioner, the black-clad ISIS militant later revealed to be a Kuwaiti-born British man named Mohammed Emwazi and dubbed "Jihadi John" by the press, read a prepared statement in a British accent before carrying out the ghastly execution. The video ended with Foley's severed head resting on his lifeless corpse.

A day after the video surfaced online and U.S. national security officials were able to confirm its authenticity, Obama interrupted his trip to pay tribute to the slain reporter. In a televised public statement, he called Foley "a son, a brother, and a friend" who had "reported from difficult and dangerous places, bearing witness to the lives of people a world away."

Just a few short years after the Arab Spring showcased the hope and promise that digital tools could bring to a population living under repressive and corrupt autocracies, ISIS showcased that the same online networks could just as easily be used to spread fear, celebrate death, and advocate violent martyrdom. The slick, well-produced beheading videos released by ISIS in 2014 represented the terrifying new face of jihad. Foley's murder was the first grisly beheading that drew the attention of the world, but shock value propaganda followed. And the videos worked. By December 2015, thirty thousand people from at least eighty-five countries had arrived in Iraq or Syria to fight on behalf of the group.

At its height, ISIS governed a large amount of territory in Syria and Iraq and proclaimed itself a caliphate, or an Islamic state. But it also encouraged adherents all over the world who were not able or willing to travel to the Middle East to pick up whatever weapons or tools they had at their disposal—guns, cars, trucks, bombs, knives, axes, whatever—and wage jihad that way. In practice that meant nobody was safe from the group, which between 2014 and 2018 had inspired or taken credit for 143 attacks across twenty-nine countries, costing more than two thousand people their lives.

How did they get their message out? ISIS and its adherents were full-fledged participants in the increasingly ascendant social web. In addition to the execution videos, ISIS propagandists published digital magazines called *Al-Naba*, *Dabiq*, and *Rumiyah*. And for those unwilling or unable to physically come to the battlefields of Syria and Iraq, they offered a pathway to wage informational jihad. The group circulated a document in both digital and booklet form titled "Media Operative, You Are a Mujahid, Too" that outlined the group's views of information warfare and its propaganda doctrine, encouraging followers to take up the cause in the digital world as well as the real world. "The tiniest action you do in the heart of their land is dearer to us than the biggest action by us. There are no innocents in the heart of the lands of the crusaders," said one ISIS propagandist in an audio message in 2016.

This was the paradox of ISIS. At the same time it was trying to impose a seventh-century vision of theocratic Islam on a huge population, more than ten million at its territorial peak, it was also completely fluent in the tools and techniques of modern digital life. Its propagandists and supporters would derisively refer to secular "moderns," yet only in the modern digital media environment where ideas can spread across borders in an instant outside the control of the formal gatekeepers is a story like the rise of ISIS even possible.

More than a month after Foley's death, Obama gave a major speech at the United Nations. He dubbed ISIS a "network of death," and he promised that the United States would put all its might behind eradicating it.

The U.S. military effort against ISIS was called Operation Inherent Resolve and would mostly consist of air strikes directed at ISIS targets in support of Iraqi security forces and anti-ISIS Syrian rebels who did much of the fighting on the ground. What fueled a lot of the air strikes was well-developed and timely intelligence, because never before had the United States fought an enemy so willing to give away crucial operational details about themselves. Gallant Phoenix was one part of a multipronged international digital intelligence and psychological operations campaign against ISIS that helped provide fodder to the pilots and special operators who were the most visible manifestation of Inherent Resolve.

The military was understandably averse to talking publicly about how deeply it had penetrated jihadi social networks—sometimes just by monitoring the open web, but also sometimes by infiltrating closed forums under false personas. But some hints have surfaced over the years. The U.S. Air Force general Hawk Carlisle, at the time the commander of Air Combat Command, recounted in a 2015 speech at the height of the military's anti-ISIS campaign how quickly air force intelligence analysts were able to go from an online tip to bombs falling out of the sky. "They see some moron standing at this command," Carlisle said. "And in some social media, open forum, bragging about command-and-control capabilities for Daesh, ISIL. . . . Bombs on target in 22 hours."

In concept, these intelligence efforts were not all that different from what Stanley McChrystal and JSOC had set up in Iraq in the 2000s to dismantle Zarqawi's network, but there were key differences. The United States would now bring in a sprawling array of international partners beyond its traditional Anglosphere intelligence partners called the Five Eyes that included the U.K., Canada, Australia, and New Zealand. And second, under McChrystal a lot of the intelligence capabilities were highly classified technical systems—largely signals intelligence equipment and capabilities that gave the United States the ability to tap into phone systems or break into computers. Those were difficult to share with some partners outside the Five Eyes.

But Gallant Phoenix would rely in part on the wide array of publicly available information that was pouring onto the internet about the ISIS threat—mostly from people like Mark John Taylor. In time, the operation would also come to exploit material taken from computers and devices abroad, as well as biometric information about foreign fighters collected in war zones. This information was far easier to share than secret signals intelligence intercepts or information gleaned from America's network of human agents, because social media and other unclassified technical intelligence did not risk compromising sensitive sources and methods such as the identity of America's spies or the kinds of technical capabilities it had developed to eavesdrop. Gallant Phoenix was also a way to bring together countries that were not used to cooperating with each other: Arabs and Israelis; Europeans and Middle Eastern nations that had never had strong law enforcement or intelligence partnerships with the United States or one another. The United States would be the pass-through for these countries to cooperate and collaborate in new ways against a common threat.

In the early days, the operation was very focused on the kind of military targeting that the United States had been conducting for more than a decade against terrorists and insurgents—putting "warheads on foreheads," in the parlance of people who worked on the effort. And it was tremendously successful at doing that. The military, particularly analysts supporting U.S. special operators, had been lurking around on web forums or nascent social media sites for intelligence clues for as long as those kinds of digital properties had existed. But the operation against ISIS showcased something new: that social media could be used for what the military called actionable intelligence, meaning that a tidbit or a clue from a photograph posted on Instagram could be quickly turned around into something that could be fed to operations planners.

Jade Parker, a contractor who was part of a task force that supported U.S. special operations, described in a podcast interview an incident where a fairly senior ISIS figure came to an unexpected end, strongly implying that he was lured by a Defense Department operation into an ambush. "He decided to sell his car on the internet. And he sold the car to the wrong person," Parker said. "It was the end of him. It was the last thing he ever sold, for sure. . . . He definitely got smoked."

Parker's job was to interact with ISIS figures using personas, she explained, often in order to get them to provide information or to alter their behavior to make it easier to target them. "It's particularly convenient if you can get them in a specific spot and to stay there for a little while," she said about her work.

Various U.S. agencies—the U.S. Central Command that had responsibility for the Middle East, Joint Warfare Analysis Center, the National Security Agency, National Counterterrorism Center, and the FBI, among others—were involved in cyber operations against ISIS, as well as a huge number of foreign partners. U.S. anti-ISIS efforts would also involve more than two dozen countries at its height. Much of the information sharing was powered by SUNet, where Gallant Phoenix had been given part of the network for its efforts. And much of the social media intelligence was gathered using the tools that made up the Berber Hunter Tool Kit: Babel Street, Flashpoint, OpeniO, and the many other open-source intelligence products that were now a standard part of the military's arsenal. These vendors would frequently send training representatives to the operation's headquarters at the airfield in Jordan where hundreds of analysts from around the world all sat together.

Of these tools, Flashpoint, in particular, specialized in penetrating obscure jihadi forums using fictitious personas. It briefly disappeared from the list of tools approved for SOCOM because military lawyers were concerned that it did not constitute open-source intelligence. The lawyers debated whether a private company infiltrating such forums was really gathering publicly available information. Eventually, the situation was resolved: Flashpoint could come back in, but the government could not direct it to collect anything.

Gallant Phoenix and other U.S. cyber-operations efforts grew and matured as ISIS increasingly lost more and more territory. And the

United States and its allies would even branch into psychological and influence operations to help shape the narrative online.

And it would also develop some sophisticated cyber-intelligence capabilities. For example, on August 24, 2017, a device with the IP address 122.61.118.145 began accessing a cornucopia of extremist content online: Islamist propaganda, the sprawling hate-filled manifesto published by the Norwegian terrorist Anders Behring Breivik, and some pages related to weapons. The browsing continued for the next eleven days before abruptly stopping.

An IP address is a unique identifier generated when a device connects to a computer network. Everything that touches the internet or any other kind of computer network has an IP address: cell phones, computers, smartwatches, routers, servers, home Internet of Things devices—everything. The addresses are the basic protocols for how data moves around digitally. If you take no precautions at all, your IP address on your mobile phone is assigned by your carrier, and the IP address on your router or modem is assigned by your internet service provider. As such it can serve as a clue to your identity as you browse the web and can be captured by any number of parties: search engines, the websites you visit, internet service providers, and governments. If you take extra precautions, such as running what's called a virtual private network, or VPN, you can essentially mask your true IP address as you move around the web—though then you're trusting that your VPN provider isn't snooping on your traffic.

More than a year after 122.61.118.145 began perusing some of the darkest corners of the web, the New Zealand Security Intelligence Service opened an investigation into the browsing activity. Investigators believed that the IP address was coming from a device in Dunedin, New Zealand, a city on the southeast coast of the South Island. They believed the address was assigned to a DSL subscriber of the internet service provider Spark New Zealand Limited, but the company wasn't able to tell them much more than that. Given that it was more than a year after the address was seen browsing extremist content, the company didn't have records dating back that far.

The Security Intelligence Service dropped the matter. It had reached a dead end and couldn't find a specific individual to link to the browsing. However, investigators in New Zealand a year later began wondering: Did that IP address belong to Brenton Harrison Tarrant, the man who had just committed one of the worst atrocities in New Zealand history? Tarrant, an Australian transplant, right-wing extremist, and white supremacist, stormed two mosques in Christchurch and killed fifty-one people and injured forty others in March 2019. The investigation would be inconclusive; there was strong circumstantial evidence that 122.61.118.145 might have been Tarrant but also some countervailing evidence.

What had powered this tip in the first place was Gallant Phoenix, a report later revealed. New Zealand had been involved in Gallant Phoenix as early as 2014 and had authorized a deployment of its own forces to the task force by 2016.

This ability to analyze who was accessing certain pieces of terrorist propaganda hinted at a tremendously powerful capability to peer into the internet browsing activity of people around the world.

CHAPTER 11

Like a Real Person

AMERICA IN THE 2020s

A t the height of the nationwide protests beginning in May 2020 sparked by the murder of George Floyd at the hands of police in Minneapolis, a twenty-six-year-old Arizona man named Loren Reed who lives in the small city of Page, Arizona, took to Facebook to vent about the police. He posted a status update inviting others to join him in a "riot" planned for the following evening.

A handful of his friends and neighbors joined him in a Facebook group called Fuck 12. In dozens of messages spanning the course of a few days (the "riot" needed to be postponed a few times), Reed said he was going to walk into a bar in the town and yell, "ACAB," an acronym for "All Cops Are Bastards!" and "Fuck cops" until someone wanted to fight him. He and the others in the group also discussed burning down the local courthouse, looting local pharmacies, and setting fire to the local police department. He discussed acquiring gasoline, fireworks, and Molotov cocktails and made disparaging comments about local police officers and politicians. "Arson, Assault, Conspiracy, here we come," Reed said in one message.

Reed was arrested a few days after creating the group. In the eyes of federal prosecutors and the Page Police Department, Reed had unlawfully threatened to destroy a municipal building. He faced a string of serious charges, carrying the possibility of years in jail or a big fine if a judge decided to throw the book at him.*

But according to Reed's lawyer and his friends, this was an overly emotional young man with a dark, provocative sense of humor caught up in the moment and being taken completely out of context by law enforcement. The hundreds of Facebook messages were largely angry fantasy, Reed's defense lawyer argued. Nobody showed up to burn the courthouse. Reed never went into a bar to instigate a brawl. "Loren oscillated between saying he *wanted* to burn the courthouse, and that he would actually do it.... Wanting to see the courthouse burn, of course, is a far cry from truly threatening to do it," his lawyer wrote. Reed's legal team also argued that messages such as "I really wanna remain peaceful" were left out of the criminal complaint as well as messages that seemed to suggest what Reed wanted to organize was a *protest* but he believed that law enforcement might respond with violence and cause it to escalate into a riot.

Whatever interpretation you take of what unfolded in Page, what led to Reed's arrest and indictment was the fact that he inadvertently added an "undercover" Facebook account controlled by the Page police officer Christopher Seamster to his private Facebook group with a handful of friends. And so for dozens of pages of messages over the

---

* After nearly a year in detention prior to his trial, Reed eventually reached an agreement with the government. If he pleaded guilty, they would allow him to enter into what's called a diversion program. He'd officially be on probation and be required to obey certain conditions that required him to stay out of legal trouble, seek mental health treatment, and submit to regular drug testing, among other things. In exchange the government would drop the felony charge. In January 2023, the government dismissed the entire case against him after he successfully abided by the restrictions placed on him.

course of a few days, a space that Reed and some of his friends and neighbors perceived as private was being monitored by authorities in real time.

By 2020, these undercover accounts had become the favorite tool of police departments of all sizes—from big-city police departments like the LAPD to the tiny twenty-three-officer force that is responsible for public safety in Page, Arizona, population of about seventy-five hundred. A tactic once used to keep ISIS terrorists in place while a fighter plane locked on target had trickled down to all levels of domestic law enforcement. These accounts involve nothing like the risks of real in-person operations involving informants or undercover officers. All that's required is a little time and some manpower. Like a fine whiskey, these accounts are often "aged" to give them a long posting history and the veneer of being a real person. Contractors or government employees spend years in character to establish a long posting history and make the account seem genuine. When they're compromised as part of an investigation like the one into Reed, police shut them down and create a new account.

A few years earlier, the Memphis Police Department had been running an account with the name Bob Smith, a self-described "man of color" purportedly living in the Memphis area. The account friended local activists and journalists and routinely RSVP'd to various events being held in the Memphis area. It also would post politically tinged status updates like "Entitlement programs like welfare, food stamps, free cellphones has crippled America. Rather than be forced to find work, people are staying in and refusing to work." Another read, "My party, the Democrat party, has turned its back on helping us get out, instead they have enabled us to stay down and have brainwashed many to believe the handouts are handups."

The account was entirely the work of Sergeant Timothy Reynolds, who was not a man of color but in fact a middle-aged white employee of the Memphis Police Department's Office of Homeland Security. Upon questioning as part of a lawsuit brought by the American Civil Liberties Union against police surveillance in the city, Reynolds described his tactics using the Bob Smith account: "You have to make this look like a real person."

Gathering intelligence from behind the safety of a computer screen poses its own problem: context collapse on steroids. Internet spaces are full of exaggeration, bravado, posturing, and outright lies. People on the internet are famous for their "keyboard courage"—the willingness to say nasty things in the digital sphere they would never dream of saying face-to-face. Lots of jokes people make online or in private would not look good when collated into an indictment and presented to a grand jury. The same thing carries over to organizing and planning. Sending nastygrams by email or social media is common in the twenty-first century, but actually planning, organizing, and executing a plot of violence or destruction is exceedingly rare. At the same time, it's also clear that very occasionally extremism bred in online spaces has led to real-world tragedies like mass shootings or terrorist attacks. Sussing out the difference between idle dark internet banter and a legitimate threat is not easy.

And such tasks were increasingly being left to a bureaucracy—one with little appetite for humor or nuance. After Elon Musk bought Twitter in 2022, he let a number of journalists comb through the company's internal files in a project that was dubbed the Twitter Files. The records Musk released revealed extensive contact between the FBI, DHS, and Twitter, including requests from federal agencies to obtain bulk Twitter user data directly from the company. Twitter demurred. One user tweeting under the handle @ClaireFosterPHD, who said she was a ballot counter on Election Day, tweeted, "If you're not wearing a mask, I am not counting your vote." She followed it up with a tweet that said, "For every negative comment on this post, I'm adding another vote for the democrats." The FBI flagged her tweets for review despite both being obvious jokes.

Bureaucracies are not good at discerning satire and will always lean toward the most cautious possible interpretation. They'll push to remove @ClaireFosterPHD's dumb jokes on the grounds that they are spreading election misinformation. And they're not going to take any chances in letting Loren Reed walk around in the middle of an outbreak of civil unrest making provocative comments on Facebook.

But the question remains: Left to his own devices to stew in a private internet space with like-minded friends and neighbors during a stressful period in American history, would Reed and the others in his group chat have burned the courthouse? Or was this all talk—provocative discussion about the proper response to police brutality in America? Was Fuck 12 a place to vent and fantasize about things that nobody was ever going to do? And when does this kind of chatter in private spaces cross into criminal territory?

There is a vast gulf between the rules around police use of social media and the U.S. military's and intelligence community's rules. After many fits and starts, the military and the intelligence community created fairly robust guidelines, policies, and procedures around access to social media in the years after Zezima's Japanese earthquake demo. What Sergeant Reynolds and Officer Seamster were running in Memphis and Page would count as a "level 3" PAI operation under military and intelligence community guidelines, which would require intensive training and detailed legal supervision. Such operations are generally run only by "three-letter agencies," said one person who works on open-source intelligence, and are subject to extremely strict oversight similar to any other cover operation involving in-person informants, agents, or officials operating under false personas.

By contrast, there are nearly eighteen thousand law enforcement agencies in the United States. These organizations are as varied as the communities they patrol. Some are giant urban police forces; others are tiny sheriff's departments responsible for rural counties. They vary widely in training, policies, and oversight. And unlike the military's and the intelligence community's, their public safety mission is directed at the U.S. population.

As a result, there is very little in the way of law or public policy restraining the use of undercover accounts or police use of social media for surveillance purposes. Policies are written on a department-by-department basis and vary widely.

Once these accounts are created, they are a law enforcement presence in what are essentially private spaces: closed Facebook groups, locked profiles, group chats. These are conversations that would otherwise require a warrant to access. And yet when people accidentally let an undercover informant into their private spaces, all bets are off. They have forfeited any expectation of privacy under the prevailing interpretation of the Constitution. The Supreme Court has protected the use of police informants in most circumstances, and that protection is presumed to extend to fictitious social media personas until the high court says otherwise.

How Americans view these tools seems entirely contingent on the politics of the moment—with those whose side is out of power inclined to fear the government and those whose side is in power ready to trust the government. First, in the summer of 2020, police aggressively used social media to monitor the protests, and that included employing undercover accounts to observe activist spaces. Like the protests from a few years earlier in Ferguson and Baltimore, the racial justice movement sparked by Floyd's death put police departments in a difficult spot. On the one hand, a small percentage of protesters was genuinely willing to torch buildings or engage in violence. On the other, they have the First Amendment right to protest, and in fact aggressive tactics by the police might have sparked some of the violence and mayhem.

Whatever the root causes, the insurance industry's trade group would later report that the Floyd protests were the single most expensive episode of civil disorder in American history. The industry estimated it would have to pay out between $1 billion and $2 billion in claims stemming from property damage to buildings across the country. In addition, more than a dozen people were killed during the two weeks of unrest. In the aftermath of those protests, police came under pressure from activists for heavy-handed tactics: monitoring lawful protests, infiltrating activist spaces under false pretenses, and using social media footage to track down and arrest protesters suspected of vandalism or violence.

Then, a few months later, on January 6, 2021, Trump supporters stormed the U.S. Capitol, intending to disrupt the certification of the 2020 election. They came to D.C. for a number of "Stop the Steal" events and rallies around Congress's ceremonial certification of the election, egged on by Trump's repeated false claims that the election was tainted or stolen. After Trump spoke at an event on the Ellipse near the White House, a riled-up crowd overwhelmed law enforcement and breached the Capitol complex.

Suddenly those same tools that had been demonized by left-leaning activists seemed necessary to fight the growing threat of right-wing violence. Social media sleuths dubbing themselves the Sedition Hunters would comb through the massive volumes of available online material to hunt down the Capitol rioters. And after January 6, the FBI would expand its social media monitoring efforts. It would purchase five thousand licenses to Babel Street—a contract that could be worth as much as $27 million over five years. In a contracting document, the FBI wrote that tools such as Babel Street "provide critical information without being intrusive because the data they return is publicly available."

How should law enforcement approach the question of monitoring social media, a technology that has become the new public square? This is a complicated question, and there is no easy answer. Aggressively police public and private digital spaces, and you risk chilling speech or curtailing First Amendment–protected protest movements. And the same tools that Western social media surveillance companies develop for public safety programs in the United States can easily be repurposed by authoritarian regimes to map out networks of activists and curtail political dissent against undemocratic or corrupt governments.

But there is an equal danger to ignoring digital spaces. Pay no attention to rhetoric on them, and you miss the warning signs of violence and radicalization. A sprawling array of new forms of online radicalism have sprung up in recent years: the devotees of a self-styled government "insider" who call themselves QAnon, "incels" who foment hateful, misogynistic speech, white nationalists who advocate for turning the United States into an ethno-state, and much more. Most members of these communities are engaging in legally protected speech, no matter how bizarre or extreme it may seem to outsiders. But occasionally, members of these communities do spill over into real-world violence. When they do, officials responsible for public safety come under intense pressure for their failures to keep tabs on dangerous individuals.

And so law enforcement is caught in a difficult position. Surveil online speech too heavily, and they are accused of violating the constitutional rights of Americans to voice edgy, provocative opinions. But if they miss the online warning signs of a terrorist attack or mass shooting, they are accused of failing to protect the public.

With legislatures moving at their typical glacial pace when it comes to new technology, the social media platforms themselves have emerged as the only entities with any plausible ability to enforce rules. Twitter and Facebook have policies against inauthentic behavior on their platforms, but their efforts have not stopped undercover accounts from becoming a widespread practice. Facebook will occasionally send letters to police departments demanding they stop creating fake profiles, but there is little it can do to make departments comply. There is even an entire industry of companies that set up, age, and then sometimes sell fake profiles in bulk to the government. But Twitter in particular has cracked down on the use of its platform to monitor protests—though most of these conversations about what the rules are have taken place largely outside the public's view between the social media platform and the vendors that buy its data.

In February 2022, U.S. military intelligence officials stationed in Japan were testing out a product made by a company called Echosec, one of Babel Street's competitors. Trying out the platform on live data, they discovered that when searching Twitter through Echosec's platform, they were unable to search for the term "protests."

Echosec's internal policies instructed service members not to do anything illegal or evil using the platform. "I don't understand how searching for protest activity could be either when looking at a US social media platform," the military official wrote after his search didn't work.

The Echosec sales rep explained that Twitter prevented anyone from searching the term "protest" "due to the fact that searching this term may be to follow or monitor individuals." If Echosec didn't want to be cut off like Babel Street, it had to follow Twitter's rules.

Caught between a restive user base and governments hungry to buy data, Twitter was choosing its users.[*]

Yet the questions raised by easy acquisition of data on the global population were about to get thornier. Social media often was public. What kind of expectation of privacy do you have when you live stream yourself breaching the Capitol, for example? But what happens when highly revealing data is generated merely as a by-product of using the web—bought, sold, and traded by companies the general public has no idea even exist?

---

[*]   In October 2022, the billionaire Elon Musk completed his purchase of Twitter. He would later rename it X. As this chapter deals with historical events, I have called it by what it was called at the time: Twitter. How Musk will deal with these thorny questions remains to be seen. I was in months-long discussions with Twitter to speak about its policies on these questions as part of my reporting for this book. After Musk's acquisition, the company stopped replying to journalists. The email account that reporters used to ask the company for comment now replies with a poop emoji.

PART III

EXHAUST

CHAPTER 12

They Know How Bad
You Are at *Angry Birds*

THE U.S. INTELLIGENCE COMMUNITY, 2013–2015

For a few minutes on January 28, 2014, anyone who visited the website of the mobile game *Angry Birds* would have seen a puzzling sight. The quirky and wildly popular game, developed by the Finnish developer Rovio Entertainment, involves flinging a variety of flightless birds to destroy evil green pigs and had accrued tens of millions of downloads since being launched in late 2009.

For a short time that day on the home page of angrybirds.com, however, visitors were greeted by an unusual illustration. Emblazoned above the furrowed eyebrows and angry sneer of a red desert cardinal known as Red J. Bird was the logo of the U.S. National Security Agency. And underneath it, in big letters, were the words "SPYING BIRDS."

The Syrian Electronic Army—a hacking collective dedicated to causing online mischief in support of the embattled regime of the Syrian president, Bashar al-Assad—claimed on Twitter that a "friend" of the group was responsible for the defacement of Rovio's website, which the developer quickly fixed.

But what had provoked this outburst of hacker anger directed at a time-sucking mobile phone game in the first place? The answer was buried in several slide decks released by Edward Snowden, a man who had been a trusted intelligence community insider before turning vigilante whistleblower. For the last six months beginning on June 6, 2013, reporters had been writing stories based off Snowden's trove of classified documents, offering an unvarnished glimpse into the surveillance activities of the United States and its allies. And much of the global public did not like what it saw.

According to documents released by Snowden, the U.S. government was collecting metadata from the Verizon telephone network on millions of U.S. subscribers. Other revelations would continue week after week: reports into U.S. hacking of Chinese servers and German telecoms; bugging the offices of the European Union; details of how the Five Eyes intelligence alliance (the United States, the U.K., Canada, New Zealand, and Australia) collected massive amounts of telecom and internet information from across the global internet. The list of individual stories based on the Snowden disclosures went on and on—airing the sources and methods of the United States and its allied intelligence agencies on the front pages of newspapers around the world. For the first time, the global public was forced to confront the extent to which their digital privacy had been traded in the name of national security and public safety.

The latest revelation drawn from the Snowden trove had come a few hours before Rovio's website had been defaced. *The Guardian*, *The New York Times*, and the American investigative journalism outfit ProPublica all published a coordinated barrage of stories detailing how the NSA and its British counterpart, the Government Communications Headquarters (GCHQ), were taking advantage of "leaky" mobile phone apps to collect data. Or in the words of Britain's GCHQ, which created one of the slideshows that the stories were based on: "We Know How Bad You Are at 'Angry Birds.'" The slides showed that GCHQ was using a system called BADASS: the

BEGAL Automated Deployment and Survey System—though one cheeky slide referred to it as the "BEGAL Automated Development / Deployment and Something Something."

The full contours of BEGAL have never been revealed, but the slides suggest a system with the capability to collect, analyze, and run queries against large amounts of raw internet traffic—access that GCHQ was probably getting by tapping fiber-optic cables or other internet infrastructure. BEGAL appears to refer to a source or a repository of the raw internet traffic itself, and BADASS is a system to search it.

Ad exchanges and analytics firms were telling mobile device users that their data was anonymized and used only for targeting advertising. But GCHQ and other government intelligence agencies had eyeballs on that traffic, Snowden's documents suggested. One slide, called "Abusing BADASS for Fun and Profit"—with the "Ab" in "Abusing" crossed out for humorous effect to make it read "Using BADASS for Fun and Profit"—revealed that it could search for specific targets through app data. In other words, it could identify when a target opened *Angry Birds* or any other mobile app if that data transited a network GCHQ had access to.

Because the *Angry Birds* app wanted to serve ads to its users and because the advertising networks with which it partnered did not take any precautions to secure the data as it transited the internet, the app was inadvertently making all of its users' information available to spy agencies. And because those ad networks wanted to target individualized ads, they were collecting a raft of personal information from those consumers that was also ending up in the hands of the spy agencies. The problem was by no means unique to *Angry Birds;* nearly every app that transmitted data unencrypted over the web had the same problem. GCHQ boasted about its collection abilities against people making queries on Google Maps: GCHQ's collection capability "effectively means that anyone using Google Maps on a smartphone is working in support of a GCHQ system."

This was digital *exhaust*—a by-product of using the apps and internet services that was being emitted over networks that the NSA and GCHQ had backdoor access to. These intelligence agencies, operating in secret, had figured out a way to turn that exhaust into a potent tracking tool.

Edward Snowden didn't only reveal that the government had access to data on the global population; he also showed exactly how that data was procured. First, as he demonstrated, huge amounts of data were being collected from some of the nation's largest technology companies. This is called downstream collection because it was coming from the providers of consumer-facing internet services like email, digital messaging, and videoconferencing. The biggest downstream collection program, PRISM, was aimed at nine major U.S. technology companies: Microsoft, Yahoo, Google, Facebook, Paltalk, YouTube, Skype, AOL, and Apple. The NSA obtained secret court orders that required these companies to search their servers for keywords or messages to and from certain accounts or users, and the companies in question were prohibited from telling the public. But unlike search warrants, which must be issued on a case-by-case basis, four secret court orders signed between 2004 and 2007 were enough to authorize surveillance on nearly 120,000 people through the program.

And then there was upstream collection: data from companies like AT&T and Verizon that provided internet services or infrastructure. This is the kind of surveillance that was probably being used in BEGAL that allowed GCHQ to see raw network traffic from mobile apps. In this kind of collection, spy agencies tap directly into this internet traffic, copy it, and look for certain keywords. Third, Snowden revealed the extent to which the United States and its allies were breaking into computer systems they couldn't intercept other ways through what is called computer-network exploitation, or the unauthorized hacking of devices, servers, and systems by taking advantage of flaws or errors in computer software code.

David Anderson, an independent British auditor appointed to examine U.K. terrorism laws, summed up the impact of the Snowden disclosures: "It was not shocking to discover that no means of communication is immune"; after all, spies had long opened mail or conducted covert surveillance. But the computer age offered the opportunity for spying on a "truly industrial scale," Anderson wrote.

Snowden's revelations sent shock waves through Silicon Valley. Barton Gellman, one of the reporters who cultivated Snowden as a source and broke many of the key stories based on the trove of leaked documents while writing for *The Washington Post,* recalled in his book *Dark Mirror* sitting with a Google engineer trying to understand some diagram he had obtained from Snowden and watching the engineer's eyebrows shoot up. "Mo-ther fuckers. . . . I've spent years securing this network. Fuck those guys." The situation was this: the NSA had essentially broken into Google's network through a back door—even as the search giant was cooperating with lawful demands signed by a secret surveillance court that had come in through the front door. It would be like if the police showed up with a warrant to search your house in the afternoon and then came back at 3:00 a.m., pried open a window, and climbed in to have another look around at night just for good measure.

The internet would never be the same. In response to the Snowden disclosures, tech companies made major changes. For one, internet services began encrypting more and more of the traffic they send along the internet, making it much more difficult to intercept upstream.

Some companies went further, thwarting even government efforts to obtain data from them armed with a warrant. Apple, for example, has made it impossible to read the content of its own customers' messages on the company's iMessage platform as well as many of its other services in some cases. It built that feature into the platform from the ground up, a fact that has been a sore spot in its relationship with law enforcement agencies ever since. Apple also encrypts the hard drives of its computers and phones by default—meaning the data can't be read by anyone who doesn't have the pass code.

Increasing concern about privacy and government surveillance became a selling point for some technologies, heralding a shift in consumer awareness, at least among a segment of tech-savvy consumers. Messenger services like WhatsApp and Signal began touting encryption and the fact that no one, not even the companies, could read messages between users. Services like Proton Mail and Tutanota, which offered the same benefit to email users, grew in popularity. These services could usually not be collected upstream *or* downstream. The only option for interception was for the government to hack an end-point device like a phone or a computer and try to obtain data from there—or even to seize it directly from a subject and try to break its pass code.

Almost overnight, encryption had become the norm, and the government's interception capabilities were severely diminished. The FBI director, James Comey, in a speech in October 2014 at the Brookings Institution in Washington, D.C., took U.S. tech companies to task for making it difficult or nearly impossible to unlock devices or intercept data. The FBI said terrorists and criminals were increasingly "going dark"—using technology that was very difficult to surveil.

"It's time that the post-Snowden pendulum be seen as having swung too far in one direction—in a direction of fear and mistrust," Comey said.

In his own cautious, deliberate way, Senator Ron Wyden had spent the decade since the Total Information Awareness fight trying to warn Americans about many of the things that Snowden made public.

In 2006, at a public hearing, Wyden pressed intelligence community leaders about what had happened to the Total Information Awareness program: Was it true that it had mostly survived? Wyden knew the answer; he had access to the classified annex that had secretly preserved large swaths of the research. But his aim was to get the intelligence community to answer to the American people. In response to Wyden's question, General Michael Hayden, who had been head of the NSA for six years, replied, "I'd like to answer in closed session"—meaning the classified portion of the hearing that would be held out of public view. Wyden didn't want the answer in closed session. He thought the public deserved to know.

This kind of performance would become Wyden's signature style on the Intelligence Committee: asking intelligence community leaders tough questions in open forums. He hinted at the existence of a business records program before Edward Snowden would go on to reveal it. In 2011, Wyden gave a speech on the Senate floor saying there were secret interpretations of the Patriot Act that the public did not understand. "When people learn about intelligence activities that are outside the lines of what is generally believed to be permitted, public reaction tends to be quite negative," he warned prophetically. That was exactly what would happen when Snowden went public with his documents.

In March 2013, the then director of national intelligence, James Clapper, appeared in front of the Senate Intelligence Committee.

"Does the NSA collect any type of data at all on millions, or hundreds of millions, of Americans?" Wyden asked. "No, sir," replied Clapper. "It does not?" Wyden said, eyebrows arched, in a surprised tone bordering on incredulous. "Not wittingly," Clapper said.

This entire scene was Kabuki theater. Clapper knew the answer was yes. Wyden knew the answer was yes. And neither was allowed to say it in a public hearing. Wyden didn't exactly blindside Clapper with this question: his Senate staff had provided notice to Clapper's staff that he planned to ask this well in advance of the hearing. And sure enough, months later, Snowden would reveal that the NSA had a program that collected all the phone records of every American and stored them in order to analyze whom terrorist suspects were calling. It was authorized under a very generous interpretation of the "business records" provision of the Patriot Act, which had been stretched to allow the NSA to collect *all* the telephone records—not the content of the calls, but who called whom and for how long—of everyone in America as business records.

The Clapper-Wyden exchange went mostly unnoticed at the time, but in the wake of Snowden's revelations critics accused Clapper of lying to Congress, which was a criminal offense. Some even called for him to be prosecuted. Clapper, for his part, said in hindsight his answer was the "least untruthful manner" to answer a question that calls for a classified answer and claimed to have been confused by the context of Wyden's question. He's also sometimes blamed a memory lapse—something Wyden doesn't buy. "I'm not a psychiatrist, but I find it pretty implausible that the head of national intelligence doesn't understand a question," the senator said.

After that, reporters began to pay attention to Ron Wyden's questions in public Intelligence Committee hearings the way that Cold War Soviet watchers would pay attention to the seating chart at the meetings of the Central Committee of the Communist Party or the way that Roman priests would read goat entrails for omens. *Is he trying to tell us something?* we would whisper to each other when he asked out-of-left-field questions. Snowden himself has claimed that Wyden's interaction with Clapper was a key moment in convincing him that he needed to act to make public information about the NSA's activities.*

Despite his pushes for transparency, Wyden had never unilaterally made any classified information public on his own accord. That claim to fame goes to Senator Mike Gravel, who in 1971 defied the Nixon administration's attempt to censor a classified and highly critical history of the Vietnam War and put it into the congressional record. At first, he tried to read it on the Senate floor, but the chamber lacked a quorum that evening. So he convened a panel that he chaired, the Senate Subcommittee on Public Buildings and Grounds, and read the text of the Pentagon Papers into the official record that way.

In one interview with Wyden, I asked him why he had never done what Gravel did. When these programs disturbed him, why didn't he just give a speech telling the American people about them? "I believe I can make a big difference by being somebody in the room who asks hard questions," Wyden replied. In other words, it might be *legal* for

---

* This remains disputed. The timeline of when Snowden began amassing documents does not correspond to the Wyden-Clapper interaction.

Wyden to do that—he'd be protected by the speech or debate clause of the Constitution, which gives members of Congress near-total legal immunity for actions they undertake as part of their official duties— but that would probably be the end of his tenure on the Intelligence Committee. He could be stripped of his committee post or even censured by the Senate for such an action, even if he couldn't be prosecuted.

Wyden didn't want to be thrown off the Intelligence Committee. He would find a way to comply with the rules and be a skeptical voice about intelligence programs and authorities.

"There is real value in having people in the room who are asking hard questions," he said.

In the years after 9/11, the political winds had shifted and the public's willingness to tolerate an invasive surveillance regime in the name of public safety had waned sharply.

For their part, NSA lawyers were befuddled by the Snowden fallout, insisting that the programs in question were in line with the laws that Congress had passed and fit squarely within the intelligence agency's long understanding of its constitutional limits. But it didn't matter. A judge might have signed off on these collection programs, but that didn't mean the public had been brought along. In short, the government didn't have a legal problem; it had a public relations problem. People around the world had gotten a look at the post-9/11 global surveillance regime, and they didn't like what they saw.

"The fact of the matter is that America was founded on the basic principle that we don't trust government the distance we can throw it," Ronald Marks, a former Central Intelligence Agency official and Capitol Hill staffer, told me in an interview. "When you collect information on a society, that's a very intimate act. And spying has always run right up to the line. Snowden is symptomatic of a society that doesn't trust government."

In January 2014, the same month that Rovio's website was hacked,

President Obama gave a speech at the Justice Department in the hopes of quelling the controversy. With no signs that journalists were done mining the Snowden archive for new stories about U.S. and British collection capabilities, the president's speech highlighted the growing paradox that the government was confronting. Even as the public was revolting over mass surveillance by the National Security Agency, increasing amounts of data were being compiled by the likes of Google, Facebook, Amazon, and a growing number of advertising technology companies, data brokers, and app developers.

"The challenges to our privacy do not come from government alone. Corporations of all shapes and sizes track what you buy, store and analyze our data, and use it for commercial purposes; that's how those targeted ads pop up on your computer and your smartphone periodically. But all of us understand that the standards for government surveillance must be higher. Given the unique power of the state, it is not enough for leaders to say 'trust us,'" the president said.

In other words, the issue cut both ways. The government has immense power to arrest, to incarcerate, and even to target for death. With that kind of capability, the state's activities ought to come under more scrutiny than commercial entities. On the other hand, the government's mission of rooting out terrorism, stopping crime, and ensuring public safety seemed much more important than delivering personalized advertising for kitchen appliances or compact SUVs.

For corporate America, though, Obama's remarks were an unwelcome spotlight on business practices that many consumers were beginning to find annoying at best and invasive at worst. The Direct Marketing Association, a trade group that represents many digital advertisers, put out a statement after the president's speech stating that the organization "was disappointed to see the responsible use of consumer data for marketing purposes conflated with 'government surveillance.'

"As revelations regarding NSA practices have come to light in recent months, DMA has been working hard to make it clear to policy-makers and the media that issues around government surveillance are not related to data-driven marketing," the association continued.

But that was not entirely true. By the time of Obama's speech in 2014, a quiet shift was under way. In response to the public blowback over the Snowden revelations and the increased encryption that companies were adding to all sorts of consumer services, the U.S. intelligence community was losing access to data it had long relied on for many of its surveillance programs, as Comey had noted.

But it would not take long for the government to find new ways to fill that void. And one possible solution was in the reams of consumer and behavioral data that members of the Direct Marketing Association had been amassing for years.

CHAPTER 13

Location and Motive

PLANETRISK AND U.S. SPECIAL FORCES, 2015 ONWARD

Mike Yeagley saw both the promise and the pitfalls of advertising data. After all, it was he who had run around Washington sounding the alarm about the risk of Grindr data for national security. At the same time, he had played a key role in bringing advertising data into government in the first place. Yeagley had spent years working as a technology "scout"—looking for capabilities or data sets that existed in the private sector and helping to bring them into government.

Remember my story of the wine-soaked dinner party, the one that set this reporting journey in motion—the night I first heard of the secretive program designed to take advantage of advertising data? I didn't know it at the time, but the program manager for the program I learned about that night was Yeagley. He helped pioneer a technique that some of its practitioners would jokingly come to call "ADINT"— a play on the intelligence community's jargon for different sources of intelligence. More often, though, ADINT was known in government circles as adtech data.

Adtech used the basic lifeblood of digital commerce to deliver valuable intelligence information from the trail of technical data that comes off nearly all mobile phones. One technology consultant who works on projects for the U.S. government explained it this way to me: "The advertising technology ecosystem is the largest information-gathering enterprise ever conceived by man. And it wasn't built by the government."

In the post-Snowden world, more and more traffic was being encrypted. No longer could the NSA pull data from the advertisers that serviced *Angry Birds* just by tapping fiber-optic cables. But there was perhaps a work-around: Could they just *buy it* from commercial entities?

Yeagley was part of a team that would try to find out. Over the course of several years, beginning around 2015, numerous U.S. government research and development agencies would provide funding for the effort. The result: a military program led by JSOC, the Joint Special Operations Command, with a mission to take terrorists off the battlefield using nothing more than ad data streaming from their phones.

In 2016, a company called PlaceIQ hired Yeagley. PlaceIQ was a pioneer in the location data market. Duncan McCall, its founder, had once participated in an overland driving race from London to Gambia across the land-mine-strewn Western Sahara. He had eschewed the usual practice of hiring an expensive Bedouin guide to help ensure safe passage through the area. Instead, he found online a GPS route that someone else had posted from a few days earlier on a message board. McCall was able to download the route, load it into his own GPS device, and follow the same safe path. On that drive through the Western Sahara, McCall recalled dreaming up the idea for what would become PlaceIQ to capture all of the geospatial data that consumers were emitting and generate insights. At first they were using data from the photo-sharing website Flickr, but eventually they would start tapping the mobile ad exchanges. It would be the start of a new business model—one that would prove highly successful.

Yeagley was hired after PlaceIQ took an investment from the CIA's venture capital arm, In-Q-Tel. Just as it had poured money into numerous social media monitoring services, In-Q-Tel had also become interested in geospatial data. The CIA was interested in software that could analyze and understand the geographic movement of people and things. It wanted to be able to answer questions like were two people trying to conceal that they were traveling together? The CIA had planned to use the software with its own proprietary data, but of course government agencies of all kinds eventually became interested in the kind of raw data that commercial entities like PlaceIQ had.

While working there, Yeagley realized that the data itself might be valuable to the government, too. PlaceIQ was fine selling software to the government but was not prepared to sell its data to the feds. So Yeagley approached a different company called PlanetRisk—one of the hundreds and hundreds of tiny start-ups with ties to the U.S. government dotted around office parks in Northern Virginia. In theory, a government defense contractor offered a more secure environment than a civilian company like PlaceIQ to do the kind of work he had in mind.

PlanetRisk straddled the corporate world and the government contracting space—building data tools and products that had national security applications as well as uses for corporate security. It was staffed by veterans of the SKOPE program, the pioneering intelligence fusion cell that had bolstered Stanley McChrystal and JSOC in Iraq. Mark Dumas, who co-founded PlanetRisk, previously ran a company called Spatial Data Analytics Corporation, which had served SKOPE's primary technology provider. PlanetRisk was building products that were aimed at helping customers understand the relative dangers of various spots around the world. For example, a company that wanted to establish a store or an office somewhere in the world might turn to PlanetRisk to analyze data on crime, civil unrest, and extreme weather as they vary geographically.

PlanetRisk hired Yeagley in 2016 as vice president of global defense—essentially a sales and business development job. The aim was for him to develop his adtech technology inside the contractor, which might try to sell it to various government agencies. Yeagley brought with him some government funding from his relationships around town in the defense and intelligence research communities.

PlanetRisk's earliest sales demo was about Syria: quantifying the crush of refugees flowing out of Syria after years of civil war and the advancing ISIS forces. From a commercial data broker called UberMedia, PlanetRisk had obtained location data on Aleppo—the besieged Syrian city that had been at the center of some of the fiercest fighting between government forces and U.S.-backed rebels. It was an experiment in understanding what was possible. Could you even obtain location information on mobile phones in Syria? It was hardly a hot spot for mobile advertising; Western data brokers wouldn't find too many interested clients trying to do ad targeting or real estate analytics on a war zone.

But to the company's surprise, the answer was yes. There were 168,786 mobile devices present in the city of Aleppo in UberMedia's data set, which measured mobile phone movements during the month of December 2015. From there, the company continued digging through the data. The data was clear: they could see the movement of refugees around the world.

The discovery that there was extensive data in Syria was a watershed. No longer was advertising merely a way to sell products; it was a way to peer into the habits and routines of billions. "Mobile devices are the lifeline for everyone, even refugees," Yeagley said.

PlanetRisk had sampled data from a range of location brokers—Cuebiq, X-Mode, SafeGraph, PlaceIQ, and Gravy Analytics—before settling on UberMedia (the company has no relation to the rideshare app Uber). UberMedia was started by the veteran technology executive Bill Gross, who had helped invent keyword-targeted ads—the kinds of ads that appear on Google when you search a specific term—when he started the search engine GoTo.com. Gross would step aside in 2015 and hand the reins to his chief technology officer, Gladys Kong. UberMedia was originally conceived as a social-media-focused company called TweetUp before Twitter complained that some of its products were trademark violations. It pivoted to becoming an advertising company and did a lot of its business on the advertising exchange that Twitter would eventually buy called MoPub—helping other customers target ads on Twitter's platform. But over time, like many other companies in this space, UberMedia would realize that it could do more than just target consumers with advertising. With access to MoPub and other ad exchanges, it could save bid requests that contained geolocation information and broker that data. Now, this was technically against the rules of most of the ad exchanges, but there was little way to police the practice. At its peak, UberMedia was collecting about 200,000 bid requests *per second* on mobile devices around the world.*

PlanetRisk had not been entirely forthright with UberMedia. To get the data, Yeagley fibbed. He told UberMedia that he needed the data as part of PlanetRisk's work with a humanitarian organization when in fact the client was a defense contractor doing research work funded by the Pentagon. (UberMedia's CEO would later learn the truth about what Mike Yeagley wanted the data for. And others in the company had their own suspicions. "Humanitarian purposes" would be said with a wink and nod around the company among employees who knew or suspected what was going on with Yeagley's data contracts.) Either way, UberMedia wasn't vetting its customers closely. It was more eager to make a sale than it was concerned about the privacy implications of selling the movement patterns of millions of people.

Yeagley called the demo for PlanetRisk's commercial phone tracking product Locomotive—a portmanteau of "location" and "motive."

---

* In 2022, UberMedia was purchased by a company called Near Intelligence. In 2023, I contacted four ad exchanges and asked them if they were aware that Near was saving bid requests and selling the data to an arm of U.S. intelligence. All four ad exchanges said they had cut Near off after my question.

Yeagley's daughter, who was then ten, helped him name it. The total cost to build out a small demo was about $600,000. They got funding from CTTSO, the same organization that funded SUNet, as well as another Pentagon research funding arm, the Defense Innovation Unit. As the PlanetRisk team put Locomotive through the paces and dug into the data, they found one interesting story after another.

In one instance they could see a device moving back and forth between Syria and the West—a potential concern given ISIS's interest in recruiting westerners, training them, and sending them back to carry out terrorist attacks. But as the PlanetRisk team took a closer look, the pattern of the device's behavior indicated that it likely belonged to a humanitarian aid worker. They could track that person's device to UN facilities and a refugee camp, unlikely locales for Islamic State fighters to hang out.

They could track world leaders through Locomotive, too. The company had acquired a data set on Russia and realized they could track phones in the Russian president Vladimir Putin's entourage. The phones moved everywhere that Putin did. They concluded the devices in question did not actually belong to Putin himself; Russian state security and counterintelligence were better than that. Instead, they believed the devices belonged to the drivers, the security personnel, the political aides, and other support staff around the Russian president; those people's phones were trackable in the advertising data. As a result, PlanetRisk knew where Putin was going and who was in his entourage.

There were other oddities. In one data set, they found one phone kept transiting between the United States and North Korea. The device would attend a Korean church in the United States on Sundays. Its owner appeared to work at a GE factory, a prominent American corporation with significant intellectual property and technology that a regime like Pyongyang would be interested in. Why was it traveling back and forth between the United States and North Korea, a regime that is not exactly known as a tourist destination? PlanetRisk considered raising the issue with either the U.S. intelligence agencies or the company but ultimately decided there wasn't much they could do. And they didn't necessarily want their phone tracking tool to be widely known. They never got to the bottom of it.

And most alarmingly, PlanetRisk began seeing evidence of the U.S. military's own missions in the Locomotive data. Phones would appear at American military installations such as Fort Bragg in North Carolina and MacDill Air Force Base in Tampa, Florida—home of some of the most skilled U.S. special operators with JSOC and other U.S. Special Operations Command units. They would then transit through third-party countries like Turkey and Canada before eventually arriving in northern Syria, where they were clustering at the abandoned Lafarge cement factory outside the town of Kobane.

It dawned on the PlanetRisk team that these were U.S. special operators converging at an unannounced military facility. Months later, their suspicions would be publicly confirmed; eventually the U.S. government would acknowledge the facility was a forward operating base for personnel deployed in the anti-ISIS campaign.

Even worse, through Locomotive, they were getting data in pretty close to real time. UberMedia's data was usually updated every twenty-four hours or so. But sometimes, they saw movement that had occurred as recently as fifteen or thirty minutes earlier. The famous World War II propaganda poster "Loose Lips Might Sink Ships" warned of this very phenomenon—that casual talk about military operations could cost lives. The twenty-first-century version was about data. Here were some of the best trained special operations units in the world operating at an unannounced base. Yet their signature was showing up in UberMedia's advertising data. While Locomotive was a closely held project meant for government use, UberMedia's data was available for purchase by anyone who could come up with a plausible excuse. It wouldn't be difficult for the Chinese or Russian government to get this kind of data by setting up a shell company with a cover story, just as Mike Yeagley had done.

Initially, PlanetRisk was sampling data country by country, but it didn't take long for the team to wonder what it would cost to buy the entire world. The sales rep at UberMedia provided the answer: for a few hundred thousand a month, the company would provide a global feed of every phone on earth that the company could collect on. The economics of that were impressive. For the military and the intelligence community, a few hundred thousand a month was essentially a rounding error—it cost $30,000 an hour to operate a modern fighter plane and more than $6 million per day to operate a carrier strike group. The FY 2020 intelligence budget was $62.7 billion. Locomotive was a powerful intelligence tool funded for peanuts.

Locomotive blew away Pentagon brass. One government official demanded midway through the demo that the rest of it be conducted inside a SCIF, a secure government facility where classified information could be discussed. Back then, in the military, anything that involved phone tracking was inherently classified. The official didn't understand how or what PlanetRisk was doing but assumed it must be a secret. A PlanetRisk employee at the briefing was mystified: "We were like, well, this is just stuff we've seen commercially. We're not doing anything wrong. We just licensed the data and sampled it and looked at it." After all, how could marketing data be classified?

Government officials were so enthralled by the capability that PlanetRisk was asked to keep Locomotive quiet. It wouldn't be classified, but the company would be asked to tightly control word of the capability to give the military time to take advantage of public ignorance of this kind of data and turn it into an operational surveillance program.

And the same executive remembered leaving another meeting with a different government official. They were on the elevator together when one official asked, could you figure out who is cheating on their spouse?

Yeah, I guess you could, the PlanetRisk executive answered.

That risk of sexual blackmail was not hypothetical.

————

Alejandro Bermudez is a well-known journalist who covers the Catholic Church for the Catholic News Agency. In 2018, a man called him on his cell phone out of the blue and asked to meet.

Bermudez claimed not to remember the man's name. He said it's not unusual for him to get phone calls from crackpots or disgruntled Catholics claiming to have explosive information about the church. He agreed to the meeting.

The man—a white male in his thirties of average build and a bit below average height—met him in Denver, where Bermudez lived. The man implied he was affiliated with the U.S. intelligence community. He claimed to have access to some kind of data source that would show top Catholic officials frequenting gay bars and saunas in violation of their vows of chastity and in defiance of the Catholic Church's condemnation of homosexual conduct. The data could identify clergy who downloaded hookup apps like Grindr and Tinder, the man said.

This man implied he had ongoing access to such data and that it was sophisticated from a technical standpoint, requiring a fair amount of data-mining skill to make sense of it. He dangled a specific tidbit to Bermudez: one well-known priest in particular could be identified easily. And he offered to keep feeding Bermudez information over time. In return, Bermudez was asked to provide the information to Catholic officials in the hopes of privately cracking down on priests who violate their vows. He declined. But he was not the only Catholic journalist being peddled this information.

Three years later, a small conservative Catholic blog named *The Pillar* founded by two former colleagues of Bermudez's published an explosive story. The site reported that Jeffrey Burrill, the top administrator for the U.S. Conference of Catholic Bishops, was a regular user of Grindr. *The Pillar*'s story, published July 20, 2021, reported that Burrill "visited gay bars and private residences while using a location-based hookup app in numerous cities from 2018 to 2020, even while traveling on assignment for the U.S. bishops' conference." The publication described its source as "commercially available records of app signal data obtained by *The Pillar*." It was later revealed that a group of

Denver-based conservative Catholics formed a group called Catholic Laity and Clergy for Renewal that funded the acquisition of the data that was given to *The Pillar.*

Burrill resigned his leadership post within the conference, and spent a year on leave, before resuming his ministry at a church in his home state of Wisconsin.

"This was something that was obtained perfectly legally and given to us perfectly legally," Ed Condon, one of the editors of *The Pillar,* said in a podcast released shortly after their story published. That was the exact same justification the government used.

But the question remains: Who was the man involved in a national security project who approached Bermudez? Was he part of the program Mike Yeagley had been running? Was UberMedia the source of all this data? It's hard to know for sure, but UberMedia is one of the few that openly offered a commercial data set that included the name of the app that the data was drawn from. Bermudez's source perfectly described the Locomotive project, which was going from a demo to an operational program at this time.

None of this is an abstract concern. I'm here to tell you if you've ever been on a dating app that wanted your location or if you ever granted a weather app permission to know where you are 24/7, there is a good chance a detailed log of your precise movement patterns has been vacuumed up and saved in some data bank somewhere that tens of thousands of total strangers have access to. That includes intelligence agencies. It includes foreign governments. It includes private investigators. It even includes nosy journalists.

If you cheated on your spouse in the last few years and you were careless about your location data settings, there is a good chance there is evidence of that in data that is available for purchase. If you checked yourself into a mental hospital or inpatient drug rehab, that data is probably sitting in a data bank somewhere. Are you being treated for erectile dysfunction at a sexual health clinic? That data is obtainable by strangers. If you told your boss you took a sick day and went to the beach or interviewed at a rival company, that could be in there. If you visited a divorce lawyer's office but then decided not to go through with it and reconciled with your spouse, your visit might nevertheless be logged. If you frequent gay bars or boutique sex shops and aren't open about your habits or lifestyle, someone could figure it all out. If you let emotion get the best of you and threw a brick through a store-front window during the George Floyd protests, well, your cell phone might link you to that bit of vandalism. And if you once had a few pints before causing a car crash and drove off without calling the po-lice, data telling that story likely still exists somewhere.

We all have a vague sense that our cell phone carriers have this data about us. But law enforcement generally needs to go obtain a court order to get that. And it takes evidence of a crime to get such an order. But this is a different kind of privacy nightmare.

To illustrate this point, I once met a disgruntled former employee of a company that competed against UberMedia and PlaceIQ. He had absconded with several gigabytes of data from his former company. It was only a small sampling of data, but it represented the comprehen-sive movements of tens of thousands of people for a few weeks. Lots of those people could be traced back to a residential address with a great deal of confidence. He offered me the data so I could see how invasive and powerful it was.

What can I do with this—*hypothetically*? I asked. In theory, could you help me draw geofences around mental hospitals? Abortion clin-ics? Could you look at phones that checked into a motel midday and stayed for less than two hours?

Easily, he answered.

I never went down that road.

Mike Yeagley wouldn't last at PlanetRisk.

As the company looked to turn Locomotive from a demo into a live product, Yeagley started to believe that his employer was taking the wrong approach. It was looking to build a data visualization plat-form for the government—something like what Babel Street had, but for location data. Yeagley thought it would be better to provide the raw data to the government and let them visualize it in any way they chose. Babel Street and other tool vendors make their money by the number of users inside government that buy a software license. Mike Yeagley wanted to just sell the government the data for a flat fee.

So Yeagley and PlanetRisk parted ways. He took his business relationship with UberMedia with him. PlanetRisk moved on to other lines of work and was eventually sold off in pieces to other defense contractors. Yeagley would land at a company called Aelius Exploitation Technologies, where he would go about trying to turn Locomotive into an actual government program for the Joint Special Operations Command—the terrorist-hunting elite special operations force that had killed bin Laden and Zarqawi and spent the last few years dismantling the ISIS foreign fighter flow.

Aelius Exploitation Technologies would win the contract to service the first version of the program. Locomotive was renamed VISR, which stood for Virtual Intelligence, Surveillance, and Reconnaissance. It would be used as part of an interagency program and would be shared widely inside the U.S. intelligence community. In the *find, fix, finish, exploit, analyze,* and *disseminate* intelligence cycle, it would be used for the "find" part of the equation. It was used not to home in on a terrorist right before a drone strike but rather to generate leads. Basically, the presence of a phone in VISR might be a tipping system that intelligence analysts could use, but they would need to definitively confirm the presence of their target in some other way.

But it was used domestically, too—at least for a short period of time when the FBI wanted to test its usefulness in domestic criminal cases. In October 2017, a man named Stephen Paddock unleashed more than a thousand rounds of ammunition from room 32-135 of the Mandalay Bay Resort and Casino, aiming at thousands of people gathered at a music festival on the Las Vegas Strip below his hotel. VISR data was used to try to generate leads. The FBI did analysis on the data around Paddock's house. They identified his landscaper. They identified a UPS guy. But they never got any real insights into why

Paddock did what he did. In another case, the data was unsuccessfully used to try to identify suspects in the disappearance of the college student Mollie Tibbetts. In 2018, the FBI backed out of the program. The Defense Intelligence Agency, another agency that had access to the VISR data, also acknowledged that it used VISR data on five separate occasions to look inside the United States as part of intelligence-related investigations.

I asked Yeagley at one point how his program was different from what the NSA was doing before, when it was pulling data off apps like *Angry Birds*. "The difference was that I didn't hack, engineer, or steal—I bought it," he replied.

CHAPTER 14

Where You Go Is Who You Are

GRAVY ANALYTICS AND DHS, 2011 ONWARD

In the late afternoon of August 13, 2018, Ivan Lopez was driving his pickup truck east on West County Nineteenth Street in Somerton, Arizona, when he saw behind him the flashing lights of a patrol car. Lopez dutifully pulled over his truck, a 2015 Chevy Silverado with a trailer attached to the hitch, to the side of the rural road that cuts straight through the dusty desert south of Yuma, the nearest big city.

Jose Vasquez, an officer with the San Luis Police Department, approached Lopez. He cited two reasons for the stop: Lopez's trailer didn't have working brake lights, and he appeared to be traveling nine miles per hour over the posted speed limit of fifty miles an hour.

By very slowly running his ID and plates and asking Lopez about what he had been doing that afternoon and what was in the trailer hitched to his car, Vasquez filibustered long enough for a second patrol car and a drug-sniffing dog to arrive. The dog, Laika, circled Lopez's Silverado before barking. Laika's cries gave the two officers the legal justification they needed for a search. Walking around the trailer, they could see two big fifty-gallon rolling utility boxes—the kind often used by contractors on a job site. Lopez told them he had tools stashed in there. The two officers pried open the boxes and found neatly packed rows of plastic-wrapped packages glittering in the late afternoon desert sun—later revealed in lab testing to be more than 6 pounds of fentanyl, 14 pounds of cocaine, 44 pounds of heroin, and 261 pounds of meth.

Lopez had been doing work at his restaurant, he told the officers. He owned a small ramshackle building in the nearby town of San Luis. It was once a Kentucky Fried Chicken but had long since been stripped of anything that might identify it as such and filled with detritus, trash, and construction equipment. Just beyond the restaurant looms the twenty-foot-high barrier wall that divides the small American town from its much larger sister city, San Luis Río Colorado, in the Mexican state of Sonora. When one is driving south on San Luis Plaza Drive, Lopez's restaurant is literally the last building in America.

After he was booked, federal agents got a warrant to search the vacant property. That's when they made another eye-popping discovery. Buried beneath the kitchen of Lopez's abandoned KFC was a tunnel leading to a house on the other side of the U.S.-Mexican border.

After his arrest, Lopez negotiated a plea deal with the government and was sentenced to eighty-four months behind bars. In a press conference that attracted worldwide attention, the Department of Homeland Security touted the arrest as a major blow against sophisticated cartel-linked drug traffickers. However, at the press conference announcing the arrest, federal and local officials omitted the reason San Luis police pulled Lopez over in the first place. The detail was also conspicuously absent in the court documents.

It was not the hunch of a local police officer who spotted a trailer with busted brake lights. Lopez, an American citizen, had been identified by the same kind of adtech data that Mike Yeagley used. What betrayed him and the smugglers using the tunnel were their mobile devices, which broadcast their location into the shadowy world of apps and advertisers. And hundreds of miles away, government analysts saw that phones appeared to be crossing the U.S.-Mexico border at a place where there should have been no port of entry.

All of this was done in secret. No prosecutor or investigator had ever asked a judge for permission to eavesdrop on the comings and goings of phones around Lopez's restaurant. None of the hundreds of millions of Americans whose phones were swept up by these adtech vendors and put into a database accessible by the government were ever given notice that their data may be part of a government surveillance program. Lopez's lawyers had no idea about the warrantless surveillance of Lopez until I called them in the winter of 2020 to tell them what I had learned.

I was the first journalist to reveal the existence of a pipeline of this kind of location data to the U.S. government. In February 2020, my *Wall Street Journal* colleague Michelle Hackman and I shared a first glimpse into what we knew about the Department of Homeland Security's use of adtech data in border security, criminal law enforcement, and deportation operations. The conduit I had first identified was a company called Venntel, but in the months and years to come, I would learn how deep the relationship between government and data brokers of all kinds was.

A substantial amount of time had passed since I had gotten my initial tip about using advertising to track people at the dinner party. The hangover from the wine had faded, but my eagerness to find some way to tell that story hadn't. Revealing the existence of Venntel and its relationship to DHS was the first tangible thing I had been able to publish. The story attracted a great deal of attention, at least in the community of journalists, activists, and regulators who care about privacy issues. Both *The Washington Post* and *The New York Times* wrote editorials citing our reporting on Venntel, arguing that what the government was doing was an end run around the Fourth Amendment. My story also launched an entire series in the *Journal* that would swell to more than two dozen stories and culminate in this book. At the heart of that series is the question I grapple with throughout: How did we get here, and where are we going as a society?

Mike Yeagley built VISR largely for the military and the intelligence community to use overseas. But as happened in so many of these technologies, things that start abroad rarely stay there. Soon, Venntel would start to focus on the domestic market. At first, it started selling to the major federal law enforcement agencies. But eventually, its data would trickle down to state and local police through its partnerships with other vendors. Ultimately it would become available to essentially anyone with a credit card.

And it all started because Jeff White just wanted to help people find cool stuff to do.

White grew up in the Washington, D.C., area and, a high school football star, was recruited by Virginia Tech as a quarterback. But he struggled to balance his athletic commitments with academics. He chose school. After college, White worked stints at AT&T and Caterpillar with the aim of one day becoming CEO of a major company. But he found himself relatively unsatisfied. He remembers the moment he decided he was done with corporate America. At one of his big corporate employers, someone came into his office one day to count the number of ceiling tiles. Apparently, there was a big office reorganization under way, and offices would be doled out according to the quantity of an office's ceiling tiles. That was the last straw. He wasn't going to spend his career at a company worried about ceiling tiles.

So he threw his hat into the fertile Washington, D.C., start-up scene. Few realize it, but the D.C. area is chock-full of technologists, coders, and aspiring entrepreneurs. It's been estimated that there are as many programmers in the Washington, D.C., area as in Silicon Valley, if not more. The backbone of the global internet passes through the Washington area—a historical accident based on the fact that in the 1990s a few of the nascent network operators on the primitive internet decided to connect their networks together there to allow their users to connect to each other and swap data. Upwards of 70 percent of the global internet traffic is still routed through servers in the D.C. metropolitan area. Companies flocked there to take advantage of the fact that physical proximity to network resources resulted in slightly faster speeds. During its 1990s heyday, AOL was headquartered in the Virginia suburbs, and data centers had mushroomed in the surrounding suburbs and exurbs during the 1990s and 2000s.

Ultimately, what distinguishes San Francisco from Washington is the fact that a good chunk of Washington's technology sector is built around the information technology needs of the U.S. federal government, whereas the Bay Area tech scene has nurtured some of the most well-known consumer-facing digital brands of the twenty-first century. Washington is brimming with massive companies that are almost completely unknown to the general public—ManTech, CACI, Booz Allen Hamilton, Jacobs, Leidos, Carahsoft—firms, often with billions in revenue, with almost no consumer-facing brand, all reliant on public sector contracts. To boot, a good chunk of Washington, D.C.'s massive workforce of coders, system administrators, and cybersecurity analysts are bound by top-secret security clearances, standing in stark relief to Silicon Valley's culture of brash self-promotion. Driving west along Virginia's State Route 267 away from Washington, one can see how these contractors have taken over the sea of anonymous officer towers and low-slung suburban office parks that dot the landscape between the Pentagon and Dulles International Airport. They're also clustered in the Maryland exurbs around Fort Meade, where the National Security Agency is based.

White, who still looks every bit the recovering football quarterback, was determined to break into this market. He founded a couple of small companies in the years after 9/11—Blue Canopy, which worked on technology issues for the federal government, and mySBX, which aimed to help other contractors win government business—and sold them both. But by 2011, White had grown tired of the federal contracting world with its byzantine acquisition rules and years-long sales cycles.

So White and a few associates founded a company called TimeRazor with the aim of capitalizing on the burgeoning smartphone revolution. They set up shop in Leesburg, Virginia, a bedroom community about thirty miles outside Washington. TimeRazor pledged to be a smartphone app that would help users find events near them—a sort of Yelp for live events such as concerts, happy hours, and pottery classes. They'd build in features like a drop-down menu of moods that would suggest events to match that mood—maybe a wine tasting if you felt "classy" or a pub quiz night if you wanted something "brainy."

White had good business instincts. He had entered the homeland security and defense market after 9/11, just as Congress was directing hundreds of billions of new spending into the industries. Ten years later, White also correctly foresaw that mobile phones would usher in a revolutionary change in how people communicated, shopped, and moved around the world. He positioned himself to capture a piece of the market. But the company would go in a very unexpected direction.

TimeRazor raised a few million dollars in its first funding round. In a breathless press release, the company announced that it was working with brands like L'Oréal, Universal Pictures, GAP, and Eddie Bauer and with musical acts like Blondie and Mötley Crüe. TimeRazor helped market the Anna Kendrick movie *Pitch Perfect* by offering access to early screenings and collectible memorabilia. The company's developers built some features into its app suggesting events to fill blank spaces in people's calendars in places where they might be. By the end of 2012, TimeRazor had raised a combined $6.4 million across two funding rounds and claimed to have hit one million downloads and aggregated more than 100 million events. It also changed its name to Gravy—first under the branding Find Gravy and then later Gravy Analytics. White explained the new name to *The Washington Post*. What they were offering was "not this thing that dominates your plate, but it's this thing that makes what's on it special. . . . It's the good stuff," he said. (Behind the scenes, concerns had grown about a trademark conflict with Razor, the scooter brand.)

Despite the cheery press releases and the buoyant media interviews, Gravy was struggling to find its footing in the world of mobile apps and events aggregators. What did it want to be? White and his business partners would discover there wasn't all that much money in curating cool events. And mobile apps would prove notoriously hard to monetize.

But one thing Gravy did have was a peek into its users' habits, routines, and interests. This was something that app developers around the world were beginning to take notice of as they wrote software that would run on millions of Android or Apple phones. Most users wouldn't download an app if it cost 99 cents, but they'd happily hand over reams of intricate behavioral details on cost-free apps. That often included the user's precise hour-by-hour location but also so much more: what kind of phone they were using, what language their keyboard was in, what direction their phone was pointed in based on the gyroscope and accelerometer, all of the contacts in their digital address book, all of the photographs on their phone's camera roll, and their daily calendar.

App developers had an unexpected window into the lives of millions of people. Dating apps, navigation apps, social media sites, and even silly mobile games were getting people to opt in to sharing their precise location and a raft of other information on their phones, because hundreds of millions were oblivious to what exactly they were agreeing to when a little pop-up asked if they wanted to grant an app access to their calendar, contacts, photo roll, precise location, and much more. One person who coded a very popular location-based app remembered the epiphany moment one day when he realized he had a window into the lives of people he knew in real life. "I could literally see my neighbors coming and going," he recalled. He never sold the data his app collected, but even years later he remembers a deep feeling of unease about having such an intimate portal into the lives of other people. "It was creepy," he recalled.

But to the Gravy team, this was a possible lifeline. Maybe the way to make money was in *data;* collecting data and getting insights from the user base of their app were going to be much more profitable than

running an events aggregator. Gravy had some permissions on mobile
devices to access the calendars of many of its users. And it also began
to build a tool that would allow it to collect location data as well.
It had been working on a deal with the newspaper publisher Gannett, the owner of *USA Today* and many local publications around the
country. Gannett had invested in Gravy, and in turn Gravy was trying
to help the newspaper publisher build an events app. In exchange,
Gravy was trying to negotiate a partnership that would allow it to insert software into the Gannett app that would allow it to see and collect the real-time movements of the newspaper app's users. That would
allow it to offer insight into what those people were interested in, their
habits and routines. This was far more intimate and detailed information than companies like Acxiom and Seisint had ever imagined they
might be able to one day collect when they started vacuuming up
phone book records and marriage licenses. This was a window into the
lives of billions. And it would quickly be commercialized.

Gravy wasn't the only company that had come to this realization.
Others had jumped into the fray with the same idea: that app data exhaust had real value if packaged correctly. But Gravy would distinguish
itself from the many other companies that were entering the location
data space because it could fuse its detailed calendar of goings-on in
major metropolitan areas with location data. For example, consider
the multisport arena in downtown Washington, D.C., called Capital
One Arena. Some nights the Washington Wizards basketball team
played there. Other evenings, it was the Capitals hockey team. Yet
other nights, the venue would host a Lady Gaga concert or a monster
truck rally. Merely knowing that a consumer was at the arena was not
enough; in order to understand whether that consumer was a hockey
fan or one of Gaga's Little Monsters required understanding what
event was happening there on a given night.

Gravy's belief was that where a person went in the world was the
key to understanding them; it revealed their interests and affinities.
And a phone was a proxy for a person. If that data streaming off

phones could be captured, organized, and analyzed, it would be of tremendous value.

Gravy ended up smack in the middle of arguments over where advertising was going—criticized by some while being hailed as pioneering by others. One early experiment it ran on behalf of the restaurant chain TGI Fridays involved serving ads to consumers based on their location. With Gravy's data, Fridays advertising managers were able to measure the effectiveness of the ad campaign by understanding the foot traffic inside a Fridays before, during, and after the campaign. This scared the hell out of some of the nation's largest advertising firms—the ones that bought ad space on TV, radio, billboards, and web publications by the billions on behalf of Fortune 50 companies. What upstart location companies like Gravy were offering was a scientific way of measuring how effective advertising campaigns were, potentially threatening their core business. Over time, this resistance would fade, but in the early days of the location data business it posed a serious challenge for traditional advertising agencies that were deeply fearful of the idea that a client might be able to actively measure the success of an advertising campaign.

What Gravy and its competitors were offering fit into a larger trend in advertising toward more rigorous measurement and accountability. An old Madison Avenue saying goes, "Half my advertising spend is wasted; the trouble is, I don't know which half." The rise of digital technologies offered a new way to gauge the effectiveness of the billions directed at influencing consumer spending.

Consumer insight-based advertising was not a new idea. For twenty years, the internet browsing habits of consumers have been tracked by marketers in detail through tiny packets of data called cookies. In addition, the effectiveness of web display ads could be measured by how many clicks an ad generated and how many of those clicks were converted to purchases. Advertising could be increasingly personalized and tailored to the specific interests of an individual based on their purchase histories, web browsing, and keywords in their emails. But the explosion of smartphones offered even more options for personalization—and tracking. Suddenly nearly every person carried a device with GPS on it. Advertisers could know where a consumer was in the world and serve them an ad for a nearby store. They could learn where consumers shopped and dined. Retailers could measure foot traffic near proposed retail locations. Gravy's proposition is that it wanted to be the mobile phone equivalent of web cookies.

The company's thesis was that "where you go is who you are," White would say in interviews. "We felt the most powerful signal of who we are as individuals was not the websites we visit, but the places we visit in the events we attend."

Gravy's transition from events calendar to advertising and location analytics was not smooth. Early on, it obtained some low-quality data from real-time bidding networks—the kind Mike Yeagley had obtained to set up Locomotive and VISR. That kind of data is very difficult to make usable because of the sheer amount of fraud and inaccuracies in the real-time bidding networks. It was extremely resource intensive to clean up.

Gravy's initial vision was to build out something called a software development kit, or SDK. Basically, an SDK is a few lines of prewritten code that app developers can take and insert into their own app. When inserted into an app, it would pass the user's location back to Gravy. And in exchange for getting data from the app's user base, Gravy would pay the developer based on the number of users with location permissions enabled. It was win-win for both parties—except, of course, the consumer, who had effectively no way to understand that there was a third-party company secretly lurking in the app they were using, collecting their data. The consumer got a free app or discounted services in some cases, but the "cost" they were paying was hidden in the code of the app, and the true nature of the transaction was obscured behind terms and conditions written in legalese that few bothered to read. Gravy had been in talks with Gannett, eBay, and

Marriott as potential partners to host the Gravy SDK inside their apps. It estimated it would be able to collect the location data of about ten million people with those apps.

But in 2016, Gravy abandoned the idea of building its own SDK. It was expensive and time consuming to run its own collection platform. And it required a great deal of effort to develop the relationships necessary to establish partnerships with companies for access to their apps. Instead, Gravy would buy data from other companies that were springing up to cater to the exploding location data market. It was a risky strategy. Gravy would no longer be a supplier of data; rather, it would be a data aggregator. On the one hand, Acxiom and Seisint built billion-dollar businesses aggregating public records and other companies' marketing data. On the other hand, Gnip's competitors had been chased out of business when Twitter executives decided to become more hands-on with sales of the platform's data. To be a middleman could be profitable, but it could also be dangerous.

White portrayed the company as offering some additional value: Gravy could *clean up* other people's messy data. White would compare the business model they settled on—buying other companies' data wholesale and reselling it—to being a gristmill. Gravy would take the raw location data coming in, and like a mill it would grind it into a finished product. So Gravy launched what it called the "geo-signals cloud," basically cleaning up and validating the location data. Because there was now money in data exhaust, lots of apps broadcast fake location data. In other words, they falsify the locations of their users, or invent fake users out of whole cloth, in order to try to make more money off their apps. But a little data science could easily detect a lot of that. It's not easy to completely fake an entire phone's movement patterns and make it look real enough. Gravy and other companies can use software to detect data that looks forged.

After Gravy began buying data from other sources, its supply of data exploded. At its peak, it had location data on about 250 million mobile devices a month inside the United States. Some of that data was spotty or inconsistent; it was getting daily data from only a fraction of those devices. Sometimes it would see a device only once or twice a month. But in total, Gravy claimed to be collecting about seventeen billion location pings globally a day—a decent-sized sample of the global population. Not everyone with a smartphone would show up in such a data set. But enough people would that it could be a useful tool.

Gravy was entirely self-aware about privacy as it was building out these location data products. Prophetically, Gravy's CTO, Guy DeCorte, criticized the burgeoning location data market in a 2015 blog post. Some companies, he said, are collecting and reselling user data without users being aware. "This data could eventually be used in either an unintended or malicious way, causing a backlash to not only the involved company, but also to every company which gathers data on users."

Ironically, it was Gravy that would help pioneer the sale of location data to the U.S. government, becoming one of the largest and most visible vendors. It was Gravy that would use data in unintended ways, pushing data that consumers were told was being collected for advertising into new markets. And it was Gravy that would elicit a backlash against the entire industry.

White began to recognize the value of Gravy's data to the government market when one day he heard secondhand that the FBI was looking for a girl who had been kidnapped. An FBI contact wondered if someone at Gravy could run a query and locate her phone. He complied. A few months later it happened again: the FBI was looking for someone who had stolen tactical gear. A third time, they were looking at a shooting suspect. Eventually, White asked: Why don't you guys just license this data and run your own queries, just like all the commercial entities we cater to?

White was not the only CEO getting visits by representatives from various three-letter U.S. government agencies. No fewer than six executives whose work gave them access to large stores of consumer data separately told me stories of being visited by representatives from various U.S. government agencies during the early and mid-2010s—all wondering about the possibility of obtaining data. In most cases, there wasn't any talk of licensing it or buying it. It was a closely held meeting that involved only a small number of people in the company. "Their pitch was basically: 'Do what's right for your country,'" one executive recalled. Most companies demurred, uncomfortable with the request and uncertain about the propriety of handing over their user base's data in bulk for surveillance.

But not everyone felt that way. White saw a market opportunity. And so a separate entity called Venntel was born in early 2017—a wholly owned subsidiary of Gravy that would cater to the defense, intelligence, and law enforcement market. Gravy was the consumer-friendly brand that could be trotted out at marketing technology conferences and on podcasts. Venntel would be lower profile. The initial version of its website would describe the company as "a pioneer in mobile location information" that "supports our national interests through technology innovation, data reliability and proven results." It sketched out uses for corporate security, event security, incident response, defense, and national security but said little else about itself. The site had no outward links to Gravy. The only way anyone could know the two companies were related was by going to the Virginia secretary of state and pulling the corporate records that showed that Gravy Analytics and Venntel shared numerous corporate officers.

White would spend the next few years playing down the implications of the new market he had entered. He would routinely use the phrase "privacy-friendly" to describe the kind of data that Gravy was collecting. He'd also insist it was anonymized and 100 percent opt in—meaning it is collected with users' consent. Of course, this was the paradox at the heart of Venntel's business. No person who was of interest to the Department of Homeland Security would opt in to location tracking. And the Department of Homeland Security wouldn't be purchasing it if it was truly 100 percent anonymized; of course there was fairly basic tradecraft they could use to identify the phone's owner. Remember, your patterns are unique to you. It's trivial to figure out who you are in a data set by where your phone "sleeps" at night.

White was putting a happy face on what was warrantless mass surveillance of Americans by their own government. And as his own CTO had said a few years earlier, the users of the apps Gravy was partnering with were "not being adequately made aware" of who was getting their data and why. But Gravy knew just how invasive the data it had was. The company's Venntel subsidiary did a product demo at one point during the Trump years where it ran all the phones that were at the White House and all the phones that were also at Mar-a-Lago and then watched them distribute across the world.

As Mike Yeagley, the creator of the Grindr demo and a rival of White's in the small world of federal contractors, put it, "If Gravy didn't think they were doing anything wrong, or anything shadowy, why did they need a stand-alone entity to support a new line of business?"

He had a point.

CHAPTER 15

The Fun House of Mirrors

THE DEPARTMENT OF HOMELAND SECURITY
AND VENNTEL, 2019 ONWARD

I t was around lunchtime on June 19, 2021, a hot, sticky Washington, D.C., late-spring day, when a directive arrived by email to a group of technologists and scientists at the Department of Homeland Security, bringing their work to a halt: "At this time, due to the unanswered privacy and legal concerns that have been raised please stop all projects involving Venntel data." A privacy lawyer inside DHS had suddenly gotten wind of what was going on inside the department and believed that the department might be engaged in a massive program of unconstitutional surveillance.

The research team housed within the Department of Homeland Security's Science and Technology Directorate, a sort of internal research organization, had been knee-deep in experiments involving Venntel's data. Seemingly inspired by Lin-Manuel Miranda's hit musical about the nation's first Treasury secretary, the team had given their research code names such as Project Alexander and Project Hamilton. One project sought to determine how effective the company's data was at tracking down individuals on behalf of U.S. Immigration and

Customs Enforcement. Another was an attempt to respond to the nationwide opioid crisis. Could advertising data drawn from apps be used for these problems and more?

Now, after months of work, they were suddenly being told to stop.

A controversy that had been brewing within DHS had finally boiled over. For months, the DHS privacy officers at headquarters had been receiving reports about a new source of data being used all over DHS: in the Science and Technology Directorate, at Immigration and Customs Enforcement, at Customs and Border Protection, and elsewhere in the department.

The DHS privacy office was a group of lawyers and other specialists whose mission was to assess the effects of the department's work on the privacy of Americans. It was the same office that years earlier had asked Paul Rosenzweig to chair an advisory committee on data. The office had received what's called a privacy threshold analysis, or PTA, from the Science and Technology Directorate almost a year earlier requesting its blessing to use Venntel's data. Other agencies housed within the department, ICE and CBP, had never bothered to make such a request. They went ahead and started using Venntel's data without consulting with the privacy officials at headquarters. The Science and Technology Directorate's PTA had lingered for a year without being approved while privacy officers puzzled over what to make of this new source of data and whether it was lawful and appropriate for the department to use. (Nobody at DHS consulted DHS's Office for Civil Rights and Civil Liberties; emails show its director would find out about the data usage from a story I published in *The Wall Street Journal*.)

By the summer of 2019, a privacy officer at DHS headquarters named Lindsay Lennon Vogel had become convinced that the department might have been acting outside the bounds of the law in acquiring Venntel's data. And so that morning, she sent an email to the Science and Technology Directorate asking them point-blank if the lawyers at the DHS office of general counsel had approved the acquisition of this data or done any kind of legal analysis about the recent legal developments and how they might apply to such technology. The general counsel had the final say on legal matters in the department. "That's where the grown-up lawyers are," quipped a longtime DHS official.

"I understand that S&T has purchased information from Venntel as part of Project Alexander. The PTA was never approved because we had and continue to have significant concerns with this technology," Vogel wrote. The basis for Vogel's concern was a recent Supreme Court case called *Carpenter v. United States*. The 2018 ruling had upended nearly fifty years of court precedent on what's known as the third-party doctrine.

The third-party doctrine had held that records Americans voluntarily shared with a third party, like the phone numbers they dial, were not protected by the Fourth Amendment. New kinds of technologies were now probing the limits of the doctrine. *Carpenter* revolved around the government's obtaining large amounts of cell site location data from mobile phone carriers without a warrant. In its landmark ruling, the Supreme Court labeled such collection as searches under the Constitution. If something was a search, the government needed a warrant in most circumstances. Searching without a warrant would violate the privacy rights of criminal suspects. This was the first time that the court had said that Americans had a privacy interest in data controlled by a third party. It was a huge shift after half a century of steady legal thinking but also left significant ambiguity. Would the logic of the decision apply to purchased data? Was the court moving toward jettisoning the third-party doctrine entirely? Nobody knew.

At DHS, Vogel suggested that a legal analysis of the question was necessary before S&T's research could proceed. The S&T research team decided to address their colleague's concerns head-on. The team wound down their research pending further legal review by department higher-ups. The issue would be refereed by DHS's top lawyer, just as Vogel had requested. A meeting was set for late summer. Venntel and its representatives were invited to make their case, as were the lawyers and privacy officers from all of the groups within the department using Venntel's data: ICE, CBP, and the Science and Technology Directorate. Vogel and the other dissenters in the privacy office were invited as well.

Venntel's adtech data had spread like wildfire through DHS and then throughout the rest of the government. But this new hurdle was an existential challenge to its ability to sell into the government. Venntel relied on the legal interpretation that its data was a form of publicly available information containing no personally identifiable information. For it to be a useful law enforcement tool, it also relied on some level of widespread ignorance of how much data cell phones were generating. In other words, it was in the government's interest to keep citizens in the dark about the adtech data being used at the highest levels of domestic federal law enforcement and border security for the warrantless tracking of Americans.

After it was launched in early 2017, Venntel's data had flowed into every nook and cranny of DHS. It would be embraced by CBP for examining patterns of illegal immigration. Partnering with the Drug Enforcement Administration, U.S. law enforcement tried to locate a Tijuana kidnapping victim using Venntel's data. It would be used as part of a pilot program to hunt down unauthorized immigrants who had violated the terms of their supervised release. Agents would use it to try to identify suspects in the shooting of a Border Patrol agent in Arizona. They would query Venntel's data to try to gather intelligence about who might be responsible for a bombing in Sri Lanka. The U.S. Secret Service used it as part of an effort to identify suspects in a credit card skimming investigation. Department of Homeland Security investigators "were able to identify specific stash houses, suspicious trucking firms in North Carolina, links to Native American Reservations in Arizona, connections in Mexico and Central America which were not known and possible [accomplices] and international links to MS-13 gang homicides." And it would flow through DHS to a host of local police and sheriff's departments in the D.C. area and the wider mid-Atlantic: Prince William County, Maryland; Fauquier County and Fairfax, Virginia; Richmond, Norfolk, and Newport News police in southeast Virginia as well as the Northern Virginia Regional Gang Task Force; and others.

In short, the adtech data that Venntel and Babel were brokering was a gold mine for law enforcement. For one, it freed law enforcement from having to do pesky paperwork to get a subpoena or a warrant approved by a judge. There was also little public awareness that this kind of data was even for sale, so few people were opting out. Like me, most people had no idea about the "Limit Ad Tracking" menu on their iPhones or the AAID that Google had given even Android devices. Many still don't.

Law enforcement had long relied on the cell phone tracking capabilities that the cell carriers offered. But cell carriers actually had much less precise data than Venntel. A cell carrier calculates the position of a customer's phone through a process called triangulation. Apps derive mobile phone location data from GPS, a satellite-based system that is far more precise than determining position based on cell towers. A DHS official said that the first time he played with Venntel's data, he looked himself up. It was precise enough to show which side of the bed his wife slept on and which side he slept on.[*]

Venntel wasn't suited for every possible use. The nature of Venntel's data was that it be as granular as getting a warrant to attach a GPS tracker to a suspect's vehicle or getting a month's worth of their phone's precise location history from their cell carrier. Police could do that with probable cause of a crime. Venntel's data was more of a tipping and queuing system—a place to look for potential clues as to who was in the area of a crime and to look for patterns and leads.

[*]   Today, the situation is very different. First, Apple has made major privacy changes that have sharply degraded the amount of data that can be collected from its phones. Second, there is a larger public awareness of these issues, meaning that far more people are opting out of location tracking. Finally, 5G cell networks require a larger number of lower-powered transmitters than previous generations of cell technology, meaning carriers today often have location data that's as good as GPS.

What phones keep popping up near a suspected drug stash house or a way station on human trafficking routes. It could also look at "known associates"—what devices did a device spend its time in proximity to? Those were probably friends, family, and colleagues. In this way, Venntel could help reveal networks and patterns of association. Finally, with a little simple tradecraft, Venntel could also be used to track social media users who left geographic clues or coordinates attached to their posts. Did an Instagram user upload a photo taken at a certain locale at a certain time? Or did a Twitter user leave GPS coordinates attached to a tweet? An analyst could cross-check the Venntel data to see if there were any phones that appeared in that location during that time. If they got a match, they could now track that user through Venntel's data. The same trick would be pulled with an IP address. Did an analyst have an IP address associated with a bad actor online? Venntel could be a useful tool to see if their phone was trackable in the open-source data. All of this could be done warrantlessly—without ever going to a judge.

For all its sudden popularity as a tool, the reviews within government on using Venntel's data were mixed. The chief of ICE's fugitive operations program enforcement division wrote, "I see a lot of value here" during one of the pilots. ICE in Nashville was impressed, using the tool for leads in numerous investigations. But HSI Detroit found there were "significant gaps in collection," since Venntel was reliant on consumers to keep apps with permission running on their phones.

But on the whole, the capability was popular inside the department. Inside DHS, officials clamored to get access to the data. And Venntel had a multipronged business strategy to get it to them. It had built its own software platform and was trying to win government contracts in its own right. If the government wanted to do business with Venntel, and run queries inside Venntel's software platform, it could do that. But if the government already had another OSINT tool and wanted to add geolocation to it, that was fine too.

Babel Street became one of Venntel's earliest partners. Babel, which already had deep relationships with U.S. special forces through its work with ECS, had followed the development of Mike Yeagley's VISR program and started building out its own version of the product in 2016. It was called Locate X, and it would rely on Venntel's data but be integrated into Babel's flagship Babel X platform.

The existence of Locate X would be a closely guarded secret from the general public. Even some employees internally didn't know the source of the company's location data was Venntel. Babel would make no mention of Locate X on its website. Its contracts with customers would specify that even the existence of the product was considered confidential information. In fact, Babel's contracts explicitly said that Locate X's data could never be mentioned in court records or introduced into legal proceedings as evidence. In part, this was to prevent Babel Street's employees from being put on the stand and having to explain or vouch for the provenance of the adtech data, which of course they couldn't do in a court, because they had no idea what apps it was derived from or if it was fraudulent or not. But this raised its own problems. In intelligence gathering, analysts could assess how confident they were in a particular data source and base any judgments on that confidence level. But typically, criminal defendants are given an opportunity to review the evidence against them as part of criminal discovery. In effect, Babel was depriving them of that by instructing law enforcement to keep secret the techniques they were using to generate leads.

Babel's secrecy around Locate X as a law enforcement tool mirrored the history of an earlier technology called an IMSI (International Mobile Subscriber Identity) catcher, often referred to as a Stingray after a particular brand manufactured by the Harris Corporation. IMSI catchers were once secret intelligence intercept equipment— developed for use by the military and intelligence agencies to collect cell phone signals in war zones. They're essentially fake mobile phone towers—they persuade nearby cell phones to connect to them instead of the legitimate cell phone network. From there, they allow eavesdropping on phone calls and data being transmitted between phones and the tower. In the mid-2000s, law enforcement began to obtain access to IMSI catchers as technologies once secretly deployed in war zones began to trickle down to civilian agencies. But vendors demanded that they never reveal the existence of the use of the technology in criminal cases. And law enforcement has by and large complied—sometimes going so far as to drop criminal charges entirely rather than allow a defendant to challenge their use in court. As a result, U.S. courts have never definitively settled the legal status of the IMSI catcher in criminal law.

Babel, Venntel, and other adtech vendors in conjunction with their government customers were running the same playbook. By preventing law enforcement from revealing they were using a warrantless tracking technology based on advertising data, they deprived U.S. courts of the ability to answer the question that Lindsay Lennon Vogel in the DHS privacy office had asked: *Is this even legal?* And they were preventing consumers, companies, and regulators from weighing in on the question of whether this practice was consistent with our values as a society.

The meeting over the legality of DHS's using Venntel took place in early September 2019. It included members of the major components that had been using Venntel's data, as well as privacy officers and lawyers. The decision would ultimately be made by the office of the DHS general counsel. Each side made its case. ICE in particular was looking for ways to preserve its access to Venntel's data. As they awaited the verdict from the DHS lawyers, one ICE project manager and analyst named Nicole LaCicero asked her colleagues, "I have a silly question regarding next steps. If DHS decides not to use geolocation, does ICE have to comply?" floating the idea that the agency could go ahead and ignore whatever the department leadership decided.

The task of drafting the opinion fell to a lawyer named Alex Wood, who asked all of ICE, CBP, and others to send material that might inform his opinion. He would ultimately conclude that yes, DHS's purchase of cell phone location data was consistent with the Fourth Amendment and could continue. Quietly and without fanfare, this became the operational policy of the department.

Venntel had won the most significant challenge to its survival as a company. But DHS had approved use of the data under the theory that people had opted in and had been notified that their data might be used by government entities.

That was a lie.

Trying to figure out where Venntel or any of its competitors get data from is to enter a fun house of mirrors. The company's data suppliers—which iPhone or Android apps it partners with—are confidential. Venntel claims to derive data from eighty thousand apps, though that number is less impressive than it seems. Many apps have only a small number of users, and the largest apps are developed by large companies like Facebook, Twitter, TikTok, and Google that collect lots of user data for their own internal purposes but don't sell it on the open market to entities like Gravy. The supply of location data that ends up with Gravy and its Venntel subsidiary more often flows from small app developers on the margins of the tech economy to obscure data brokers and aggregators to Gravy's servers and then on to government entities.

Venntel also claims the data it collects is 100 percent opt in. In Venntel's telling, its business model is explained transparently in the privacy policies of those apps. These privacy policies are legal documents that are supposed to spell out how a website or a service uses its customers' data. However, in recent years, they've swelled to unimaginable size and complexity. A *Washington Post* reporter tried in 2022 to read the privacy policies of all the apps on his phone. They amounted to one million words, written in dense jargon. No wonder most consumers never bother to read them.

No mobile app privacy policy that I've ever found discloses that a government intelligence agency or security service may be buying the data. Many do acknowledge they might have to turn over user data in response to a warrant, but in general privacy policies around data sales and sharing make two claims: first, that user data is anonymized if it's transferred and no personally identifiable information is shared; second, the purpose of that data is for analytics or advertising or commerce. Neither is true. Both the user and the app developer cannot definitively say what the uses are after the data leaves their control. They cannot guarantee that the data will be used only for commerce or analytics. Once data is collected and sold, what happens with it cannot be guaranteed by anyone.

In short, nobody can knowingly consent to Venntel's data collection because Venntel has no consumer-facing relationship and the apps it partners with are trade secrets. If anything, Venntel and other adtech companies that cater to the government market have taken extraordinary steps to conceal their place in the data collection ecosystem. This is the paradox at the heart of Venntel's legal position—and one of the questions that the DHS privacy office raised. *Was this really consent?* For example, CBP's privacy officer at one point set conditions on the use of Venntel's data. One of those conditions was that commercial phone data could be used if "*the terms of service under which the data was collected* discloses that the data may be sold to a customer base that includes public sector customers, and the user must accept the terms of service prior to using/accessing a service or product." (Emphasis mine.) Few if any of the apps that Venntel was partnering with met that standard. App developers did not even know their data was going to Venntel. It was passed through numerous intermediaries before it ever showed up on a computer in front of a CBP or ICE analyst. At the point of collection, the consumer is left totally in the dark that a government entity may be using this information for surveillance.

Early in my reporting, it occurred to me that I might be able to use a landmark new California privacy law as a way to try to understand the flow of data from apps to Venntel. In 2018, the California legislature passed the California Consumer Privacy Act, the first comprehensive attempt to regulate data flows in the United States. The law included a provision entitling California residents to the right of access to data about themselves. I wasn't a California resident, but *The Wall Street Journal* had bureaus in San Francisco and Los Angeles. I quickly enlisted two of my colleagues, Yoree Koh and Asa Fitch, as guinea pigs. Both submitted identical requests under the right of access to both Venntel and Gravy. Neither company had anything on Fitch, but both reported having data on Koh. But because they knew her only by her mobile ad ID number, they asked for verification of her identity. "Please provide us with the following information. A few of your recently visited locations, including name of location and a full street address ... e.g. Starbucks, 555 Main Street, City, State zip; or for locations that don't have names, just the complete street address; and At your option, you may also provide us with a frequently used IP address." Koh did that, sending them her home address in Oakland, her phone's IP address, and the Safeway supermarket she usually frequented. Two days later, Gravy told her that the information she had provided was not enough to verify that she really was the owner of the phone. A lawyer friend advising me during this quest suggested Koh draw up a sworn statement, a lawyerly document swearing that the ad ID belonged to her, and send it to Gravy. Again she was denied. CCPA did not provide a mechanism for using sworn statements to verify identity, Gravy argued. Venntel replied separately with the same result. Fearing I was testing my colleague's patience, I gave up. California's landmark privacy law had failed in its basic task of allowing a citizen to easily obtain information about what data brokers knew about them.

On the other side of the world, an enterprising team of reporters at Norway's public broadcaster, NRK, had the same idea. Europe had passed a law similar to California's called the General Data Protection Regulation, or GDPR. A reporter named Martin Gundersen had wondered if he could use GDPR to force some measure of transparency on these app brokers. Like CCPA, the European privacy law contained a "right of access." At NRK, they had an old Android smartphone lying around. So Gundersen loaded the phone up with about a hundred different apps. And then he waited. Beginning in February 2020, he began carrying this second phone around with him, giving it access to his precise location 24/7. He sent ninety companies that he suspected of brokering data demands under the GDPR for an inventory of his data, including Venntel and Gravy Analytics. A lot responded that they had his data but they hadn't passed it on to any other vendors. Some said they had passed along his data but refused to tell him to whom. But Venntel actually responded, saying they had 75,406 location points corresponding to Gundersen's movements. Most of them were clustered around his home in Oslo or NRK's offices in the Marienlyst section of the city. But some of them showed him out on a hike, having a drink at a bar, and visiting his grandmother in southern Norway.

And more intriguingly, Gundersen managed to piece together a tiny smidgen of information about the flow of data from his phone: From the documents he got back, he found that two navigation apps from a Slovak app developer named Sygic as well as an app called Fu*** Weather, which delivered forecasts such as "Don't look at the shitty sky unless you want to fuck up your mood!" were passing data through two separate intermediaries to Venntel. And that was all Gundersen could really figure out. There were likely many more apps passing data to Venntel on his baited phone. But companies interpreted their GDPR and CCPA obligations in different ways. And so the trail went dead.

"There are open questions about how well the GDPR functions," Gundersen told me. Many companies may violate it in spirit or in practice. But because the data protection authorities don't know where to look, many companies can skate by, he said. "I think that opaqueness of the industry helps to avoid scrutiny," he said.

These two laws have been heralded as landmark efforts by legislatures to bring new privacy rights to consumers in Europe and California. But in reality, any consumer who wants to meaningfully exercise those rights often ends up frustrated. Websites have mastered the art of getting people to click "I accept," burying a consumer's right to decline tracking deep in screens that you must click through. And neither law meaningfully allowed even professional reporters from well-resourced media outlets to trace the flow of data through the advertising data ecosystem.

What hope is there for an ordinary person?

CHAPTER 16

Success Lies in the Secrecy

AMERICA IN THE 2020s

I n the summer of 2021, I was sitting with a longtime U.S. intelligence official in a coffee shop in downtown Washington, D.C., when I sprang my favorite question on him. "So," I asked, leaning in close and lowering my voice, "have you ever heard about the U.S. government using online ads to track people's movement in the real world?"

We had been talking for some time, and while he wasn't exactly spilling state secrets, he had been gamely answering many of my questions as I nursed an iced coffee. He was doing a delicate dance: trying to be as candid as possible without imperiling the safety of U.S. spies or ending up in handcuffs for disclosing classified information to a journalist. But my question about the nexus between advertising and national security was one question he was not prepared to answer. He chuckled nervously and said, "Next! Next question!"

And with that, my relatively chatty source clammed up—at least on that topic. Our conversation moved on to other things. I didn't.

Beyond the commercial vendors like UberMedia and Venntel that were collecting and reselling large amounts of information from apps and ad exchanges as a service, I was still trying to figure out what else was happening in the bizarre world of online targeted ads. And how did we get to a place as a society where advertising had become so intertwined with surveillance?

It would take a long time for me to piece together a rough understanding of the scale of what was happening and why. Venntel and UberMedia were just two manifestations of a larger phenomenon; there are more programs buried inside three-letter government agencies and more suppliers providing data about the global population. In fact, it was becoming big business as government agencies became hungrier for commercially available data sets beyond just advertising. Data brokers had grown from scanning the phone book and marrying the information with census records to creating detailed logs about the precise movement of people around the world. And the government appetite for movement data didn't end with phones.

Along with every other military and intelligence agency on earth, the U.S. government had come to see the hyper-connected modern landscape of social media, information technology, and advertising technology as a *domain* for future conflict and competition with other nations. The Pentagon called it the information environment, or the IE. According to one Pentagon strategy study, the information environment was "the aggregate of individuals, organizations, and systems that collect, process, disseminate, or act on information: The IE is a heterogeneous global environment where humans and automated systems observe, orient, decide, and act on data, information, and knowledge."

Aspects of this conflict have been well documented: the rise of the techniques of hacking, trolling, and digital sabotage as elements of national power has been the subject of a great deal of journalism and academic study. But there is another aspect of that same conflict: the use of open networks like ad exchanges and social networks that don't need to be hacked for information warfare, manipulation, dissemination of propaganda, or covert tracking. For example, anywhere U.S.

forces now operate, they need to be aware of an adversary's capacity to manipulate the information environment with propaganda or disinformation—and push back with counter-messaging. The United States is routinely accused of killing civilians while conducting military operations against terrorist groups like ISIS, for example, and indeed sometimes the United States does kill civilians inadvertently as the by-product of strikes against legitimate targets. But in other instances, it's false propaganda meant to embarrass the United States and make it seem as if a legitimate strike against terrorists killed civilians. The United States needs to counter that message. In addition, modern governments are dependent on public opinion, both at home and abroad. And nations have grown increasingly concerned—and some might say paranoid—about the ease with which their rivals, adversaries, or internal dissenters are able to sway public opinion using information networks.

As the nature of conflict and national power changed in the last two decades, the U.S. government became increasingly involved in a global power struggle over *information* and the networks through which that information flowed. These conflicts fall short of the definition of war but are nevertheless part of a growing international struggle over power and supremacy that is increasingly encompassing digital networks of all kinds. In such conflicts, big armies and technologically capable navies will still remain important, but the real frontline warriors are special operators and intelligence agencies.

And because unique and clever information warfare capabilities—the ability to target specific users through advertising technologies or social media tools and techniques that most people don't even know exist—were useful in this new kind of conflict, they were a tightly guarded secret.

That's why when I sued U.S. Special Operations Command in 2021 over its failure to turn over to me documents related to its use of social media and advertising data under the Freedom of Information Act, it cited the need to protect "critical infrastructure security information," "intelligence sources and methods," and "investigative techniques and procedures for law enforcement investigations" as reasons to deny providing the documents. This was data that anyone with a credit card and a plausible excuse could get, yet America's special operators were loath to talk about what they were doing with it. To them, the internet was a battlefield. And you don't give away your position on a battlefield. The twenty-first-century version of "loose lips might sink ships" is the far less snappy "FOIA exemption b(7)E" and Title 5, Section 552 of the U.S. Code.

And so a truly public conversation about the ways in which the modern internet leaves us all vulnerable to forces that we can't see or understand is being subordinated to the very narrow mission requirements of the U.S. special forces and intelligence agencies. Their missions are important, but so is the global public's understanding of exactly what they're signing up for when they use modern technology. Did they know they were signing up for a system where governments and corporations would use the means of delivering advertising for manipulation and surveillance?

And tools created for the intelligence and special forces world never stay there—a pattern that repeats throughout this book. Mike Yeagley had created VISR to support the top-tier U.S. special forces units. Just a few short years after his demo, a similar tool would be marketed to the local police—creating what the technologist and civil libertarian Bennett Cyphers would call "a mass surveillance program on a budget."

In the same way that Stingrays had gone from secret phone intercept technology to a tool that police departments were using domestically, so too would adtech data come to dozens of police departments. A company called Fog Data Science LLC packaged up Venntel's data and offered it to hundreds of local police forces, where it would be used for the same kind of warrantless tracking that the Department of Homeland Security did in the Ivan Lopez drug-tunnel case. Fog would even sell data to private researchers. Whenever Venntel fielded requests for its data from a private investigator or research company, it would steer them to Fog Data Science.

The ability to rewind the clock and look at a suspect's entire history—without getting a search warrant or generating any sort of paper trail that would need to be disclosed to judges or defense attorneys—was one of the selling points. Fog would remind clients logging into its service that "this portal provides access to sensitive data which should be appropriately safeguarded."

"Picture getting a suspect's phone then in the extraction being able to see everyplace they'd been in the last 18 months plotted on a map you filter by date ranges," wrote one sergeant with the Maryland State Police about Fog. "The success lies in the secrecy."

UberMedia, Venntel, Babel Street—these vendors offered easy commercial, off-the-shelf solutions for tracking people or understanding patterns of activity around specific spots on the earth. They source their data in slightly different ways. UberMedia largely got data from ad exchanges, which were quicker and more real time. Gravy at one point was getting ad exchange data, but its lawyers nixed it at some point after Europe and California passed privacy laws. So now Gravy's business model is to partner with other brokers who had relationships with app developers. Both companies have about a twenty-four-hour lag in delivering data to customers, though for some of Gravy's app partners, the lag can be longer.

But the government wasn't satisfied. From poring over a dozen contracting documents, conducting halting and vague interviews with people eager to help without violating their obligation to protect classified information or their nondisclosure agreements, and observing a pattern of résumés, job vacancy announcements, and LinkedIn profiles, I realized that the government needed more than what these data vendors could offer it. Hidden behind a maze of shell companies, contractors, proxies, and shadowy business arrangements, our government itself is lurking in the global networks that serve ads to consumers worldwide for a wide variety of purposes. In other words, the government had found ways to penetrate the ad networks themselves—to be on the systems that buy and sell in ways that I never quite figured out other than that they were happening.

And it's not just the United States; any foreign government with a halfway decent cyber-intelligence capability was doing the same on behalf of its nation's intelligence services. For example, several UberMedia employees described to me suspicious activities on the company's data platform that seemed government linked. In one instance, they found a client had been geofencing Ukrainian airfields at the start of the conflict with Russia—something that sure didn't look as if it had any advertising purpose.

Sometimes this activity is for tracking purposes. Sometimes it's to serve an ad to a group of people as part of a government-backed psychological operation, or what the military calls psyops. And sometimes targeted advertising is being enlisted in some sort of cyber operation—to deliver malware to a specific phone, for example.

I've found more than half a dozen defense contractors or intelligence officials who boast on LinkedIn about having built or used tools for government to ingest or use advertising data. I've met service members who described to me tours of duty buried deep in paperwork trying to understand the terms of service of half a dozen of the world's advertising exchanges and how those could be manipulated to the military's end. And I've observed major defense contractors posting jobs seeking candidates with experience in "social media monitoring, digital marketing, sentiment analysis, or background in data analytics."

From what I can tell, all of these military or intelligence community programs that take advantage of this data are run carefully and overseen by lawyers, and the resulting surveillance is aimed primarily at non-Americans overseas. But all of them aim to take advantage of the modern ad-supported digital economy to create a form of mass surveillance: the modern ad-supported internet. And of course, these capabilities never stay with the intelligence community and the military. They're trickling down to law enforcement agencies and even private investigators.

America's largest corporations don't like to acknowledge that their billion-dollar advertising budgets are being repurposed as a delivery mechanism to target bombs or government malware as well. But that's the reality. Yes, there are some privacy mechanisms baked into this system (pseudonymized advertising IDs, for example), but they're easily breakable by entities with sufficient skills because no part of advertising technology was designed with security, privacy, or anonymity in mind. If anything, it was the opposite. The system was designed as a transparent open system connecting consumers with advertisers and ad buyers with ad space sellers. It was naive from the beginning to believe that such an intricate system of linking every device in the world to a consumer profile would spring into existence and then be used only for commercial purposes.

When you start to look at the advertising industry as a small portion of a larger battlefield raging for our attention, certain things make a lot more sense. For years, I've tried to understand why the giant defense contractor Sierra Nevada Corporation owns and operates a tiny marketing company called nContext as a subsidiary. Sierra Nevada is a nearly $2.5 billion defense contractor whose website is adorned with pictures of futuristic planes and orbiting space systems. On the other hand, nContext's website looks like every other small-to-midsized anonymous marketing firm. The company says on its website that it "was born from the need to analyze data from the thousands of sources that capture information from our everyday activities. nContext enables understanding and business application of the volumes of data." It boasts case studies about how it helped a Philadelphia performing arts venue, the 92nd Street Y in New York City, and a large pharmaceutical company with their marketing needs.

nContext also secured six federal contracts to provide data to the most secretive parts of government. This tiny marketing company is providing data in support of the National Security Agency, the U.S. Air Force's cyber operations, the Defense Counterintelligence and Security Agency, and an intelligence-community-wide cloud computing project called IC ITE. I once tried to request information about an nContext contract that was ostensibly funded by the U.S. Army. After being shuffled around agencies a few times, I got a letter back saying the records in question belonged to the National Security Agency. *Dead end.*

The real reason to use shell companies and cutouts like nContext is that governments and their contractors need a plausible veneer to be on advertising networks to be collecting data or serving ads. Most of the time, the National Security Agency or the CIA cannot call up an advertising exchange and ask for an account for the purposes of conducting mass surveillance. Asking around about nContext is a fool's errand—dead end after dead end of stonewalling or nonresponses from Sierra Nevada, nContext, its former employees, and the U.S. government. The best I ever got was a well-placed rival contractor who described it as "a shell company—and not a very good one." I would eventually find out that it too was getting data from UberMedia, the same data broker that Mike Yeagley used.

Tiny nContext is not unique. There are half a dozen vendors that seem to be offering the same services. Some are heavyweight U.S. defense contractors who appear to be working on major intelligence programs that are aimed at ingesting global consumer data on massive scales. Others are just data vendors or advertising companies that will either offer up data for sale or volunteer it out of their patriotic obligation. Sometimes they slip up and reveal at conferences or to others in their industries that they provide data to three-letter U.S. government agencies.

Over beers one night in Washington, D.C., a former government insider pushed his phone across the table to me. On it was a list of all of the advertising exchanges that America's intelligence agencies had access to in one way or another—through cutouts, intermediaries, research agreements, shell companies, or other means. The list included nearly every major exchange. These were the real-time bidding networks that UberMedia was siphoning data off. They delivered targeted advertising to nearly every phone on earth. Somehow, the U.S. government through a maze of contractors, shell companies, or proxies was able to collect data from all the major ad exchanges. Or they could serve ads or malware using those networks. It's probably no exaggeration to say that every smartphone, tablet, and computer on earth is passing data back to these exchanges in some way. Worse, the source told me that China, Russia, North Korea—all these nations—were sitting on the same networks. They were using shells and cutouts like nContext to obtain data on Americans by the petabyte. And nobody wanted to talk about it because America does the same thing.

And collection of information is only part of the information warfare equation. The *dissemination* of America's message to every corner of the internet is now part of the war that America's special operators are waging. Another special forces document I've seen solicited a contractor who could create and maintain two hundred fictitious social media personas with the capability to disseminate messages on behalf of the U.S.-led task force fighting ISIS. The personas "should appear to be based in Iraq, Syria, Jordan, or regional diaspora." The aim of this was to spread covert U.S. propaganda messages to ten thousand to twenty thousand people daily, with no links back to the U.S. government.

This is the very same kind of activity that the U.S. government spent several years blasting Russia for engaging in during the 2016 U.S. elections, where Moscow used a social media "troll farm" that created divisive social media content and bought targeted advertising to inflame U.S. public opinion. This was done with the intention of denigrating Hillary Clinton and boosting Donald Trump. The true effect of those operations on the outcome of the election may never be known, but the consequences of them on American public life are clear. Trump spent nearly his entire term in office under investigation about whether his campaign was connected to the Russian-led effort. Trump by all accounts was deeply resentful of the suggestion of the illegitimacy of his election, and conversely many Democratic diehards were convinced that Trump's defiance of preelection poll odds could only have been the work of a foreign plot.

That the U.S. government engages in the same activities on behalf of its own national objectives raises more questions than answers.

Even if the United States isn't interfering in a democratic election—and is instead targeting a terrorist group and its supporters—what is the principle here? Is it wrong to use social media sock puppets to manipulate global public opinion with propaganda? Or is it only wrong to do so on behalf of a covert campaign to undermine a democratic election? Under what circumstances do U.S. special forces contractors deploy these "personas" to disseminate messaging?

Special operators in particular, in conjunction with their intelligence agency partners, have become frontline soldiers in this new information conflict. That mission is transforming the special forces in unusual ways: the organization now hosts a cadre of highly trained, disciplined combat soldiers alongside experts in psychological operations, civil affairs, hacking, and intelligence.

Left unexamined in all of this geopolitical back-and-forth is whether any of this is effective at all. Can tweets from U.S. special forces and their contractors pretending to be Arabic influencers really change hearts and minds? Whatever the Russian social media campaign in 2016 accomplished, it was most effective at amplifying pre-existing divisions in American society. That, and breeding cynicism that everyone and everything you don't like online is part of an information operation.

Notably absent from much of this book are the tech companies that run those consumer services and are household names and international brands: Facebook, Apple, Google, Twitter, and the rest of the tech giants. They don't sell raw consumer data to the government per se in the same way that Acxiom or Venntel does. All do have huge compliance departments geared around responding to law enforcement and intelligence agency requests for user data, but they typically require some sort of court order for that. All have mind-numbingly complicated privacy policies that assure users of their commitment to privacy.

But there are ways to get data off each of their networks other than knocking on the door with a subpoena in hand. Each of them played a role in enabling this kind of surveillance, whether inadvertently or on purpose. Apple created the very idea of a pseudonymized advertising identifier, though it did so to stop developers from collecting more invasive information. Google and Facebook run massive platforms that enable the targeting of advertising and consumer messaging. Google's smartphone operating system, Android, is a data collection machine—meant to seamlessly help connect advertisers to users. Twitter until 2022 owned the advertising exchange MoPub, from which UberMedia was acquiring some of its data. The "Twitter Files" that Elon Musk released in late 2022 and early 2023 to handpicked reporters after he bought the company also show a cozy relationship with the FBI and Twitter's acquiescence to the U.S. military employing its platform to disseminate propaganda using fake accounts, even as it cracked down on other countries doing so. These platforms aren't built to protect users from surveillance. If anything, they're all bringing thousands of minimally vetted companies together under one roof and giving them access to data coming off billions of mobile devices. Silicon Valley has built this entire world. The military and the intelligence community are just living in it.

"People are worried about mass surveillance. Well, you're all carrying around the world's greatest surveillance device and I've got news for you. It's not government controlled," said one former intelligence officer. "You and your data are the product. That's why they're willing to do it for free. Google's not in it for the good of humanity."

These tech giants are not naive about what is happening on their platforms but have largely found it in their commercial interests to look away. Conducting due diligence on the thousands of entities that have accounts on their ad exchanges would take resources. Curtailing the consumer data available on them would cost them revenue. Digital advertising is projected to potentially be a trillion-dollar market by 2027. Information collection for targeted advertising subsidizes the overwhelming amount of content on the internet. To unwind it would be an economic project of epic proportions.

On the advertising and social media networks of these companies, great power competition is playing out every day. Government and corporations alike are participants in the same ongoing battle for their attention and their data.

Transparency about this is being subordinated to the special and specific needs of a narrow class of intelligence and military professionals. In the kind of conflict the United States is now waging, the needs of special operators and intelligence personnel are obscuring a huge cost to the public in democracies and non-democracies alike. How many Americans are quietly being swept up in foreign information operations or are being tracked through platforms that they are being told are for commerce? How many millions or billions of people are receiving social media messaging or targeted advertising that is really part of a nation-state's propaganda efforts? How many social media users are actually government sock puppets, and how are those used to manipulate the public? And finally, is any of this even effective? Or are the costs worth the benefits? Does the United States want to contribute to an internet that is dominated by nation-state propaganda campaigns and an increasingly angry, bitter, and cynical public?

We'll never know the answer to any of these questions as long as the needs of intelligence agencies and special operators continue to take precedence over the kind of world that we want our technology to create.

And the collection of data would not stop at advertising data. Technology continues to change rapidly—far faster than even the smartest lawmaker or forward-looking regulator could possibly keep up with. Peer deep enough into any modern technology, and there are 1s and 0s logging every behavior. And increasingly everything in modern life is becoming interconnected: your car, your washing machine, your wireless headphones. Data is the by-product of those connections. And so long as there is data, there are eager customers.

PART IV

GRAY DATA

CHAPTER 17

Going Gray

WASHINGTON, D.C., 2022

There are a lot of small indignities and absurdities in the careers of public servants, but the time Eliot Jardines spent watching the U.S. Interagency Gray Literature Working Group, or IGLWG, debate whether to spell the word "gray" with an *a* or an *e* sticks out.

"It's G-R-A-Y. You laugh but that's two hours of my life I'll never get back," said Jardines, who spent his career inside and outside government as a champion of open-source intelligence before rising to become the assistant deputy director of national intelligence for open source.

Gray literature describes material that exists outside traditional publication distribution channels. IGLWG, an unwieldy acronym pronounced "Iggle-Wig" when spoken aloud, defined it as "foreign or domestic open-source material that usually is available through specialized channels and may not enter normal channels or systems of publication, distribution, bibliographic control, or acquisition by booksellers or subscription agents." Think: the volumes of government reports that every modern country generates, working drafts of research papers by academics or think tanks, marketing material distributed by corporations about their products, research reports produced by nonprofits or nongovernmental organizations, surveys conducted by pollsters, economic reports by chambers of commerce, and so on. None of these items are secret. But they vary in how widely they are distributed: some may be publicly available and some are distributed to only a very narrow audience. What they all have in common is the fact that none are published and distributed by traditional academic or trade publishers.

Jardines left government in 2008, going to work for a few big defense and technology providers before setting up his own consulting shop. I went to visit him in his small office in a bedroom community of Washington, D.C., in the winter of 2022. We were engaged in a lengthy discussion about how open-source intelligence had changed dramatically in the fourteen years since he had left government. OSINT once meant collecting books, reports, brochures, and foreign news reports. It now seemed much murkier and involved a wider array of material, including data that people don't even know exists.

I told Jardines, for example, that I had been chasing rumors that the intelligence community had learned how to exploit the fact that modern car tires broadcast a unique identifier. Ever wondered how your car's computer knows the pressure of each tire? Well, those aren't hardwired sensors. There is a tiny wireless tire pressure monitoring sensor, or TPMS, device inside each tire. And it is constantly broadcasting something like "I'm Acura tire k192e3bc and my tire pressure is 42 psi." The message is meant for the central computer of your own car, but anybody with an antenna can listen in. Car manufacturers have never bothered to secure the transmission with encryption or any other kind of privacy mechanism.

In 2020, a Finnish programmer named Tero Mononen placed a digital radio near his window that was programmed to capture transmissions in a certain frequency for seventy-five days—just to see what he might get back. The answer was 1.5 million rows of data, mostly from devices in his own home like car keys and smoke detectors. But to his surprise, he was able to capture 75,000 readings from 10,000 unique tires from passing cars. He concluded in a blog post that "TPMS data capture could be utilized by researchers, spies and people who are being followed." He was right.

Multiple officials have told me that the intelligence community and the military have figured out how to collect tire pressure data from specialized sensors for tracking purposes—usually just by placing a software-defined radio somewhere, often on choke points like bridges or tunnels where a target must cross. How far has this capability penetrated into a mass surveillance technology? I never quite got the answer. One contractor, which claimed to be doing work in Ukraine, sold a system that it promised could detect TPMS transmissions, along with more than a hundred other common kinds of wireless signals including the low-frequency signals emitted by modern tap-to-pay credit cards and the kinds of key fob entry cards we all use to get into our offices or apartment buildings. The same vendor sold "emerging radio frequency sensor nodes" to the Department of Homeland Security's Border Patrol. Another company, based in Utah, is blanketing cities and counties in the United States with sensors attached to lampposts that detect TPMS and other wireless signals ostensibly for the purpose of studying how traffic flows—but there is serious surveillance potential for that kind of data. It even promises local governments that it can pinpoint the origin and destination of car trips based only on the wireless data. But don't worry, the company is committed to protecting privacy by giving everyone a random identifier devoid of personally identifiable information.

And it's not just modern cars. All those Bluetooth devices that people are carrying around? They're constantly broadcasting unique identifiers called a MAC address. Another enterprising Scandinavian took it upon himself to show the privacy risks. A Norwegian tech enthusiast named Bjørn Martin Hegnes biked more than 175 miles around Oslo over twelve days, carrying a bundle of radio equipment that could suck up all the Bluetooth and wireless signals from about a hundred-yard radius. He ended up collecting 1.7 million Bluetooth identifiers during this time period. He picked up signals from almost 10,000 pairs of headphones and other Bluetooth devices at least twice at two separate locations—meaning that Hegnes had encountered many of the same people at different locations around Oslo on his long bike ride.

Even if I disable the GPS sensor on my phone, an app might still know where I am. Wi-Fi networks themselves can be used as proxies for location. Sitting in my bedroom in my Washington, D.C., home has a unique ambient signature, based on the distance from my wireless router, my neighbor's wireless router, my wireless printer, my Apple TV in my living room, and so on. All of those markers indicate to anyone who is listening exactly where I am. And because half a dozen apps on my phone require access to my Bluetooth sensors, that's half a dozen apps that know where I am without my ever turning on GPS.

Is collecting all this really open-source intelligence? I asked Jardines. Was OSINT now really vacuuming up car tire identifiers?

"It's gray literature," Jardines said. "It's a subset of OSINT provided it's publicly available."

"Or gray data?" I volunteered.

"Yeah, gray data," he said.

What we termed gray data is the next growth area of OSINT. It's the by-product of a world in which everything is becoming networked and everything is generating data, much of it wireless and lots of it for sale in increasingly bizarre marketplaces.

For example, to understand the weird world of radio-frequency signals, it's important to recognize the different ways devices broadcast identifiers. First, Bluetooth devices are constantly looking for other known Bluetooth devices to pair with and are sending out a Bluetooth Device Address, a unique forty-eight-bit identifier given to the device by its manufacturer. Second, phones, smartwatches, computers, and wireless routers are scanning constantly for Wi-Fi signals and are sharing a MAC address with anything that is nearby. Some devices change the MAC address they broadcast at certain intervals for privacy purposes, but many do not. Third, anything with a cellular connection is looking for nearby towers. Cellular phones broadcast something called an IMEI, or International Mobile Equipment Identity. And the tiny little SIM card in the cell phone that gives it access to a carrier's network broadcasts a second identifier, the IMSI.

All of these identifiers can be intercepted and mapped using the right kind of antenna. But this kind of radio-frequency information is messy, chaotic data. It's hard to collect in bulk. It's hard to make sense of. There's no giant registry of what identifiers belong to whom—at least not yet. But in this new era characterized by increasingly invasive forms of "surveillance capitalism"—to invoke the term coined by the Harvard professor Shoshana Zuboff—that hasn't stopped corporations from collecting this data and trying to make sense of it for their own business purposes. We got a hint of this when the website *Politico* reported in 2022 that Kamala Harris refused to use Bluetooth headphones. *Politico* took the opportunity to poke fun at Harris as technophobic, rather than acknowledging that maybe the vice president and former member of the Senate Intelligence Committee knew something the rest of us didn't about security and privacy vulnerabilities in Bluetooth connections.

Retailers have started embedding Bluetooth and Wi-Fi sensors all around their stores to better understand who is inside and what they're doing. Those sensors can sometimes interact with computer code embedded in mobile phone apps to help identify people as they shop in stores. You, of course, opted into this tracking. It's right there in the privacy policy of whatever app the code is running in. In 2013, the city of London even briefly contracted with a company called Renew London that used Wi-Fi-enabled trash cans—yes, you read that correctly—to deliver advertisements to pedestrians as they passed. The trash cans were also using Wi-Fi to detect the phones of passersby and understand their behavior and movements. An outcry over privacy prompted the end of the pilot program.

Of course, governments know these capabilities as well—not for personalized advertising, but for tracking and man hunting. It once required very specialized equipment to scan the environment for signals—an activity that the military and the intelligence community refer to as doing a wireless survey. It's also sometimes informally called sniffing, wardriving, or battledriving. At first, such scanning was done for specific cell phones, using very expensive and highly classified pieces of equipment that were mounted on aircraft and in trucks. They could be preprogrammed to scan for certain cell phones—identifying the presence of a high-value target in a specific area. But eventually, this technology would come down in price and size.

An $11,500 device called the Nemo Handy put some of those capabilities in a small handset. One person involved in intelligence operations recalled that using special equipment like the Nemo Handy, an operative might visit the lavatory at the back of a plane as a ruse to capture the identifiers of everyone on board—perhaps to confirm the presence of a target on the plane or to capture the digital information of a person of interest. Just carrying the phone with them up the aisle was enough to do a survey. But today, you don't need an expensive piece of equipment to do that. The ability to scan the ambient Wi-Fi and Bluetooth signal environment around a device is embedded into virtually every modern smartphone and tablet.

Cars are an excellent way to illustrate the concept of gray data, and the problem goes far beyond sensors in tires.

For example, in 2021, *Vice* reported that a government contractor called the Ulysses Group was marketing a product to government agencies that could provide the real-time location of cars for intelligence-gathering purposes. Your car transmits its location to numerous parties, few of which are explicitly disclosed. In-car security and emergency services like OnStar and its competitors have car locations, as do the companies that make the vehicle infotainment systems. And, just as with smartphone data, there is a rich market for vehicle data.

Ulysses boasted that its data sets were useful for "whether you want to geo-locate one vehicle or 25,000,000." The company claimed to be able to collect fifteen billion vehicle location data points every month. The exact sources of Ulysses data are unknown, but specialized data brokers exist that aggregate all this data. For example, an Israeli company called Otonomo is the Gravy Analytics of car data. It gets data from either the car manufacturers, built-in navigation systems, or mobile phone apps designed to provide vehicle navigation services. On a smartphone, you can ban apps from accessing the GPS. But there is no easy way to opt out of car data transmission. And manufacturers are fighting proposed laws that would let consumers opt out as easily as they can with smartphones. A spokesman for a trade group representing automakers told the Associated Press that it had safety concerns about letting consumers opt out of data collection—though, of course, car manufacturers didn't collect any data about their customers from the dawn of the automobile age until just a few short years ago. In fact, there is no easy way to even *understand* what data is being generated from a car. I know. I have tried.

In the summer of 2021, I found myself in the market for a new car. Buried deep in the reporting that would become this book, I couldn't help but consider potential privacy vulnerabilities in new vehicles. The Hyundai dealer I walked into had no idea what they were in for. First, I told them I was interested in an Ioniq hybrid but I wanted one without Hyundai's Bluelink service. *Oh, you can disable that by just not subscribing after your free trial period,* the sales manager patiently explained. Hyundai, to its credit, is actually pretty explicit about what it will do with your Bluelink data if you sign up. "We may share Covered Information, including vehicle, performance and driving data, as well as geolocation data, with authorized dealers and select third parties," the car company states in its privacy policy. But the policy also repeats the lie that geolocation data can be made anonymous or non-identifiable. But remember, your movements through the world are unique to you.

Unless you also work alongside your spouse, your roommate, or your children, you are the only person in the world who wakes up at your home and drives to your workplace. There is no way to anonymize your precise movements through the world. Yet Hyundai says it will provide that non-identifiable data "for marketing, advertising, research, compliance, or other purposes." Not that anyone aside from freaks like me read the privacy policy, though. And Hyundai is not even the worst offender. Nissan's privacy policy states that the company reserves the right to collect "driver's license number, national or state identification number, citizenship status, immigration status, race, national origin, religious or philosophical beliefs, sexual orientation, sexual activity, precise geolocation, health diagnosis data, and genetic information." How Nissan knows anything about your sex life is left unexplained.

Entire government surveillance programs have lurked behind language like "other purposes." So there was no way I was signing up for Bluelink. In fact, I told the dealer, I wouldn't even buy a car from them that had the Bluelink cellular antenna built in. If they had the base model car without the antenna, I would take that. The lower-end models don't even give consumers the *choice* to subscribe to Bluelink because they don't have the hardware installed that the service needs. The dealer said he could get me one from a dealer in Pennsylvania in a few days and then confessed—after I explained that I was a reporter covering national security—that it *was* "crazy" the amount of data the cars he sold now collected.

When my new car arrived, however, I realized I had shut down only one vector for data collection. Ripping out TPMS sensors—the sensors in your tires—is much easier said than done. Reputable mechanics won't do it for you: it's a federal requirement that cars have them and has been since 2007. You could theoretically do it yourself, but only if you were capable of jacking up a car, deflating four tires, finding the TMPS sensors, removing them, and reinflating the tires. A source described a garage near the special operations hub of Fort Bragg in North Carolina that could maybe rip all of the signal-emitting devices out of my car, but he wasn't sure they would do it for a civilian like me. Beyond that, the car had a satellite radio receiver and other telematics systems used for diagnostics and maintenance that could not easily be removed. If I want to use maps or play music, the infotainment system pairs with my phone and I have no way of fully understanding how they interact and who can collect the data.

Even if you did succeed in removing tire sensors and other potential surveillance systems, you'll face another privacy challenge when driving around. The entire country is increasingly blanketed with license plate readers. Private companies have sprung up to collect and sell license plate data. One company called Vigilant mounts cameras in public places. It also partners with tow-truck operators and garbage trucks—mounting its license plate readers on vehicles to capture the movement patterns of cars. Other companies like Vigilant partner with parking garages or private companies to get license plate data.

Finally, consider the evolution of the highway tollbooth. Until recently, drivers like me who hadn't bothered or didn't wish to get a toll transponder still had the option to hand cash to a toll collector sitting in a booth. But during the pandemic, many states with toll roads removed those remaining booths and humans in favor of automatic license plate reader toll systems that scanned your plate and mailed you a bill. Thus, on many American toll roads today there is no longer any way to legally drive in anonymity. Your location will be captured and documented, whether you like it or not. And, of course, those toll transponders like E-ZPass are yet another radio-frequency device, like a cell phone or a Bluetooth headphone. And again, they can be read in places where there are no tolls for tracking purposes.

In 2013, a hacker who identified himself with the online handle "pukingmonkey" gave a presentation at the security conference Def Con showing how he'd modified an E-ZPass to alert him every time it was read. He did this by wiring the device's circuits to a toy cow that made a "Moo!" noise every time the transponder was read. On a drive between Times Square and Madison Square Garden, where there are no tolls, his E-ZPass mooed six times. New York City claims it uses the transponders to measure traffic flow anonymously, but if you've read this far into the book, you'll recognize the surveillance potential. The "live free or die" state of New Hampshire offers the option of obtaining an "anonymous" E-ZPass, but still requires you to hand over your license plate, which doesn't offer a tremendous privacy benefit. And in order to replenish the funds on your anonymous New Hampshire E-ZPass account without giving up your credit card, you have to physically go to the Granite State in person and pay in cash.

And so I surrendered, ordering an E-ZPass, determining there was no privacy benefit whatsoever to not having one. For a while, I put mine in a Faraday bag that blocked the signals to avoid it being read when I'm not on the highway. But one day, my Faraday bag disappeared out of my car. Perhaps it was a deep state plot to make sure I was trackable and a team of agents covertly broke into my car to seize it from me. But more likely, I dropped it in a parking lot somewhere when opening my door.

I never replaced it. I had surrendered to the car tracking, just like the rest of us.

CHAPTER 18

We're All Signal Collectors Now

In 2012, on the University of Virginia campus, an undergraduate named Joshua Anton had an idea: what he called a "condom for your phone." He built an app called Drunk Mode that would keep you from humiliating yourself while intoxicated. Before a person set out for a night of drinking, Drunk Mode could be set to block certain apps like Snapchat and Facebook; it could remind you not to drunk dial specific people like your ex; and it had a location tracking feature that let you keep track of your friends and make sure they got home safely. It even had a feature called Breadcrumbs that allowed you to reconstruct your movements from the night before when you woke up in the morning. Another feature showed the girl-to-guy ratio at parties.

Anton spent his formative years growing up in the Virginia suburbs of Washington, D.C. In his teenage years, he had a strained relationship with his parents and was thrown out of the house as a senior in high school. While at Northern Virginia Community College, he set his sights on transferring to the University of Virginia's McIntire School of Commerce, one of the top business schools in the country. He set about building the entrepreneurial chops that he thought might impress an admissions officer. His first-ever business was called Awesome Ideas, a start-up to help other people launch start-ups— "not the greatest idea," he would acknowledge, looking back years later. He also resold used textbooks and even cheap scarves, which he and his brother would buy from New York City street vendors for $3 and then resell for $10 in the community college lounge, but their profit margins weren't enough to live on. He would also launch a T-shirt printing company and then a school supplies company.

All of these early businesses would flop, but they'd lay the groundwork for Anton's application to business school. He was so set on getting into UVA that when he realized he misspelled the name of the business school as "MacIntyre" instead of "McIntire" on his application, he took drastic measures. He made the trip from D.C. to Charlottesville and showed up at the admissions office at 8:00 a.m. to personally apologize to the school's admissions staff. UVA overlooked the slight and accepted him in 2012 as a transfer student.

His first fall on campus, a girl he had a crush on, after imbibing a few drinks too many, called Anton up one night to invite him over. While this was not exactly an unwelcome development, Anton, ever the entrepreneur, considered the development through the lens of a business opportunity. His first year at UVA, he had moved on from reselling scarves and was self-publishing e-books with titles like *Inve$ting: Blunt and to the Point* and *Mug Breakfasts: Quick & Easy*. But the burgeoning market for mobile phone software might enable him to level up. The idea was this: What about an app that stops people from making regrettable mistakes while intoxicated?

Drunk Mode was born. Anton didn't code, so he paid an eighteen-year-old undergraduate on Virginia's campus to turn his idea into reality. In addition to being a way to make some money, Anton thought the app had the potential to keep his classmates safe. He didn't drink in college, but UVA was a hard-partying school with all the consequences that entailed for the student body: trips to the ER for alcohol poisoning, general campus disorder, fuzzy morning-after memories, and the occasional tragedy. While Anton was a student, one of his undergraduate classmates at the school left a Charlottesville bar with a stranger and was later found murdered. Anton thought the app could be a way for friends to look after one another and prevent such tragedies.

The initial version of Drunk Mode launched in 2013 and cost 99 cents. It was a modest success and attracted a user base of about ten thousand people. But it was not without glitches. An early version accidentally erased the entire address book of a few hundred of its earliest users. But by the time he graduated, the app had switched to being free and had about ninety thousand users—a decent user base for a first-time app developer but nothing earth-shattering in the growing app economy.

As graduation loomed in the spring of 2014, Anton faced a choice. He had job offers from Google and Unilever; he could go the direction of a safe entry-level corporate job. Or he could try to build out Drunk Mode into a real business. He picked Drunk Mode. In diving into the world of start-up culture, Anton set a goal for himself: he wanted to double the user base of Drunk Mode and be able to pay himself a livable salary after two years.

In the early months, Anton would get creative in trying to gin up buzz for his app. He looked up lists of the top party schools and would create pages on Facebook like "UC Santa Barbara—Class of 2015" and invite people to join them. Then he would harvest all of the emails of the users who signed up and blast out Drunk Mode invites. (This was back in the time of fairly loose Facebook data collection rules; this is a no-no today.) A University of Alabama student named Jake Ellenburg replied to one of Anton's emails and said that he thought he could help market the app. He'd keep up the marketing stunts that Anton had pioneered, blasting Drunk Mode press releases to reporters with subject lines like "not porn" and "sober email." Ellenburg's persistence paid off when MTV and *The Huffington Post* both did write-ups on the app the same week—driving a surge of more than 150,000 new downloads in the days that followed.

But like so many other companies, the siren call of being paid money in exchange for user data changed the course of Drunk Mode's development. Early on, a company called Placed.com reached out and offered the app money to install its SDK inside Drunk Mode. Placed would then be allowed to collect location data from Drunk Mode's users, and in exchange the app would get badly needed revenue: a few thousand dollars a month. This was an eye-opening experience for a young company. Anton took the revenue from Placed and went out and raised about $1.5 million on a total valuation of Drunk Mode of about $8 million. Not bad for a novelty app.

At the same time, Drunk Mode was plagued by glitches. One of the app's features—the location tracking code that allowed users to track their inebriated friends or reconstruct where they went the night before—was causing technical problems. The piece of code it was using—from another company called Parkour Method—was quickly draining the batteries of users. It turned out Parkour Method's SDK was recording the location of the phones running the app once every second—a power-intensive operation that was causing problems for the app. Drunk Mode risked losing users or destroying the very usefulness of the app. You can't keep track of people and make sure they get home safely if their phones are dead, after all.

These two developments—the welcome cash infusion from Placed and the issues running Parkour Method's code—helped coalesce a new idea in Anton and his young management team. They gradually came to see that the real opportunity for growth lay not in building an app but in brokering data. Charging users 99 cents a download had sharply limited the app's growth potential. So they needed another way to monetize the app. As a first step, they thought they could make a better location SDK that wouldn't drain the batteries of users so aggressively. And second, they believed they could take that SDK and use it to make money on Drunk Mode and to help other young, fledgling app makers make money as well. Instead of being in the app business, they would build a data business.

Drunk Mode would morph into X-Mode Social, and Anton's goal became trying to create a suite of location-based lifestyle apps that could take advantage of the new X-Mode SDK they had built. One proposed app was called High Mode—a sort of Drunk Mode designed around the specific needs of cannabis users. The adults at X-Mode talked Anton out of that one. He explored building a family-tracking app called Family Mode, which would let family members keep tabs on each other; an app that he described as Waze for Humans, sort of Yelp meets *Pokémon Go;* and Walk Against Humanity, a fitness app with attitude that would track steps and running distance. This one actually came to fruition. Walking one mile would prompt the app to say, "Congrats on finishing your first mile! Did you know that Adolf Hitler had only one testicle?" Meanwhile, X-Mode could collect that user location data and sell it.

X-Mode the lifestyle app company didn't really catch on. Instead, the company's specialty would be partnering with other apps and paying them to embed X-Mode's new battery-friendly SDK. It first partnered with a handful of goofy apps in the vein of Drunk Mode: two alcohol-related apps, a soccer app, a weather app. But over time, it would get better at targeting apps that had a good reason to have 24/7 location permissions from users. For a long time its biggest data source would be Life360, a family safety app that allowed parents and children to keep track of each other. There were many others: app-based travel guides for cities like Amsterdam, Barcelona, and Istanbul; a GPS speedometer; transportation apps for major cities that would look up train and bus timetables; numerous dating apps, including some competitors of Grindr, that catered to an LGBTQ audience. There was even an app called Catwang that superimposed ridiculous cat faces on your selfies and other photographs. The Peel Universal

Smart TV Remote let people control their televisions with their phones. All told, X-Mode got inside hundreds of these medium-sized apps, with an aggregate user base that totaled millions of users.

X-Mode had found a distinct business model from Gravy, the company that started out as an events and calendar aggregator before pivoting to the location data business and launching a federal government subsidiary called Venntel. To put it simply, X-Mode was hunting for apps that might sell it data. Gravy was hunting for companies like X-Mode that might sell it data.

As a young business, it's hard to say no to money.

Placed.com wasn't the only company that approached the Drunk Mode team in search of data. A company called SignalFrame first approached Josh Anton before the company became X-Mode in 2014. But, unlike Placed.com, SignalFrame didn't just want location data on users. SignalFrame wanted to essentially rent access to the app to do something far more extensive: to tap the millions of people running Drunk Mode on their phones or tablets to conduct persistent scans of the signal environment around the user's device and record all of the Bluetooth and wireless information observed there.

And, at first, SignalFrame couldn't pay; rather, it wanted to trade X-Mode's SDK for access to some of the company's analytical tools. Such exchanges are pretty common in the mobile app ecosystem, but at the time Anton was looking for revenue—not data insights. However, in November 2017, SignalFrame came back to Anton with a different proposition: Would X-Mode be willing to use its burgeoning network of partnerships with apps to do signals collection for it? This time it could pay. A lot.

Both SignalFrame and X-Mode came out of the small, tight-knit Washington, D.C.–area tech community. SignalFrame was founded in 2014, the same year that Drunk Mode transitioned from being a campus project to a real company. The company was originally called the Wireless Registry, and it aimed to map out the world of wireless signals, encouraging people to "register" their wireless identifiers such as their phones, routers, and vehicles in order to provide them with personalized services. Getting few takers, the team pivoted toward collecting these identifiers from the ambient environment without user permission and mapping them out. SignalFrame at first hoped this data would be valuable to potential clients who wanted to better understand the world of consumer devices. For example, SignalFrame's software could distinguish a Tesla from a Fitbit from a Nest smart home thermostat. Just as location data could give Wall Street firms insight into how well a certain retailer was doing by measuring the ebb and flow of foot traffic in its outposts, SignalFrame might be used to guide investment decisions by offering a picture of the evolution of the kinds of devices being used in the world and how that might change over time. Was the number of Fitbits being seen in the wild increasing or decreasing? Could you compare that with the number of Apple Watches spotted and make a guess about market share? Such information could in theory be valuable commercial information. SignalFrame could also be used for security and identity verification. If you were trying to log in to a company network, were you in a place where the wireless signals like Wi-Fi networks and nearby printers corresponded to a company property?

But by the second time it approached Anton, SignalFrame had begun working for the government like so many other companies that started out working on a commercial product but found Washington's deep pockets and bottomless appetite for data alluring. SignalFrame told Anton it had a handful of federal clients who were looking to use the signals data for things like counterterrorism and facility security and were eager to obtain Bluetooth data at the kind of scale X-Mode could offer.

SignalFrame had a new twist on an old idea. Remember the Nemo Handy? The handset that an operative might carry to the back of a plane to confirm the presence of a target or gather information about a crowd? In essence, with the advent of the modern smartphone in 2007, we are all now carrying something like a Nemo Handy, and all it takes is a few lines of code in a time-wasting app to turn our phone into a government surveillance tool. Scanning the signal environment is what the government calls doing a wireless survey, and the tactic has become an increasingly important part of intelligence gathering as the number of devices and accessories that emit unique signals has increased. The ability to geolocate someone's phone or Apple Watch is an important and powerful intelligence tool.

SignalFrame wanted to turn a distributed network of millions of phones into what it used to take a highly classified $11,500 piece of equipment to do. It was as if it had put a secret piece of signals intelligence equipment into the hands of millions of unwitting people. In the 2008 superhero film *The Dark Knight*, Batman uses a sophisticated computer virus to turn on the microphone of every single phone in Gotham, allowing him to locate the Joker using high-frequency pulses emitted from everyone's devices as an echolocation tool. Batman later decides that such a system is too powerful and invasive and orders it destroyed. SignalFrame was proposing to do something similar with the Bluetooth sensors on the phones of millions of people walking around with X-Mode's SDK. The X-Mode SDK usually collected location. But it could just as easily also be programmed to collect Bluetooth and wireless information.

Anton and the rest of the young leadership team were at first unsure. Did they want to get into the business of helping to collect data for the government? But Anton eventually agreed to the relationship, believing that the data could genuinely play the same role in society that he hoped Drunk Mode might play on the UVA campus. He thought that in the right hands inside government it might help keep people safe, but in this case from terrorism, war, natural disasters, and famine.

Here's where a familiar figure reenters the narrative. The wireless data that X-Mode was helping SignalFrame collect would end up going to the data program that Mike Yeagley set up for the Joint Special Operations Command. From its PlanetRisk incubation as a demo called Locomotive, it had by now morphed fully into VISR, a "virtual" intelligence, surveillance, and reconnaissance tool created for special operators and intelligence analysts.

Like when he was at PlanetRisk, Yeagley was looking for a way to get adtech data without fully explaining what he was doing. *Success lies in the secrecy,* after all. At PlanetRisk, Yeagley had told UberMedia that he was working with a humanitarian organization that needed this global data feed as part of its work. When VISR got up and running, Yeagley simply used SignalFrame as a cutout. SignalFrame went out and acquired the data from UberMedia, saying it needed it for commercial purposes. It then passed the UberMedia adtech data and all the wireless data SignalFrame had collected to the VISR program.

As he had done at PlanetRisk when he acquired data under the pretense of humanitarian relief, Yeagley was trying to limit UberMedia's reputational risk and knowledge of what was actually taking place. Would UberMedia have done the deal with him to begin with if it knew the data was going to the government? It's unclear. UberMedia had a young liberal staff based in Pasadena, California, and a self-image of being a start-up that wanted to provide data for socially beneficial purposes, not surveillance or military operations. But once UberMedia had become accustomed to the hundreds of thousands of dollars a month coming in from a government contractor, it was harder to cut off the relationship with VISR.

But Yeagley's cover story would eventually unravel—not because of a whistleblowing government insider, but rather thanks to a stunt pulled by a competing data business CEO. Jeff White, the CEO of Gravy Analytics and Venntel, somehow found out that UberMedia was covertly providing data to the Joint Special Operations Command through SignalFrame. So he did a strategic head fake—the kind of mind game that's not uncommon in the cutthroat world of Washington, D.C., contracting. In April 2018, he sent a concerned email to an executive at UberMedia saying its participation in VISR was about to be revealed through a Freedom of Information Act request. White also said in a confiding tone that he thought government work was too controversial to pursue given all the privacy concerns and that Gravy wouldn't be entering that market. Both were a lie. There was no public records request that was going to reveal anything about UberMedia. And White himself had set up Venntel a year earlier and was making a serious push into the government market, but that wasn't widely known yet.*

UberMedia was then forced to confront head-on the reality that they were providing data to a government entity for a secretive national security program. Yeagley came clean with them. He told them that he was a government contractor and that he wanted to keep licensing UberMedia's data for use in a secretive federal government counterterrorism program. In August 2019, UberMedia cut out the middleman, SignalFrame. They signed an agreement to license its adtech data to Aelius Exploitation Technologies, the defense contractor with offices in Virginia and North Carolina, where Yeagley was now employed. The contract allowed Aelius to use the data "in the areas of national security and personnel protection." Only UberMedia's top executives were ever fully aware of what Aelius really was. The rest of the company's workforce was told the data was being provided for humanitarian purposes.

And thanks to its new relationship with X-Mode, SignalFrame had a platform to surreptitiously collect Bluetooth and wireless identifiers from hundreds of millions of people's devices all around the world. There were as many as ten million people a day walking around the world with SignalFrame's software on their phones who were now scanning the signal environment around them. In dense urban areas, a phone running X-Mode's code might see the radiofrequency signals from thousands or even tens of thousands of people every day. Remember the Norwegian who biked around Oslo and collected nearly

---

* Out of revenge, SignalFrame offered X-Mode $150,000 not to do business with Jeff White at Gravy Analytics. Bad blood ran deep in this industry. X-Mode and Gravy would never work together.

1.7 million Bluetooth signals over twelve days? SignalFrame was now able to replicate that kind of collection at scale. It had several million Bjørn Martin Hegneses walking around cities all over the world—unaware that their navigation apps, games, and goofy time wasters had turned their phones into surveillance devices. In total, SignalFrame would brag of being able to see 2.5 billion wireless signals a day.

The users of the Peel Universal Smart TV Remote were now signal collectors for JSOC.

After agreeing to work with SignalFrame, X-Mode would offer its location data on millions of people worldwide to other government-linked clients. And it would get plenty of takers: the defense contractor Sierra Nevada's nContext unit; another defense contractor called CACI, and yet another called Systems and Technology Research; a satellite mapping company with ties to the U.S. intelligence community called Maxar. At its peak, about 30 percent of X-Mode's revenue would be from clients working for or with the U.S. government, and another 30 percent would come from advertisers. The rest was from either hedge funds looking for data that would give them insights into markets or cybersecurity firms that were trying to use X-Mode's data to hunt down online threats.

In time, Anton would become a trusted partner in the community of government contractors working on location data acquisition. Mark Dumas, the founder of PlanetRisk, even made an investment in X-Mode.

But Anton also had reservations about the industry. In order to get comfortable working with government and its contractors, X-Mode put a number of restrictions on the use of its data. First, it would refuse to partner with law enforcement entities because Anton didn't feel it was right to make arrests based on his data. Second, even for contracts involving the military or intelligence agencies, X-Mode would insist that the data not be used to track specific individuals. In theory, X-Mode's data was supposed to provide a lens for understanding what was going on at a physical spot on earth or for understanding the behavior of cohorts of people in the aggregate. Of course, X-Mode was providing raw data and had no visibility into what its customers were doing after the data left the company's servers. UberMedia had written the same prohibitions into its contracts on tracking individuals, but analysts who have used this kind of data have described using it to track individual devices.

X-Mode was occasionally nudged to do data collection favors on behalf of the government. In one case, the company was asked to try to get X-Mode's SDK into two apps that government contractors were interested in: the hiking app AllTrails and the chat app Viber. Apparently, AllTrails was being used by people of interest to navigate certain areas with rugged terrain, and Viber was popular among Russians. Anton never managed to do either.[*]

But the one thing that Anton really did differently was insist on transparency. He listed *all* of his clients on X-Mode's website, including the ones with significant government contracts. He even listed SignalFrame. No other location company working with the government had done anything like that. This was something of a faux pas. Remember: *success lies in the secrecy*. But Anton wanted to chart a different course. He wanted X-Mode to be at the forefront of responsible uses of location data. He wanted to be transparent with the public about what X-Mode was, what it was doing, and whom it was working with out of the belief that transparency was good for the industry and the consumer.

That would be the company's undoing.

---

[*] AllTrails said it has never provided user data to any data broker.

CHAPTER 19

Mini-spies

PREMISE AND THE DEPARTMENT OF DEFENSE,
2012 ONWARD

"**W**rong"

A lengthy email with that subject line landed in my inbox at 9:54 p.m. on February 25, 2022. It was from Lanny Davis, a well-known Washington crisis communications expert. It was addressed to *The Wall Street Journal*'s Washington bureau chief, Paul Beckett, with me copied in.

It was day two of Russia's extraordinary and unprovoked invasion of Ukraine, and like many Americans I was glued to coverage of the war. And what was circulating on Twitter that evening was an incredible claim: that Russian forces were using freelance gig workers from an American market research company called Premise Data to mark targets for destruction by Russian warplanes. This rumor had gone viral on Ukrainian social media—sparked by a few users who claimed they saw people being told on the Premise app to paint markings with fluorescent paint. The reports had been given legitimacy by the General Staff of the Armed Forces of Ukraine, which warned in a Facebook post that the Kremlin was using the app to target artillery strikes. The rumors set off a panic in Ukraine—a country that was already on edge after being invaded by its powerful neighbor and whose very existence was under threat.

Premise was founded as something akin to TaskRabbit or Handy for the developing world: a way for organizations to collect data or do basic observational tasks from afar. The app had a globally distributed workforce of hundreds of thousands of freelance contributors or gig workers, all using their smartphones to collect data—usually examining the price of food or other goods, answering surveys, and taking photographs.

Premise was different from TaskRabbit in one crucial respect. The Russian military couldn't just download the app and start putting up tasks; instead, Premise vets its customers and helps them design the tasks. And with the outbreak of the war in Ukraine, the entire world's attention was suddenly focused on a new hot spot. Premise was eager to help, asking its contributor network in Ukraine to do things in the midst of the outbreak of war: take pictures of hospitals, bridges, roads, and even bomb damage. But it was not asking them to mark targets with paint; that was just rumor and misinformation born from the fog of war.[*]

I was interested in this rumor even though I knew it to be false, because I had spent the last few months investigating Premise and I knew something else. Part of Premise's business was serving as a government data collection operation—yet another way of obtaining gray data. It was offering up *people* as a service—freelance mini-spies that could take reconnaissance photos or collect signals without ever knowing who they were working for.[†]

---

[*]   Premise says it paused tasks in Ukraine after concerns were raised and that all of them were designed with contributor safety in mind. It eventually restarted them after the company believed it was safe to do so. Premise said it is unaware of any contributor being harmed as part of its Ukraine work.

[†]   Premise said in a statement: "In addition to the surveys and polls that can be completed from the comfort of one's own couch, Premise's contributors gather only publicly accessible data through photos of public places, as any tourist or other citi-

In Ukraine, Premise was not working for the Russians. Rather, its clients were the U.S. and British governments. Dating back to 2019, Premise had a network of more than 1,000 gig workers in the country that were being asked to do tasks that they believed were innocuous market research or corporate data collection but were actually secret intelligence-gathering projects for American and other Western allied governments. In Ukraine, Premise contributors were being asked to photograph crops as part of experiments to better hone American satellite imagery capabilities. Their phones were running software in the background that was secretly mapping out Ukraine's telecommunications system and its Wi-Fi access points. At least one Premise gig worker was actually a Ukrainian servicemember—and without his knowledge, his phone was inadvertently helping gather data for U.S. intelligence even as he served in his country's armed forces. In a sales presentation given in 2019 to U.S. defense officials, Premise touted its ability to track that Ukrainian soldier's movements in and out of military facilities. "Guilty by Geography," the slide deck read, boasting of how easy it was to identify the person's occupation thanks to their real-world movements.

On that February evening, however, I was keen to understand why Premise was being accused of something else. What was happening on the ground in Ukraine? Lacking any other way to get in touch with civilians in Ukraine on a Friday night, I started tweeting at the accounts, presumably Ukrainian Twitter users, who were claiming Premise Data was a Russian spy app. I wanted to try to interview them and figure out more. Lanny Davis saw these tweets and went ballistic.

---

zen can do. The tasks that contributors choose from are all publicly available and accessible from the Premise application, which is available for free to all to view on the app stores. Further, Premise discloses to its contributors in its terms of service that the data they collect can be sold to Premise's customers. Characterizations of Premise as a covert tool for intelligence agencies are rooted in fantasy, not reality. Premise provides insights and data so that its customers, including private companies, nonprofits, and government departments, can better understand the world."

"Paul," he wrote to my bureau chief, who unbeknownst to both me and Davis was trying to enjoy a long weekend away from Washington in the Bahamas. "Hate to disturb on a night like this. Earlier today Premise was targeted with a misinformation campaign falsely accusing the company that its paid contributors were helping Russians to target Ukrainians. . . . Yet Byron Tau actually went online today to ask at least one person who believed the vicious lie to call him." He added, "May I call you over [the] weekend or Monday before I issue a press statement calling Byron out for exploiting this tragedy and allowing himself to be caught up in this disinformation—without the courtesy of a phone call to me?"

For several months, Davis had been aggressively representing Premise as I dug into the company's relationship with the U.S. military. From what I could tell, it seems to have hired Davis at no small expense just to deal with me. He had gone up and down the *Journal*'s organization to complain about my reporting. Trained as a lawyer, Davis rose to partner at a prominent D.C. law firm, becoming active in Democratic politics at the same time. He met and befriended Hillary Clinton at Yale Law School and became a special counsel to the Clinton White House. But his specialty during his time in government was aggressive media relations—rising to become one of President Clinton's chief communications advisers during some of the lowest moments of his presidency, including the 1999 impeachment trial. After leaving government, Davis held a series of lucrative positions at high-powered law firms, lobbying shops, and PR agencies, taking on foreign governments that needed their images polished as clients. He also dabbled in representing people like Harvey Weinstein when they found themselves facing press scrutiny.

Davis's most aggressive action on behalf of Premise had come several months before, on November 17, 2021, when he sent a ten-page letter addressed to the general counsel of the newspaper. It began with the subject line "False and Misleading Statements Made by *Wall Street Journal* Reporter Byron Tau." It included a litany of complaints against my process of reporting. Premise had obtained some LinkedIn messages that I had sent to their former employees whom I was trying to cultivate as sources. I was using a tried-and-true journalism technique called a "spray-and-pray," where you message a huge number of ex-employees (spray), offer to have a confidential conversation, and wait (pray). I was pretty candid in those messages that I was working on some critical reporting about Premise and wanted to confirm a few details with them. Some of those ex-employees were uncomfortable with my out-of-the-blue outreach and had forwarded Premise my messages—a common hazard of the tactic. Davis was claiming that by merely asking questions, some of which he claimed were loaded or contained unverified information that I was trying to confirm, I was somehow defaming Premise. Our lawyers quickly set him straight about how journalism works: we contact people and ask them questions for a living.

Premise was waging this scorched-earth PR campaign against me because I was a threat to its business model of presenting itself as a normal market intelligence company while covertly offering its services to the military and the intelligence community.

Far from being just a survey app, Premise had become an intelligence, reconnaissance, and surveillance tool for government agencies: a way to collect information of all kinds from afar. Part of its pitch was that its local gig workers could go places where it would be hard or dangerous to send government operatives. At the same time, its work in Ukraine was like a match to tinder in a scared and overwhelmed society that was already primed to see conspiracies and plots lurking everywhere. As a result of asking untrained people to do surveillance work in a war zone, it had gotten itself accused of being a Russian saboteur.

Digital technology has made it possible to enlist and organize thousands of people to take surveys, do tasks, and pool information at scale—solving problems faster than any individual ever could. I was following Premise because at the highest levels of the U.S. intelligence and defense community, there was tremendous interest in what was sometimes called crowdsourcing. Crowdsourcing is born from the social science idea that crowds can often be smarter, better, or faster at doing certain tasks in the aggregate than individuals.

One of the areas of research into this idea was funded by John Poindexter's Total Information Awareness program back in the early 2000s. The research proposed the creation of a "futures market" called the Policy Analysis Market that would let people wager real money on the possibility of coups, assassinations, and terrorist attacks—on the belief that such a market might generate valuable insights. Such a market, whatever its theoretical value, was too macabre for Congress, which defunded TIA shortly after the existence of the research became public. This was in fact the last straw for Poindexter. He resigned in 2003 shortly after Senator Wyden and others on Capitol Hill began blasting the idea of wagering real money on terrorist attacks or political assassinations as "ridiculous," "grotesque," "morally offensive," and "wrong-headed."

But DARPA never lost interest in crowdsourcing. In 2009, DARPA would run something called the Red Balloon Challenge, where it would place ten eight-foot-tall weather balloons all around the country. The first team to identify the location of all ten balloons and report their locations to DARPA would win $40,000. DARPA expected that the competition could last as long as a week, but a team from the Massachusetts Institute of Technology won in just nine hours by tapping social media and other open sources of data. And this kind of crowdsourcing eventually became part of operational programs: one U.S. intelligence community project used gig workers to take photographs of bomb damage during the Syrian civil war to assess the scale and scope of the devastation there.

Premise was founded in 2012 on the idea of collecting good-quality data on the prices of consumer goods in the developing world. The original aim was to be able to provide price trend data to businesses, nonprofits, and international development organizations. In less formal economies where cash is the primary method of payment and a "retailer" could be anything from a full-fledged supermarket to a street vendor, finding reliable price data was difficult. The company's early leadership saw it as a way to monitor supply chain issues and give humanitarian organizations high-quality data in order to help alleviate problems like food insecurity. But there was a more commercial dimension to it, too: one of its founders, David Soloff, had been an investment analyst (and before that, a punk rock musician in New York City during the 1980s and 1990s) and realized that a lot of the data being used in business decisions was inaccurate or out of date. Premise's initial bet was that there would be enough of a market among traders, investors, and international development organizations for the kind of economic data it would generate.

Early on, Premise attracted considerable interest among deep-pocketed Silicon Valley investors, with backers including some of the biggest names in the Bay Area tech VC scene, among them Google Ventures, Social Capital, and Andreessen Horowitz. The former Treasury secretary Larry Summers briefly joined the board of directors. Premise also got glowing write-ups in *Wired* and *The New Yorker*. The Gates Foundation and USAID would become clients. It would branch beyond just collecting price data and offer its gig-working services to companies or organizations to collect any kind of data they wanted. Western Union, for example, hired the company's contributors to photograph the location and conditions at the company's sprawling array of international locations. And eventually, Premise would branch into sentiment surveys, asking people to complete polls about how they felt about all manner of social and political issues as well as measuring consumer and brand sentiment.

During its first few years, Premise's mission and focus attracted a young, idealistic workforce—the kind of socially progressive young college graduates who believed firmly that technology could make a difference and improve lives all over the world. But over the years, Premise found there wasn't a huge market for corporate data collection in the developing world. By the time I got interested in it, Premise was no longer primarily a company catering to nonprofits or financial traders. Its website still boasted of ties to the World Bank, USAID, the Rockefeller Foundation, and Bloomberg. And it had contracts with those organizations. But Premise had quietly come to derive the majority of its revenue from the Defense Department. It would target the kinds of units that did intelligence-gathering and mission-planning operations—U.S. Army Intelligence in Europe and the special operations task force that operated in Afghanistan, for example. It would advertise itself and its internationally dispersed workforce of workers for hire to the Pentagon and the U.S. intelligence agencies as an intelligence, surveillance, and reconnaissance tool—freelancers armed with cell phones who could be deployed to be the eyes and ears of the U.S. military in far-flung places, all without its low-paid developing-world workforce's knowledge. Premise would boast in meetings and in pitch decks to the Department of Defense that it was the only company that could gather intelligence under the guise of doing commercial tasks. In some briefings to government agencies, it suggested that it could be used to vet or recruit potential human spies for the military.

To support these claims, Premise took extraordinary steps to disguise the extent to which it was transitioning to be a defense contractor—even in some cases from its own workforce.

"And if you're going to throw up, make sure you throw up on the homeless people!"

It was December 2019 and Premise's CEO, Maury Blackman, was fumbling his way through a year-end speech aimed at celebrating his workforce just before he was to cut his employees loose to unwind at the company's annual holiday party. His joke warning employees about not drinking landed with a thud among his company's young, idealistic workforce gathered in the company's headquarters in the SoMa neighborhood of downtown San Francisco. *That's fucked up,* one employee thought to herself. (Blackman remembers it differently—

claiming he warned the staff they "should be careful not to vomit on any homeless persons if they drank too much.")

The company's co-founder David Soloff had spent several years as CEO before stepping aside in favor of new leadership. He would technically remain on the board as chairman, but his attention would be focused elsewhere. He'd start a new company and leave Premise in the hands of Blackman.

Blackman—a buff, fifty-something tech executive and former U.S. Army artillery officer—had spent the majority of his career marinating in the San Francisco Bay Area tech start-up scene. He had been named the Premise CEO two years earlier, inheriting a company that had a bold vision and had attracted big investors but was struggling to deliver on its potential.

At the time of the 2019 holiday party, Premise was at something of a crossroads. Enough of the staff who had joined what they thought was a data-for-good start-up with clients in the international development space remained on payroll, but it had slowly dawned on many of them that their employer was rebranding itself as an intelligence and surveillance tool for a variety of military clients. This was a small company, and it wasn't easy to hide things. Those gathered around as Blackman joked about vomiting on the homeless were the ragged survivors of various purges and mass exoduses that had roiled the company in the months since Blackman took over as he tried to mold an international development tool into a surveillance platform without really telling the bulk of his workforce what he was doing.

When Soloff, the co-founder, had been CEO, he had been liked well enough by the staff. He was described as polite and transparent. He earned high marks for the way he conducted weekly staff meetings where he would forthrightly discuss the state of the company, including its constant struggles with money. One employee remembered asking Soloff in a job interview how the company decided whom to work for and what the ethics were of what they were doing. Soloff said he wanted everyone to be fully read in on projects and that anyone—

engineers, project managers, operations staff—should not hesitate to ask questions or raise concerns about clients and projects. But under Soloff's management, the company was not making money. In fact, it was turning a negative gross profit on some projects; the more work it did, the more money it was going to lose for many clients. Beyond that, its technology and data analytics sometimes struggled to do what the company wanted or needed them to do as the company scaled up and users joined the platform. But in terms of management style, Soloff largely had the respect of his staff.

Blackman had been brought in by the board after it realized that to survive, the company needed to branch out from nonprofit clients. His task was to turn the company around and justify the $66 million in venture funding that had been poured into Premise with precious little to show in return. Accordingly, he and the people he brought in with him set a different tone. Secrecy became the hallmark of his management style. At the all-hands meetings he would lead, people would ask: So how are we doing? What's the financial state? What's in the pipeline? Don't worry about that, Blackman would say. That's my business.

One of Blackman's new lieutenants, the chief revenue officer, Ted Pardee, took a trip to Portland, Oregon, a few months into the Blackman era to meet the tight-knit team of engineers in the offices there who were emerging as vocal critics of the new direction of the company. One new prospective client, in particular, began causing a lot of friction internally, and it had nothing to do with defense work: Philip Morris, the cigarette giant. Employees began questioning the ethics of working for a tobacco company. The Bill & Melinda Gates Foundation was another Premise client, and reducing tobacco use had been a major public health initiative of the foundation. Employees in Portland wanted to know whether this was a conflict and how it squared with the company's general mission statement. Grow up, was Pardee's message to the developers. Stop acting like children. Do your jobs and don't worry about who the clients are. Unsurprisingly, the Philip Morris work would continue to rankle, especially for those who had worked hard to make the Gates contract happen. Some employees, aghast at these developments, decided to leave or to look for new work.

Meanwhile, employees in San Francisco were also growing increasingly restive. Premise had long been collecting data from its contributors' phones, mostly as a way to validate that the gig workers were who they said they were. The company had dealt with instances of fraud: contributors would create multiple accounts and do the same task under different accounts, for example. As a result, the company had built algorithms into the app over the past few years to try to defeat fraud attempts like this one. For one, Premise would make contributors take photographs of the goods they were collecting prices on. (Although this didn't always work: one enterprising user in Nigeria set up a fake storefront with all the provisions that Premise typically asked people to collect price data on and was charging *other* Nigerian Premise users for the right to enter his fake store and photograph his produce.) It would ask them to turn their GPS location on when they did so. It would begin collecting lots of metadata from the phone in order to fight the use of "emulators," or software that could make it seem as if the Premise app were running on a phone when it was really installed on a desktop computer. As a result, Premise was sitting on a boatload of data about its contributors that was going unused for anything other than task validation and fraud prevention.

But increasingly, under Blackman, the company was looking to that data as a potential resource. Like SignalFrame, Premise believed that there was a market to sell this kind of wireless data to the government. At some point in 2018, Premise staff began to get wind of a particularly sensitive client whose name was rarely spoken aloud by senior managers. That client was asking Premise contributors to walk a route with the app open—that's it. But in the background, the app was collecting detailed information about the signal environment around the phone—namely, what cell towers it was connected to and what the signal strength of those connections was.

Employees at Premise heard a senior manager refer to the client as "NexGen" and began calling it that. They started digging into what the company was and made a bizarre find. A California corporation named NexGen Discoveries LLC was registered listing Blackman as an officer a few months earlier. It had a parent company in Delaware with the same name. One employee responsible for finance and contracting told his colleague with a chuckle, "You'll never believe who is behind that." I never found out, and neither did they. It was, however, precisely the kind of signal data that the military was interested in buying around this time, and it was widely believed internally to be a front for a government agency.

Premise would eventually offer this exact capability to government clients: the ability to look at all the signals from Wi-Fi and cell towers within a city. In a JSOC task force document that I obtained, Premise said its network of several thousand Afghan contributors could do "continuous" cell tower and Wi-Fi monitoring in a hundred-square-kilometer radius. It was also offering the capability of understanding the signal strength at a specific location of interest. In its presentation, Premise gave the example of an internet café, a popular way of accessing the web in many countries. Its contributors could collect the basics such as the name and location of the café as well as details about and photographs of the location. But it could also passively collect which Wi-Fi networks and cell towers were reachable from that internet café.

Even before Blackman joined, it was clear that the public sector was going to be a major part of the future of the company given that its growth in the international development and corporate world had stalled. But the company's workforce believed that their government work would be about sentiment surveys or other support for the civil society, not the surreptitious collection of user data or the use of the company's gig workers in intelligence, surveillance, and reconnaissance work. But now a steady stream of proposed projects began to draw lots of concerns. Work in the Philippines, for example, where President Rodrigo Duterte was then engaged in a campaign of extrajudicial killings. Projects that proposed taking pictures of ports, including the comings and goings of ships. Assignments that might ask a contributor to photograph terrorist safe houses. All sorts of new tasks raised alarm bells among the San Francisco staff.

Their concerns were not unjustified. Premise had issues with contributor safety long before Blackman came on board and started pivoting the company into being an actual surveillance tool. Even when Premise served primarily as a corporate price-monitoring tool, its contributors would occasionally be detained and arrested. Often, shopkeepers did not want their wares photographed. The company had a long trail of contributor arrests across the globe, including a Malawian who was accused of witchcraft; a Palestinian man who was arrested by the authorities and given a hefty fine; a Zambian arrested for taking pictures of chicken; others arrested for photographing gas stations, banks, and so on. During the COVID-19 lockdowns, some people were arrested for violating curfews or stay-home orders. One Rwandan ended up in a two-week-long detention. The commonality in all these stories was usually photography: that certain authorities in certain places saw it as inherently suspicious or dangerous, made worse by the fact that some of Premise's untrained contributors would get scared and escalate the situation or try to flee.[*]

By the summer of 2018, Premise was in a bind. Blackman had grown wildly unpopular; the direction of the company no longer seemed tenable to its longtime employees. Government contracting was often a long process to land business, and it wasn't until later that the company would start to derive the majority of its revenue from defense work. In short, the company was in the middle of a dangerous period of instability. Blackman's new direction had yet to pay dividends, and staff morale was sinking rapidly. Moreover, the company had dwindling cash reserves—just enough to get it through the fall of 2018. Blackman announced at a July 27, 2018, all-hands meeting that the company would need an emergency loan to sustain its operations

---

[*]   Premise says that it has records of only thirty security incidents affecting fewer than 40 contributors out of a total of 5.5 million contributors. It says it has no records of some of the incidents described to me by employees.

until a new round of funding closed. At the same time, concerns about data privacy, clients, tasks, and the overall direction of the company were coming to a head. What emerged was a stew of toxic dissatisfaction that sank employee morale just as the company was struggling to close a bridge loan to shore up its financial condition. People began resigning en masse. In August, the company would lose its chief operating officer, senior vice president of technology, a people operations partner, a technical recruiter, and a growth analyst. In September, the company would lose its VP of engineering, its VP of data science, a senior manager of operations, a growth analyst, and a user experience designer.

In the midst of the turmoil, employees turned to various online forums to commiserate. Employees had created Slack channels outside the company's computer systems. One was called Dark Slack; another, Axiom. There was Prexit and yet another called lesmiserables. There was also the Signal group chat titled Dumpster Fire. The groups were a mix of current and former employees—giving one another advice, support, and leads on new jobs and encouragement to stay in touch. After the dust cleared, nearly thirty people would leave or be fired between May and November 2018—venting their anger in various online and in-person forums at Blackman, at Premise, and at the direction that the company had chosen to go. The company at the time had about a hundred people, meaning that close to a third of the staff vanished. And many were senior leaders who had been with the company since the beginning.

One of the company's growth analysts went further. After resigning from Premise for a new job at Facebook, Alex Pompe casually mentioned to some of his contacts at the Gates Foundation that Premise had become a very different kind of company over the last few months.

It would earn him a world of trouble. Premise filed an eleven-count civil lawsuit against him a few weeks later in California state court—alleging breach of contract, intentional interference with contractual relations, slander, and false light, among other things. Never mind that what Pompe, a thirtysomething who had come out of the international development space and joined Premise making $60,000 a year, had told the Gates Foundation was true: that Premise had begun working with U.S. government clients and that there were serious internal concerns about the safety and ethics of such work. In May, Premise would file a similar suit against the company's former director of data science, alleging that he had breached his contract by inducing other employees to leave. Both men would be tied up in years of litigation stemming from this.

As a warning to any other employee who might speak out, Premise framed both lawsuits as part of a widespread conspiracy. It named a hundred "Doe" defendants in both suits—meaning it could add any other former employee at any time as a defendant in either suit. To the diaspora of employees who had quit in frustration about the change in direction, the message was received loud and clear.

Shut your fucking mouths.

CHAPTER 20

Rhamnousia, the Goddess
Who Punishes Hubris

GEORGIA TECH AND DARPA, 2016 ONWARD

I n 1969, a scientist working on a project for DARPA—then known as ARPA—successfully transmitted a message between one computer at the University of California in Los Angeles to another computer at Stanford in Silicon Valley. It was a breakthrough that helped pave the way to the modern internet. In the years that followed, computer scientists often working with government funding hammered out the protocols and technologies that today enable every smartphone, watch, car, thermostat, and dishwasher to all exchange information nearly instantaneously on a global network of interconnected computers.

But the basic protocols of the web were designed by technologists who didn't anticipate that billions of people would move intimate details of their lives onto something that began life as a research network. Early internet architecture was designed in a trusting academic environment. What possible gain was there in hacking a research project? None of the internet's basic technologies were designed for either security or privacy. That gap—between the internet's original design and how we use it today—has given rise to a giant cybersecurity industry. Any improvements in the fifty years since that first network connection had to be welded on to an existing technical superstructure— a cumbersome and technically difficult task.

Much of the attention in the cybersecurity world today focuses on fixing or exploiting bugs, or unpatched flaws in software that enable the theft of data, the remote hijacking of devices, and cyber espionage of all kinds. The most valuable kinds of bugs are called zero days because they have never been publicly revealed—hence they've been known to the public for zero days. Intelligence agencies and spyware vendors pay millions to hackers for details about unknown vulnerabilities and build entire surveillance systems on those secret bugs. But beyond this trade in exploits, there is a secretive gray market for other kinds of internet data—as I discovered by accident when doing my day job.

In the spring of 2022, I was one of the reporters at the *Journal* assigned to cover a bizarre, contentious criminal trial that shined a light into the little-known practice of the buying, selling, and trading of huge quantities of a certain kind of obscure but important internet data. But as I dug through the details, I realized that it was just another example of the same phenomenon that I had seen when reporting on Venntel and UberMedia, the use of yet another kind of gray data that the public didn't even know existed and whose use the government didn't want publicized.

On trial that spring was a well-respected cybersecurity lawyer named Michael Sussmann, charged with a single count of lying to the FBI. The facts of the trial revolved around questions so technical that the prosecution as their first witness had to put an FBI cyber expert on the stand with a PowerPoint presentation to explain networking concepts to the jury. The jargon-laden proceedings featured a sprawling cast of characters and accusations of political intrigue, which might explain why the prosecution suffered an embarrassing loss when the jury acquitted Sussmann after just a few hours of deliberation.

Let's back up. The criminal case against Sussmann had its origins in the final days of the 2016 election between Donald Trump and Hillary Clinton. In the summer of 2016, a tight-knit group of academic researchers, tech company executives, and online threat hunters began combing through a massive trove of highly technical internet data to look for links between Trump and Russia after Kremlin-linked hackers had targeted Democratic organizations. They were looking to see if there was any evidence that attackers were probing GOP computer systems. Their purpose may have been two-fold: some of these researchers had also grown suspicious about the Republican presidential candidate's constant praise for Vladimir Putin's strongman regime and some of the ties that his staff seemed to have to Moscow. These researchers were mining what is called DNS data. DNS, or the Domain Name System, is basically a global address book for the web; it's how a computer knows that when you type google.com into your web browser, what you are really asking is to connect with the web address with the internet protocol address 172.217.9.206. Your computer relies on an architecture of DNS servers to deliver that information, translating a text web URL readable by a human to a numerical IP address readable by a computer, and it happens in a blink between the time that you press "go" and the web page loads on your screen. The same process plays out when sending an email or opening a mobile app.

Certain telecommunications companies at certain internet choke points are in a position to collect large amounts of that data. Just because a computer looked up a domain does not mean it actually exchanged data with that domain—in the same way that looking up someone in the phone book does not mean you actually called them. This kind of data is messy and incomplete; it's able to capture only a small share of individual user queries. But a large enough store of DNS data can *sometimes* let you infer things about internet activities of individuals or organizations, particularly in combination with other kinds of data. And sometimes those telecommunications companies sell or trade that data. Naturally, all of this is done in the shadows— with few having any idea who has access to these large pools of data and how they're being exchanged between government, industry, and even private individuals.

At the center of this research project into Trump and his connections to Russia was a longtime cybersecurity executive named Rodney Joffe. Joffe had tapped his business associates, employees, and contacts in the cybersecurity community to help with an investigation into whether computer systems belonging to Trump were showing any connection to Russian entities. There is some evidence suggesting Joffe was under consideration for a cybersecurity job in the Clinton administration, though he later denied it. And he seemed to view Trump as a national security risk.

Either way, what these cyber sleuths found was a strange series of lookups from a web domain called mail1.trump-email.com to domains belonging to the Russian Alfa-Bank. They ended up producing a white paper that alleged that an email server belonging to the Trump Organization seemed to be looking up computers at the bank in highly unusual ways. In the fall of 2016 as Election Day approached, their research was given to the FBI, the Clinton campaign and its operatives, and some of the country's top investigative reporters. The attorney who would later be put on trial, Sussmann, ended up in this mess because he was acting as a lawyer to Joffe at the same time his firm was also representing the Clinton presidential campaign. Sussmann was the one who took the research to the FBI, telling a friend at the law enforcement agency, "I'm coming on my own—not on behalf of a client or company—want to help the Bureau."

That statement would, years later, result in the charges against Sussmann.

After receiving the information from Sussmann, the FBI opened an investigation but quickly concluded that it was highly unlikely that Trump or anyone else in his orbit would establish a secret communications channel with a Russian entity under a web domain branded with the business mogul's own name. The bureau deadpanned in an internal assessment: "It appears abnormal that a presidential candidate who wanted to conduct secret correspondence with the Russian government (or a Russian bank), would (1) name his secret server 'mail1.trump-email.com,' (2) use a domain (trump-email.com) registered to his own organization, and then (3) communicate directly with the Russian bank's IP address."

Even after all I've described in this book, there are still ways to have a relatively secure communications channel. Nothing is foolproof of course, but a disposable burner cell phone purchased with cash communicating through an encrypted communication app like Signal is pretty good protection in most circumstances. There have been instances where I've done exactly that to communicate with a skittish source. I walked down to Best Buy—carrying nothing on me other than enough cash to buy a burner phone and a prepaid SIM card. I left my real phone behind at home to avoid any chance that the phones' patterns of life could be associated with each other.* This is not iron-clad security by any means, but it probably was good enough—even for a little international intrigue like a brief back channel between someone in Trump's orbit and someone linked to the Russian government. So the idea that instead someone would establish an alleged back channel through such a server was hard for people familiar with secure communications to believe.

Trump would spend the next two years under investigation for his purported ties to Russia by the special counsel Robert Mueller. After Mueller's investigation concluded in 2019, the political winds shifted. Trump's loyalist attorney general, William Barr, appointed his own special counsel named John Durham to essentially investigate the investigators—to see if the FBI had been overly zealous or too credulous in its 2016 investigations of Trump. That's how Sussmann ended up on trial. Durham accused him of pretending to be going to the FBI on his own, when really he was billing his time to the Clinton

---

*   In 2013, *The New York Times* revealed that the Drug Enforcement Administration could seemingly detect "burner" phones using big data. Similar reports surfaced that the NSA has the same capability. In general, if one phone is being switched off at the same time and general location that another phone is being switched on, they could potentially be associated.

campaign and secretly trying to generate media headlines negative for Trump. Sussmann fought the charges, denying he had misled the bureau and insisting that he wasn't acting on behalf of the Clinton campaign in bringing Joffe's DNS research.

Because this entire sordid affair inflamed partisan passions on both sides, it was seen mostly through the prism of politics. Democrats saw the case as the work of an overzealous special counsel who was falling for Trump's outlandish conspiracy theories, and Republicans saw a dastardly Clinton-linked opposition research plot that had invented the entire Russian collusion narrative out of whole cloth as a political weapon. The trial quickly descended into a political circus—one more salvo in an endless shouting match that had been going on between the parties for the better part of six years over whose behavior during the 2016 election was more appalling. Most cybersecurity reporters simply ignored it.

But in reality, the trial was like lifting up a very heavy rock and seeing what was scuttling around underneath. The Sussmann trial lifted a veil on some of the ways in which the entire internet is being quietly monitored—with vast implications for both security and privacy.

The only names you need to take from this are Rodney Joffe and his employer Neustar. Joffe is an enigmatic figure who had long played a behind-the-scenes role in delivering data or technological capabilities to the U.S. intelligence community, the Defense Department, and law enforcement. He was a confidential human source to the FBI. He held a high-level security clearance from the National Security Agency. He was known within Washington as being a reliable partner to both industry and government. He founded or invested in a dizzying array of companies, many of which straddled the line between corporate data collection and government surveillance. Tens of millions of dollars in taxpayer money flowed to his companies for the highly specialized data and services that his business empire could provide law enforcement and intelligence agencies.

Not bad for a guy who early in his career was peddling cheap grandfather clocks by mail.

Born in South Africa in 1954, Joffe dropped out of college, instead training as a programmer in the 1970s at a South African insurance company. But his real vocation would be more entrepreneurial. He immigrated to the United States, where he ended up in the marketing and direct mail industry in Los Angeles during the 1980s—the same field that had birthed Acxiom more than a decade earlier. One company he co-founded blasted physical mail out to thousands of people congratulating them for winning a "world famous Bentley IX" grandfather clock. To claim it, they'd just need to mail $69.19 in shipping costs. The thousands who signed up did get a grandfather clock—a cheap model that required assembly. Consumers hadn't "won" anything. They had in reality bought a particleboard knockoff "grandfather clock" worth approximately $69.19.

Numerous state regulators were less than pleased over this mailer. "You say grandfather clocks to people, they think of these big floor models," said a spokesman for the attorney general of Rhode Island. "They thought they were getting a deal." Joffe and the U.S. Postal Service reached an agreement that would refund consumers' money and stop the promotion. A recorded message that Joffe's company put up after the settlement said, "No doubt you are calling with a question or two about the grandfather clock you ordered."

This was a strange backstory for a man who would go on in the coming decades to reinvent himself as an anti-internet-spam warrior and a security professional with deep ties to law enforcement and the intelligence community. But it's proof that there really are second acts in American life.

Joffe moved to Phoenix, where he started an internet service provider and web hosting company in the 1990s called Genuity. By his own telling, as the manager of a lot of traffic in an unregulated, freewheeling early consumer internet, Joffe could see the source of the email spam transiting his network. At the time, most data transiting the internet was not encrypted, meaning that someone running an internet service provider like Genuity could see the content moving across the network. Back then, an ISP could read your emails or watch your browsing behavior in real time. These were such early days of the web that Joffe once described literally ripping network cables out of panels to stop spammers from sending emails across his network.

Joffe had reinvented himself now as someone determined to protect the nascent network from the kind of junk he himself once sent via the postal service. In 1997, Genuity was sold to a larger company called GTE Internetworking. Now being supervised by a real team of attorneys and corporate executives under the new ownership, Joffe couldn't yank wires out of server racks to fight spam anymore. He tried to pioneer an unsuccessful universal email marketing opt-out list in the late 1990s—a sort of Do Not Call registry for the internet. He would bring lawsuits against fax spammers in small claims court, representing himself despite a lack of legal training.

Spam *really* bothered Joffe. As late as 2017, Joffe would rail on a private industry listserv against a hapless technology vendor who attended a conference and sent a polite follow-up email hawking his company's products to several members of the list. Joffe angrily demanded that the list administrators take action against such unsolicited messages. He also suggested those in the technology community with "traditional" views about spam boycott the vendor entirely for the sin of sending an unsolicited email. "Rodney, What do you suggest? Shoot them at Dawn?" another member of the forum retorted.

Joffe belonged to a generation of technologists that had watched the internet transform from a clubby insular place to a global network. For early tech adopters like them, norms about spam and expectations of privacy were set in a time when network administrators could see everything happening on their computer systems.

After selling Genuity, Joffe would pivot more toward network security issues. He developed a new technical protocol for DNS and created a new company called UltraDNS that would offer better security and services to corporations. Essentially, UltraDNS would help protect large enterprises against a certain kind of cyberattack that directed so much traffic at a website that it overwhelmed the site's servers. It also helped manage a website's presence in DNS. If you're running a website online—say amazon.com—you need a way to tell potential customers that your servers are at 54.239.28.85. That is the service that UltraDNS offered. In 2006, UltraDNS was acquired by Neustar, a telecommunications company based in the Washington, D.C., suburbs. As part of the acquisition, Joffe would go to Neustar as an executive. He would quip once that his title there was "senior vice president of nothing in particular."

Neustar was spun out of the defense contractor Lockheed Martin in 1999. It was initially created to manage the North American telephone system. It helped allocate phone numbers, managed the area code system, and was responsible for the number portability system. (This meant that, starting in the late 1990s, when people moved homes, they could take their landline numbers with them. Later they could do the same with cell phones when they switched carriers.) Neustar would later branch out into marketing data, risk, antifraud, and other security services. By the time it bought Joffe's company in the mid-2000s, it was performing important services to many businesses and government agencies but was largely unknown to the general public.

It was around this time that Joffe would increasingly be drawn into the intelligence and national security space. In 2008, when a computer worm called Conficker infected millions of computers, he was part of a working group of experts who helped tame it. A worm is just a kind of computer virus that replicates itself to spread. Joffe was able to take his DNS expertise and use those stores of data to better understand the worm's origins and behavior. Basically, the computer virus was programmed to take instructions from a certain set of computers on the internet. DNS data could show computers that were looking up those servers and thus provide evidence that a computer system was infected. This was a successful proof of concept for how DNS data was a potential way to track and mitigate online malware. Several years later, in 2013, Joffe would be given a prestigious award by the FBI for his work on a different computer virus—the first time a member of the private sector was given such a prize in the category of outstanding cyber investigation.

Joffe's success with Conficker would show the value of the data as a cybersecurity tool. Many computer viruses need to take instructions from a computer server responsible for command and control. DNS can be used to track those computers responsible for directing the activities of malware. Neustar would be given a large classified contract to provide access to huge quantities of DNS data to the FBI. Joffe would also work with the Defense Department and the intelligence community. Neustar employees remember Joffe as someone who worked all hours—often tinkering around on secretive projects outside the company's traditional marketing, antifraud, and online security work for enterprise businesses. They had little visibility into what Joffe was doing, but they all had the vague sense it was on behalf of the three-letter agencies in the government.

Joffe had the trust of top Neustar leadership and a great deal of autonomy. He was allowed to pursue outside business interests while remaining on the Neustar payroll. He started numerous other companies that catered to the defense, law enforcement, intelligence, and cybersecurity communities that were separate from Neustar.

As with his anti-spam crusade, Joffe seemed driven to root out bad behavior on the internet by tapping his access to a kind of highly technical data. He clearly cared about the security of the internet. But the research project he furnished data for in the summer of 2016 also showcased that access to raw DNS information was poorly regulated, with potentially dangerous consequences.

That summer, a young Georgia Tech professor in the college's School of Electrical and Computer Engineering named Manos Antonakakis had a unique opportunity to win a significant amount of government funding from DARPA, the same Pentagon research organization that had incubated the Total Information Awareness program years earlier.

Antonakakis had come up with the idea of using several kinds of internet metadata—including DNS data—to develop algorithms that could detect and trace the origins of cyberattacks. He would build a giant machine learning framework called Rhamnousia, named after the Greek goddess who exacts retribution against those who show hubris or arrogance, designed to analyze this data at scale to look for malware and other cyber bad actors. Neustar would be the primary source of the DNS data, selling access to its data repository to Georgia Tech with money from the DARPA research grant. And Joffe would be Antonakakis's primary contact at Neustar. He would go beyond just being a service provider; he'd often play the role of wizened, sage mentor, helping the young researcher navigate the ups and downs of the government research and contracting process.

At the time, Neustar was collecting about 150 billion DNS lookups a day and providing approximately two or three terabytes of data a day to Georgia Tech. The U.S. residential internet service providers Comcast and Cox were initially planning to participate in this research and contribute their own DNS data, though Comcast eventually dropped out. Another residential ISP, CenturyLink, offered to turn over data to Georgia Tech, but that offer never went anywhere either. It's unclear why both Comcast and CenturyLink backed out.*

Even without Comcast and CenturyLink, Antonakakis managed to get his hands on a huge store of DNS data. Once he started working on advanced, cutting-edge algorithms to sort through it for in-

---

* Comcast was named in the DARPA contract as a subcontractor but said in a statement, "Comcast has not provided DNS or NetFlow data to Georgia Tech as part of this project or in any other context. We don't track our customers' online activities through their broadband connections, nor have we ever sold that information to anyone." CenturyLink said, "We didn't share any of this Netflow or DNS data with Georgia Tech or anyone else . . . there are instances where we share highly sanitized, anonymized data for educational or network management/security purposes. In other words, the type of data that isn't connected, in any way, to a specific customer but is useful for students to gain real-life work experience, to assist in improving our network efficiency or to help keep the Internet safe." Cox declined to comment.

sights, he would field calls from three-letter U.S. government agencies for help on all sorts of things. The FBI would call for help attributing cyberattacks. The Defense Department's Cyber Command would try to reach him, as would other elements of the intelligence community. The Justice Department's lawyers would ring him up. One of his fellow researchers on the same project would be made an FBI confidential human source. And of course his primary data provider, Joffe, was also an FBI source with his own access to a huge repository of data from Neustar and the numerous other companies he had an ownership stake in.

But as the two men set about trying to win DARPA funding, they were also doing a bit of freelancing on a research project that would eventually become infamous.

The Russian president Vladimir Putin's animosity toward Hillary Clinton dates back to 2011 when the then secretary of state criticized Russian elections that year as marred by possible "fraud and manipulation." Street protests erupted, and Putin believed that they were egged on by Clinton's comments. That predisposed Moscow to be suspicious of her and to potentially prefer the election of Trump, whose foreign policy was going to be a sharp departure from the traditional bipartisan foreign policy consensus. Trump had far more isolationist and noninterventionist views and sometimes seemed to take positions that were aligned with Moscow's strategic interests. The simplest explanation was that Trump didn't share the worldview and the assumptions of the professional foreign policy class and brought an outer boroughs gut instinct to his foreign policy. But a good chunk of the national security establishment was primed to see in Trump someone who was a walking counterintelligence risk, with his messy personal life and tangled web of foreign and domestic business dealings. Such a man would be an easy target for a sophisticated intelligence agency, they reasoned.

When the Democratic National Committee's computer systems were breached in the summer of 2016 by hackers believed to be linked to Russia, a number of cybersecurity experts including Antonakakis began trying to understand if Republican candidates or organizations were also being targeted by Moscow. That eventually led them down the path of scrutinizing any servers that seemed to be linked to Trump—an effort that would dig up the Alfa-Bank connections. Joffe had helped generate a massive list of possible web domains and email addresses related to Trump, Russia, and Trump's business associates. He sent it to his employees at Neustar and other cybersecurity companies that he had an ownership stake in. They got hits between the domains of the Russian Alfa-Bank and a Trump-branded mail server controlled by a marketing company down in Florida.

Joffe was the data guy in this project, providing huge stores of DNS data that Neustar and other companies affiliated with him were capturing. Joffe once joked about his role in the cybersecurity community, saying, "I'm not the smart guy in the room. I'm really the dumb guy that carries the bags—but fortunately in those bags, I have a lot of money." Joffe was being self-deprecating; he had technical chops. But it's true that his role was more an entrepreneur than a true technical wizard. His role on the Conficker worm was acting as the chairman for the working group that eventually helped mitigate the virus, for example. Antonakakis was the real expert, a PhD computer scientist doing cutting-edge research on novel data sets and hard computing problems.

The important thing to understand about the DNS data is that it's *messy*. To use it in a report often requires making inferences that might hold up in an intelligence report but would be hard to demonstrate in a court of law. This is because intelligence analysts are permitted to offer informed speculation, essentially saying, "We believe X will happen and we have medium confidence in our assessment." Lawyers and law enforcement officers cannot do this; they must stay in the realm of fact.

Joffe thought the initial results of DNS queries they were running were damning, showing troubling connections between Russian entities and Trump's email server. He strongly supported writing up a white paper and wanted to distribute it to law enforcement and the intelligence community. Antonakakis and others weren't so sure the paper would hold up to scrutiny from other cybersecurity experts.

"Rodney, you do realize that we will have to expose every trick we have in the bag to make a very weak association?" Antonakakis wrote. "In this case we will have not only the Trump folks trying to [shoot] this down, but all the privacy freaks trying to come up with a crazy conspiracy theory on how we obtain the data."

Joffe went forward anyway. He distributed the DNS allegations in the form of a white paper to his contacts in Washington, including Sussmann. They filtered onward to the Clinton campaign, to other academic researchers, and to the media. It became an extraordinary footnote in one of the most contentious presidential elections in American history, alongside dozens of other extraordinary footnotes that historians, researchers, and journalists will be puzzling over for decades.

One of Antonakakis's colleagues, David Dagon, wrote of the data used to assemble the draft paper: "I would preface the whitepaper by noting the criminal context of the inquiry. . . . While I'm not aware of any . . . privacy rights Trump might expect, I expect they all vanish when his network is used for criminal purposes."

But there was no crime—at least involving Trump. There was only a very tenuous association that a bunch of independent cybersecurity researchers had found on their own, using their privileged access to computer data that few knew they had. When the FBI and the CIA looked at this matter, they determined there was little they could prove with the data that was provided. Antonakakis and other researchers who did the analysis *knew* it was a weak association—not invented out of whole cloth, but not strong enough to make in a public accusation without significantly more data. Joffe, Antonakakis, Dagon—everyone involved in this project had taken it upon themselves to protect a network that didn't belong to them. These self-appointed guardians of the internet had made sweeping determinations with no oversight regarding how they got those conclusions.

There were consequences for that kind of hubris—the kind the goddess that Antonakakis named his project after used to dole out in myth.

Joffe left Neustar in 2021 as the controversy around his actions during the 2016 election grew. He found himself enmeshed in a criminal investigation by the special counsel John Durham for months before he was cleared in late 2022 and the investigation into his actions closed. Even though he was not charged, his legal expenses totaled more than $2.5 million—a sum that Neustar balked at covering, despite an employment contract between Joffe and the company that covered his legal bills in connection with company work.

And Antonakakis was vaulted from an obscure computer scientist and Georgia Tech professor to a top target for harassment by the legions of Trump diehards. Trump himself put out a statement after the extensive details of this caper became public, writing that what had become known as part of the Sussmann proceedings was "indisputable evidence that my campaign and presidency were spied on by operatives paid by the Hillary Clinton Campaign." Trump was not spied upon, and the Clinton campaign did not direct this research, but a torrent of public anger and harassment rained down on Antonakakis, Joffe, and everyone else involved in this research. Antonakakis would vent to colleagues by email about how quickly he had gone from a trusted researcher working on important projects for the Defense Department to a key witness in a Justice Department special counsel investigation—as well as the target of threats and harassment from crazy people online.

"Nearly four months after I 'received' a subpoena, I still do not know what I possibly have done wrong in this case," he wrote to colleagues at Georgia Tech in one of a number of self-pitying emails. He mused openly about returning to Greece.

What to make of the computer lookups between Trump and Alfa-Bank? To this day, the whole affair remains a mystery. Years later, many of the researchers stand by their conclusion that there was something suspicious about these DNS lookups between the Russian bank and Trump-linked IP addresses—something that was far from conclusive but worth investigating. Other experts believe the data was just marketing spam or that it was even spoofed by sophisticated entities who wanted to make it look as if Trump were communicating with a Russian bank. DNS is hypothetically vulnerable to this kind of manipulation by sophisticated actors. A final theory was that the U.S. government did not want to investigate the matter because to do so would expose the amount of internet traffic it was monitoring through internet metadata. This theory was floated by an unnamed U.S. official in a 2020 *New Yorker* article that once again took a look at the Trump-Alfa server story. "It seems possible that the U.S. government decided not to pursue this because it did not want to expose an important source and method for intelligence gathering," the official told the magazine.

But to me, the interesting question is not the DNS research about Trump. Shortly before the 2016 election, Franklin Foer became the first mainstream media journalist to report on the DNS allegations. In a piece on the website *Slate* that was heavy on speculation, he wrote, "Some of the most trusted DNS specialists—an elite group of malware hunters, who work for private contractors—have access to nearly comprehensive logs of communication between servers. They work in close concert with internet service providers, the networks through which most of us connect to the internet, and the ones that are most vulnerable to massive attacks. To extend the traffic metaphor, these scientists have cameras posted on the internet's stoplights and overpasses. They are entrusted with something close to a complete record of all the servers of the world connecting with one another." But Foer showed remarkable incuriosity about this world he had briefly been allowed to peer into. To take Foer's metaphor further, if a secretive cabal of scientists had actually placed cameras at America's stoplights and overpasses and were doing pattern mining on the movement of all 330 million Americans to fight crime, that would be alarming to say the least. Even if they used those cameras for good, helping you identify some notorious criminal, the entire project should at least raise some questions. Who were these elite malware hunters? Where did they get this data? Who put them in charge of anything? What other research projects were they running out of public view with large quantities of data? Foer didn't bother to explain any of this to *Slate*'s readers.

To me, those are the interesting questions about the huge quantity of data sloshing around between the cybersecurity industry and government. Neustar is not the only provider of this kind of data. Another Joffe-linked company called Packet Forensics also collects huge troves of DNS data for the U.S. intelligence community. A company called Team Cymru brokers a different kind of internet data called netflow data that's even more powerful and revealing, alongside DNS data, which it also offers. One person in the cybersecurity industry told a *Vice* reporter that it was "kinda bonkers" that he even had access to netflow data through Team Cymru, which was even more revealing than that of DNS. DNS data shows computers looking up one another; netflow data shows if they actually connected. If you want to go to homeopathic-hemorrhoids-relief.com, DNS logs would show that your computer looked up the correct internet pathway to get there. Netflow data would show whether your computer actually connected to the domain and for how long. Neither kind of data would show what happened once you got there. The logs would not show if you made a purchase for a cooling salve or made an appointment with a specialist or just loaded the page so that you could take a screenshot and send it to a friend as a dumb joke. But such data is still quite revealing. Cymru claims to have visibility into 93 percent of the world's internet traffic—mostly getting it from internet service providers in exchange for access to the company's own threat-hunting tool.

Corners of the cybersecurity industry are based on these kinds of clubby arrangements between private companies and government agencies communicating outside the view of the public and trading massive amounts of data in ways the consumer might not expect. It took the Sussmann criminal trial to provide a small peek into how they worked. With enough data and computing power, it becomes possible to get a pretty good picture of what happens online. Though DNS data sets lack personal information such as a name, it is possible to trace things back to an individual or organization with enough time, money, and effort.

Most of the time, as we've seen with Joffe, the people trading these data sets are well intentioned. They want to secure the computer systems that are increasingly used for everything in modern life: communications, transportation, and even keeping the lights on. All of the computer systems are now interlaced with physical infrastructure, and all of them are supremely vulnerable to disruption. But the sheer lack of visibility the public has into these arrangements and the utter lack of regulation around them are causes for concern. Sometimes private entities sell data to the government. Sometimes they give it. And sometimes the government designates them a "confidential human source" and has them exploit their access to it to provide information and intelligence. These arrangements are completely opaque. If you ask questions, you're told that certain identifiers are stripped of these data sets to preserve privacy. That's a strange defense when Joffe and his band of malware hunters were able to precisely resolve computer lookups between a Trump-branded server and other entities.

In February 2021, Senator Ron Wyden sent a letter to the Defense Department asking the agency to publicly detail what kinds of netflow and DNS data the Pentagon was acquiring on Americans without a warrant. It was a shot in the dark but in line with the kinds of hard questions Wyden had been asking of the intelligence community about how its activities intersected with Americans' privacy rights. "As Congress debates important legislation to close the loopholes exploited by these data brokers and their government customers, the American people have a right to know the answer to these questions," Wyden wrote to the Pentagon. "Accordingly, I request that you clear this information for release to the public."

The Defense Department's answer was a firm but polite "no thank you." But behind the scenes, Georgia Tech's Enhanced Attribution project was being quietly transferred to the Pentagon's Cyber Command as a prototype in 2019. There was talk of merging the kinds of adtech data sold by companies like Gravy and UberMedia with this giant repository of internet data for additional insights. The government would then run giant machine learning and artificial intelligence systems on top of this pile of data to help sort through it all for anomalies or patterns. The program disappeared behind the vast curtain of the intelligence community's wall of secrecy—yet another system ingesting vast quantities of data about the global population in the shadows.

CHAPTER 21

The Apps Are Not What They Seem

MEASUREMENT SYSTEMS AND X-MODE, WASHINGTON, D.C., 2020–2022

O
ne of the five pillars of Islam is the salah, or prayer. Performed five times daily by devout Muslims, the prayers must be said facing the most important mosque in the holy city of Mecca. The prayers also must come at certain times that change throughout the year based on different astrological conditions. The prayer times also vary by location on earth, because they are set by the position and behavior of the sun. Calculating the proper prayer times in each locality is a complicated mathematical endeavor, and many mosques once employed a specialized astronomer called a *muwaqqit* who could create locally accurate timetables for the correct prayer times throughout the year for that particular geographic locale.

This being the twenty-first century, there's an app for that. Many, in fact—dozens of smartphone programs for Apple and Android devices. Al-Moazin Lite was one such app. The app has been downloaded more than ten million times. It used the GPS locations of its users to calculate accurate prayer times based on the sunrise and sun-

set at a given point on earth. It could notify users with a digital re-
minder when it was time to pray. And it also featured an integrated
digital compass that could point worshippers toward Mecca no matter
where they were. It was a digital *muwaqqit*—yet another example of
modern technology making things just a little bit easier and more
convenient.

And it represented another facet of modern life: the app was a vector for what looked like government-linked data collection from its
millions of unsuspecting users.

The Android version of Al-Moazin was secretly running a bizarre
bit of computer code that was behaving in highly unusual ways.* Beyond collecting the usual GPS location, the app could collect an exceedingly large amount of data about its users' phones and send it off
to an unknown third party. First, when a user connected to a Wi-Fi
network, Al-Moazin could collect information about every other device running on the network. It could see every other phone, tablet,
router, smart TV, and smart speaker connected to that Wi-Fi and the
special unique digital identifiers belonging to those devices. This could
enable whoever was receiving the data to map out the social network
of the phones' owners—by seeing what other phones' devices were in
proximity at a given time. Second, it could also copy the material on
the phone's clipboard—which often included sensitive information
like passwords—and the email address of the owner of the phone as
well as the phone number assigned to the phone.

This was new. Data received by companies like Gravy Analytics and
X-Mode contained no explicit personal information like an email address or a phone number. With some basic tradecraft or some additional commercial data, a name can usually be inferred. But the software

---

*   Apple's iOS operating system is both more secure in some ways and much less
transparent than Google's Android. Some of the data collection through the
Al-Moazin app and other apps with the same software that are described in this
chapter is only technically feasible on a phone running Android. At the same time,
this behavior was uncovered only because Android is a very open system that allows
technical experts to see what a phone running Android is doing at any given time.

code running inside Al-Moazin could directly map a person's identity to their movements through the world.

Most bizarrely, it had the capability to scan the WhatsApp downloads folder of any phone it was installed on. It couldn't necessarily read the contents of the files, but it seemed to take an inventory of the file names stored there. This could be a remarkably valuable intelligence-gathering tool. WhatsApp is a popular chat app owned by Facebook that is used around the world as an alternative to standard text messages. And unlike standard texts, its messages are encrypted, meaning that governments have great difficulty intercepting them. This software in Al-Moazin could circumvent some of that and see what kinds of files users were trading on WhatsApp—whether cat memes, pornography, state secrets, or terrorist propaganda.

All this data about millions of users was not being sent back to the Egypt-based developer that had created Al-Moazin more than a decade ago. In fact, the prayer app's developer, a company called Parfield, seemed to have no idea what these lines of code were doing at all. Parfield had been contacted by a tiny, obscure Panamanian company called Measurement Systems that offered it money to insert a few lines of code into the prayer app. "We are a network analytics company with hundreds of client locations worldwide where we primarily measure network speed and performance for our clients. These include some of the largest ISPs in the world as well as financial service and energy companies," Measurement Systems explained to developers in an email trying to persuade them to insert the code. In exchange for placing this software development kit in the app, a developer would get a few thousand dollars a month, depending on how many monthly active users it could deliver data on.

The software was present in other apps, too. Measurement Systems in its own marketing material would claim that it was in more than two hundred apps. An app called Speed Camera Radar that purported to help detect speed traps had the software. As did a utility app that let you use your phone as a mouse for your laptop. But many of the apps seemed to be targeting Muslims: Another digital *muwaqqit* called Qibla Compass with more than five million downloads also had the software. So did Al Quran MP3 and Full Quran MP3—audio versions of the Islamic holy book in app form.

In total, dozens of apps had Measurement Systems software running inside them—most with global user bases in geopolitical hot spots such as eastern and central Europe, the Middle East, and Asia. More bizarrely, Measurement Systems was going around telling developers it didn't want data on the United States. Typically, the United States and Europe with their hundreds of millions of wealthy consumers are the biggest target for corporate data collection and command the highest prices. Why would someone ignore those markets?

The Measurement Systems software code had been discovered in 2021 by two computer scientists, Joel Reardon and Serge Egelman, who work together to study vulnerabilities in the mobile app ecosystem. They hold academic appointments at the University of Calgary and the University of California, Berkeley, respectively, and have also started a company together called AppCensus that helps audit mobile apps for security vulnerabilities.

They had never quite seen anything like this code. They diligently filed a report with Google about the concerning behavior of the Measurement Systems software code. The tech giant didn't get back to them. But they wanted to know more about who was behind this code, a piece of software that wasn't behaving like standard-issue malware. To them, this code looked like a Swiss Army Knife of espionage. But as they dug, they discovered that the ownership of Measurement Systems was hidden behind a maze of offshore holding companies in jurisdictions with some of the strictest corporate privacy laws in the world. The company's website was registered to "Contact Privacy Inc. Customer 0163902773," using a website registration masking service that enabled people to hide the true ownership of web domains. It seemed like a dead end.

But a few months after Reardon and Egelman had first started looking into it, someone either forgot to pay a bill or forgot to renew that web-masking service. Suddenly the true owner of the Measurement Systems website was exposed. And the trail led right back to Rodney Joffe's empire of cybersecurity and surveillance enterprises in the United States.

Beyond his role at Neustar, Joffe had ties to a number of cybersecurity companies. One of those companies was Packet Forensics. Joffe founded it in 2005 and still has an ownership interest, but long ago turned the day-to-day management over to a business partner and a protégé named Victor Oppleman. As I discovered, the company's activities were cloaked behind layers of obfuscation. The Packet Forensics website advertises a handful of boring-looking devices for sale that it describes as "some of the world's most sophisticated sensors for communications networks." They look just like any ordinary piece of equipment that you might see in any server room at any company anywhere in the world. That doesn't illuminate the reality of the company's business. The most succinct explanation for what the company does came from one of Joffe's business associates during the Sussmann trial. "Packet Forensics is a cyber company filled with hardware and software devices," he explained on the witness stand under questioning from prosecutors. The company is responsible for "collecting information on the internet globally and they did that mostly in support of requirements from the U.S. government," he said.

A peek inside some of the company's work with the U.S. government came in 2010, when a PhD candidate, security researcher, and technologist named Chris Soghoian got credentials to an event called the Intelligent Support Systems conference in Washington, D.C. The conference is sometimes called the Wiretappers Ball and brings together surveillance technology vendors and government officials. Soghoian, who would go on to work for the American Civil Liberties Union and eventually be a top cybersecurity adviser and investigator to Senator Ron Wyden, picked up a Packet Forensics brochure at that year's conference. The brochure described how Packet Forensics could help the government intercept encrypted communications by forgery: tricking computers into thinking they have a secure connection with one another when really the government is in the middle of the transmission. This doesn't break the encryption itself. Rather, it's what is called a man-in-the-middle attack: Alice tries to talk to Bob, but the message must secretly pass through Eve the Eavesdropper without either Bob or Alice knowing.

Soghoian turned his findings over to *Wired* magazine, which published a story in March 2010. Packet at first denied to the magazine that the box intercepted communications. The next day, however, a spokesman changed his tune. "The technology we are using in our products has been generally discussed in internet forums and there is nothing special or unique about it," a Packet Forensics representative told *Wired*. "Our target community is the law enforcement community." That old thing? *Nothing to see here.*

More than a decade later, Reardon and Egelman followed a trail of digital breadcrumbs that linked Measurement Systems to Packet Forensics. The two men brought their initial findings about Measurement Systems to me in February 2022. At that point, I had carved out something of a niche beat as a journalist interested in these questions of government-linked data collection through the mobile app ecosystem. They thought I might be interested, and I was. But I also felt that there wasn't yet a strong enough connection to Joffe's business empire to publish. It would take more reporting. The two researchers had linked the *web domain* to a known Joffe associate: Victor Oppleman and his company, Packet Forensics. But they hadn't linked the Measurement Systems *company* to them. Ownership of a web domain technically didn't mean ownership or affiliation with the brand. If Amazon somehow messed up and forgot to renew its iconic web address, amazon.com, I could buy it up and lease it back to Amazon. That doesn't make me Jeff Bezos. What Reardon and Egelman found was certainly a very intriguing connection, but it wasn't definitive enough to allege a genuine business relationship—yet.

The breakthrough came when we decided to follow Measurement Systems' ownership structure. Measurement Systems was incorporated in Panama, but two other American companies seemed to have an ownership stake in it—one in Wyoming and one in New Mexico. Those companies shared an address in the D.C. suburbs with a Joffe-linked company. In addition, one of Joffe's associates had created a U.S.-based company with the name Measurement Systems as well. So there were now three paths that led back to Joffe and his business partners: first, the Measurement Systems web domain was owned by one of his affiliates; second, two companies that had stakes in Measurement Systems shared an address with Joffe-linked entities; and finally, a Joffe associate had started a U.S.-based corporation *with the same name.*

This was the link that we had been waiting for. Beyond the shell companies, several colleagues and I had plenty of human sources who were willing to describe Joffe's relationship to the national security establishment, even if they didn't know the specifics about Measurement Systems. We were ready to move forward. Google, which had ignored Egelman and Reardon's initial report, was interested in their findings now that a newspaper was preparing to report on the existence of this bizarre bit of software code lurking in scores of Android apps used by tens of millions of people. Google gave me a statement saying it would ban any app running Measurement Systems code from the app store until the code was removed. This would stop *new* users from downloading apps with Measurement Systems software, but it wouldn't do anything about the tens of millions with the software already installed. That would require users to update to new versions of the apps without the SDK or delete the apps from their phones themselves.

But that issue was almost immediately moot. The entire Measurement Systems operation abruptly vanished on the eve of publishing our story. As I was going around to the various parties involved telling them that the *Journal* was preparing to publish, the Measurement Systems software code running inside dozens of apps suddenly disconnected itself from the internet. It stopped sending data back to its servers in Panama and went completely dormant. At the same time, the U.S.-based LLC Measurement Systems filed the paperwork to dissolve itself as a corporation.

Measurement Systems had been blown, as they say in the spy business.

Measurement Systems wasn't the only company that would come under fire over data collection from religious-themed apps.

Josh Anton's company X-Mode, which had made a long evolution from its days as the Drunk Mode app catering to college students, differed significantly from Measurement Systems. X-Mode was in the commercial data market, along with hundreds of other players. It made most of its money from investment firms, advertisers, or other commercial players looking for location insights. Measurement Systems SDK, on the other hand, was behaving more like malware— bypassing the controls that Android had in place for how apps were supposed to behave and failing to disclose to either the vendors or the app users what exactly the SDK was doing.

Still, X-Mode would find itself in the crosshairs after *Vice* reported on the source of some of its data. Through dogged reporting, the *Vice* reporter Joseph Cox traced the flow of data from some individual apps to data companies like Babel Street and X-Mode and published a story on November 16, 2020, with the headline "How the U.S. Military Buys Location Data from Ordinary Apps."

One of the apps X-Mode was collecting data from was Muslim Pro. Cox highlighted it prominently in his article, but also made note that X-Mode was embedded in all sorts of other apps. Like Al-Moazin, Muslim Pro calculated prayer times and used the phone's compass to point toward Mecca. But it had a much larger user base. As of the time of Cox's article, it was closing in on nearly 100 million total downloads, though the number of power users who had granted the app permission to know their location was in reality much smaller.

And Cox was able to link X-Mode's work to the U.S. government because of Anton's insistence on listing its entire client base on its website, including naming the handful of large defense contractors that were taking advantage of the company's location data. (X-Mode would later start scrubbing that list after reporters began systematically calling every defense contractor on the list to ask them what exactly they were doing with X-Mode's data and what government agency was their client. Unsurprisingly, they almost all declined to answer.)

Cox's article went viral. It stoked outrage among many Muslims that an app that helped them express their faith was being targeted for data collection and that that data might be passed back to U.S. military contractors. Muslim Pro put out numerous statements disavowing any knowledge of data transmission to U.S.-government-linked entities and terminated its relationship with X-Mode. In truth, X-Mode's data collection relationship with Muslim Pro was only a few weeks old; it had started shortly before Cox's article. In addition, Muslim Pro had long been selling location data to other location companies as well, and X-Mode's defense contractor clients had nothing to do with prodding X-Mode to target that app in particular. But Apple and Google found themselves under pressure from members of Congress and activist groups to take action.

I got a tip one December day in late 2020 a few weeks after Cox's story that I should call the communications departments at both Apple and Google and ask them about X-Mode. When I reached out, both companies confirmed to me they were preparing to take action against X-Mode. They were giving apps thirty days to remove X-Mode's software code or face a total ban from the app stores.

Preparing to file a story for the *Journal* about this, I called X-Mode to get its comment. Nobody at Apple and Google had bothered to tell X-Mode that it was about to be banned. It was through my phone call that it learned it was about to be blacklisted and its business imperiled.

And this was exceedingly poor timing for the company. X-Mode had been days away from closing its series B round of funding—a major moment for a young start-up. The new funding would have given the company an influx of new cash to make strategic investments in the future: to hire more staff and ideally to grow even larger. X-Mode's series B funding vanished. Anton described this to colleagues as the worst day of his life—worse than when he was thrown out of his house his senior year of high school by his parents.

It's unclear what rule X-Mode actually broke. Apple's explanation was that X-Mode "surreptitiously builds user profiles based on collected user data." Well, okay. If Apple was going to ban every piece of software that did that, it wouldn't have many apps left in the app store. The entire digital advertising business is built on the surreptitious collection of user data to make user profiles. These are serious questions worth addressing at a systemic level by Apple and Google, which wield tremendous influence over what kind of software consumers can download through their control of their app stores. Apple and Google had swatted one small gnat as a swarm continued buzzing all around them, threatening to devour them and their users.

In the weeks after X-Mode was blacklisted, the company had to lay off about a third of its staff. It did manage to survive, figuring out a different way to collect data from apps that Apple and Google had less visibility into and almost no ability to police. It stopped being transparent about who its clients were, unless required by law. And finally, in 2021, Anton sold it to a cyber-data company called Digital Envoy at a reduced price from its series B valuation.

But the appetite for the kind of data X-Mode was offering was only growing. A few months after Anton sold it off, Gravy Analytics closed its seventh funding round. And UberMedia was bought by a Singapore-based company called Near. The combined entity went public through a blank-check merger for $1 billion. It was providing data to the U.S. government through a maze of shell companies well into 2023.

Most people are bewildered to learn that their phones and apps might be a vector for data collection. *Why would any government care about me?* they ask. But beyond being harmless time wasters, apps are a backdoor portal to doing data collection. Beneath software code running on millions or even billions of mobile devices is a world that the ordinary person can't possibly begin to unravel and understand without a PhD like Serge Egelman or Joel Reardon. Each of these apps can be a vector for delivering malware to an intelligence target or Chinese takeout to a consumer—or both at the same time.

The first time many consumers had to even confront the idea that their phones might be collecting something of value to a nation-state was the intermittent outbreaks of bipartisan alarm in Washington over TikTok that began in 2020. TikTok, the addictive social media service with more than a billion users worldwide, is owned by the Chinese internet company ByteDance, which under Chinese law is required to cooperate with demands from Beijing for data.* The Trump administration tried to ban the app from the United States in its final year in office. Two separate federal judges ruled against the administration and blocked the ban from going into effect, finding that the president's emergency economic powers did not confer the authority to ban TikTok. The Biden administration eventually withdrew the order when it came into office in 2021.

But that didn't end concerns about the app. The Biden administration kicked the problem to an interagency group that reviewed investments in the United States. In March 2023, that entity—called the Committee on Foreign Investment in the United States—recommended that TikTok's Chinese parent company be required to divest from the app. The Biden administration threw its support behind a bipartisan law being considered in the Senate that would overcome the problem Trump faced and give the president new powers to ban software services from certain adversary countries.

National security officials remain so concerned about TikTok because the United States engages in the same practice: collecting data through apps at scale to project national power. That is why Anton was nudged to try to start collecting location data from AllTrails and

---

*   TikTok claims that U.S. user data is stored on U.S.-based computer servers, a claim that has not mollified critics of the company.

Viber. That is why Measurement Systems is lurking in apps popular in eastern Europe and the Middle East. And so the United States should not be surprised that China does it. The United States had the lead for the better part of a decade when its homegrown social networks like Facebook, Instagram, and Twitter were ascendant. But national security officials woke up one day to the fact that one of the most popular social networks in the world was controlled by a Chinese company regulated under Chinese national security laws that give the state powers to access pretty much anything. And China does not let American companies store data on Chinese citizens on servers that are geographically in the United States. To China, data is a national asset that needs to be protected, and other countries' data is a resource to be exploited whenever possible. The United States has been very slow to understand this and even slower to figure out how exactly to address this problem in a free society where it might be seen as a bridge too far for a government to tell citizens they can't have a video-based social media app filled with dance videos and dumb viral trends.

Americans have already seen the effect that data can have on their own intelligence operations. For almost a decade, U.S. special operators have been getting lessons in operational security: how to avoid leaking data from their cell phones and other consumer devices into the commercial ecosystem. Not all of them have been taking those lessons to heart. In 2018, the fitness app Strava published a global "heatmap" showing all of the popular running and cycling routes that its twenty-seven million users ran. Inside that data were the internal layouts of a number of unannounced military and intelligence facilities—mapped in the data of more than a billion exercise routes collated by the company. "This is where I politely remind @Strava that it is sitting on a ton of data that most intelligence entities would literally kill to acquire," one well-known professor tweeted. In July 2023, Strava's potential use as an intelligence tool to understand the habits and routines of an adversary would come to light again after a Russian submarine commander who regularly posted his running routes on the app was killed in broad daylight on a morning run.

An even more bizarre operational security lapse came when the open-source intelligence collective Bellingcat revealed the presence of sensitive information on an app called Untappd. Untappd is used by people who like beer to keep track of and rate their favorite brews and allows users to upload photos or log where they are when they sample a new bottle. On this beer-themed social network, one U.S. Defense Department official took a picture of his beer with classified papers in the background of the photo. Another user kept logging his location at "the Farm," the CIA training facility where clandestine service officers are trained.

TikTok offers far, far more vectors for these kinds of errors.

"If Americans woke up tomorrow to stories in *The Wall Street Journal* or *Washington Post* that China had put 100 million sensors all over America, there would be alarm. But that's exactly what's happening with TikTok," the former CIA officer and technologist Klon Kitchen told me.

TikTok offers numerous ways for an adversary like China to cause trouble. For one, through a social network like TikTok, China can collect immense amounts of behavioral data on Americans. It can understand their likes, dislikes, preferences, habits, and routines. The friend networks and social circles of Americans can also be collected through TikTok by mapping out who follows whom and who interacts with whom. Finally, Americans are uploading a great deal of biometric information—their faces, for example—to these services. American law enforcement and intelligence pull facial data from social media sites, so it's hard to imagine that China would not use its unprecedented access to all data that flows through its country to do the same.

Finally, TikTok has a tremendous influence on global public opinion and online discourse. Should it be concerning that an authoritarian country decides what content billions of people see? TikTok for a time had generalized global policies in place that ban discussing topics like the Tiananmen Square massacre, the Cambodian genocide, and other parts of history that reflect poorly on communist movements. It did not permit political speech that denigrates the policies and social rules of governments, which encompasses attacks on China's lack of democracy and poor human rights record. (It now says it has lifted some of those restrictions.) That an authoritarian country regulates a platform that tens of millions of Americans use every day certainly raises profound questions, beyond just data collection.

These spy games go beyond apps. As with TikTok, the United States is concerned about how deeply Chinese telecommunications companies like Huawei have penetrated developed world communications systems, citing the risk that Chinese equipment could be used for espionage. Because we do it. They can too.

At least three people have described to me the commercial partners that for all intents and purposes allow the U.S. government to buy foreign telecommunication data—sometimes an entire country's worth at a time. Basically, an American company with hidden ties to the intelligence community finds a commercial reason to install telecommunications equipment in a foreign country or otherwise gain access to the network. Usually, it offers the foreign telecom a service: to improve network reliability or fight fraud or spam calls. Something like that. And as part of the arrangement, it gets commercial access to foreign telecommunications networks and sells that data back to the U.S. government for tens of millions of dollars. In some cases, this isn't just the metadata of who called whom; it can include the content of calls, text messages, and other data transiting the network.

American intelligence agencies have spent more than a decade running this playbook of data collection through commercial arrangements—with their antennas pointed at geopolitical hot spots like the Middle East and eastern Europe. But now another powerful country is focusing the might of its resources backed by its cultural and technological assets against *us* and our global interests.

For the first time since the dawn of the computing era, we Americans are the ones who suddenly feel vulnerable in a world awash in data.

CHAPTER 22

The Privilege of Disappearing

AMERICA IN THE 2020s

I n the twenty-first century, the privilege of disappearing is one that belongs only to the government and its employees, the very wealthy, or the very eccentric. When it comes to the rest of us, the ability to move around the world without being trackable is seen as a threat.

Consider the tale of two companies that were both broadly in the same business: securing mobile devices in order to offer privacy to their users. One is called CIS Mobile. The other is called Sky Global.

CIS Mobile makes a highly modified version of Google's Android operating system that it calls AltOS. On its standard version of Android, Google collects a wealth of information about the device: what apps are installed, the GPS location of the phone, diagnostic and technical information about the hardware and software, and much more. The original manufacturer of the phone—Samsung, Motorola, Huawei, and so on—often also installs software on the phone to collect similar data. And that's all before users even begin to install apps or browse the web, where hundreds or thousands of entities can collect data in some way, shape, or form in the marketing ecosystem and make it available for sale in opaque digital marketplaces.

AltOS puts a stop to much of this. Android is open-source software, meaning its computer code is free for public inspection and can be modified by anyone who wants to change it to suit their needs. Developed by a Canadian technologist and executive named Paul Litva, CIS Mobile's heavily modified version of Android reduces the amount of data exhaust transmitted to third parties down to zero. It breaks the advertising industry's tracking infrastructure by randomizing the device's Google-issued advertising identifier at frequent intervals, making any sort of persistent tracking of the device over time impossible. It also has a feature that partitions the device into digital "containers" and allows a user to have a hidden container that is invisible upon casual inspection even if the user is forced to unlock their device. Different containers can be set for different levels of security; for example, a user could install games and social media in one less secure container and work-related apps like email in a separate container that has stronger security. The containers are digitally isolated from one another and there is no cross-pollination, so the less secure apps have no visibility into the other apps' data. Finally, the phone can also be put into a special "secure mode" where the microphone, camera, and cellular and Bluetooth connections are disabled.

At the same time, AltOS is completely integrated with the standard Android ecosystem. It can be installed on a smartphone that looks no different from any other consumer phone. The apps that people rely on for communications, connection, and distraction can run on an AltOS phone with few of the risks that typically come with these apps when they're downloaded onto a standard consumer phone.

The other company in this tale is Sky Global. Founded in Canada in 2010, Sky Global took a much more hardware-oriented approach to the problem of secure mobile phones. Sky Global sold heavily modified Nokia, Google, Apple, and BlackBerry devices coupled with a high-end end-to-end messaging service. It would physically disable the cameras, microphones, and GPS of their mobile devices—all vectors for hacking and surveillance of one kind or another. One can't collect location data from a consumer if the phone doesn't even have GPS, after all. Having no microphone limited a device's usefulness as a "phone" in the traditional sense of being able to make voice calls, but users could communicate via an encrypted text-based messaging platform that Sky Global ran and install the standard smartphone apps that most smartphones allow. Sky Global's services had some unique features. The entire device could be wiped if the user entered "panic" as a password. And chats sent over the company's encrypted platform were set to disappear by default. Finally, Sky Global could wipe the phone for customers remotely if it was lost.

These two companies took different technical approaches to the same set of problems: that in the twenty-first century, tracking is persistent and ubiquitous; that consumer technology is entirely built to facilitate it; and that the only plausible way to avoid it is to go to extremes. Both companies came up with their own custom solutions to address this issue.

But that's where their stories and fortunes diverge sharply.

CIS Mobile is a trusted U.S. government contractor that occasionally sells its devices to high-net-worth individuals and other civilians with extreme privacy needs. It markets its phone as useful in intelligence and military operations. It is even trying to get government agencies comfortable enough with the technology to let their employees bring CIS Mobile phones into secure government work spaces—usually a big no-no in classified offices. Because CIS Mobile can enforce software restrictions such as turning off certain features of the phone in certain places or at certain times, it believes it offers a way to let government employers let their employees bring their device into work.

Sky Global's CEO, on the other hand, was indicted in 2021 for being involved in a criminal enterprise "that facilitated the transnational importation and distribution of narcotics through the sale and service of encrypted communications devices" under a law typically used to prosecute international drug cartels and mafia organizations.

Sky Global "allegedly provided a service designed to allow criminals to evade law enforcement to traffic drugs and commit acts of violent crime without detection," said the FBI agent in charge of the field office that supervised the investigation. Facing a stiff sentence that could go as high as life in prison, the CEO, Jean-François Eap, has nevertheless vowed to fight the charges, proclaiming his innocence.

The fundamental philosophical question raised here is, what's the difference, exactly? Should having access to a secure phone be limited only to government personnel such as intelligence officers and spies? Are citizens *required* to carry a tracking device that logs their every move and transmits it to dozens of parties to access the benefits and conveniences of modern life? Does the mere desire to have ephemeral communications that are not tracked, stored, logged, and searchable forever indicate criminal behavior? Is it too dangerous in the twenty-first century to let people live off the digital grid? In 2023, the U.K.'s Home Office even went so far as to propose a legislative measure that would make selling or even *possessing* an encrypted device a crime in and of itself in some cases.

These are profound and unanswered questions raised by the legal theory advanced by the prosecution in the Sky Global case. There is no doubt that drug dealers and other criminals were using Sky Global devices to communicate in furtherance of some very nasty things. But drug dealers and other criminals also use Apple and Samsung devices. They use encrypted software chat apps like WhatsApp and Signal that millions of law-abiding people also use. They also sometimes use Ford cars and Williams-Sonoma kitchen knives in furtherance of nasty things, for that matter. There was plenty of evidence that Sky Global was simply making a tool—one that perhaps it knew could be used by drug dealers but one that was fundamentally still just a tool to communicate privately. At one point, its sales reps offered Canadian law enforcement officials a demo of the device in the hopes of selling Sky Global phones to police officers and prosecutors who might need secure communication. Sky Global's lawyers filed in court paperwork instances in which Sky Global refused requests to sell the phones to known criminals or refused to remotely wipe phones that had been seized as part of a law enforcement investigation. That's not exactly the mark of a transnational criminal organization.

The government knows the dangers a phone can pose to its own operations, officials, and service members. But it increasingly takes the position that it wants its citizens trackable at all times and that anything that thwarts that is suspect, dangerous, and possibly illegal. Want to build an ultra-secure phone? That could lead to lucrative federal contracts—or jail.

The one place where there is a small but thriving market for ultra-high-end privacy services that has not yet been shut down by authorities is among the very wealthy.

In September 2022, I spoke to two executives from a small Maryland-based firm called Glacier Security. Like the former intelligence officers they are, they asked me not to use their names. The two had met while serving in government, working on the problem of securing mobile devices for federal employees. After leaving government service, they founded a consulting firm aimed at helping high-risk individuals with their privacy and security needs. Their primary clientele are wealthy individuals and their families, though they also provide services to entire corporate executive teams.

Glacier also has government customers; its corporate offices are adjacent to Fort Meade, Maryland, the home of the National Security Agency. They told me they don't get a lot of criminals seeking their services. That's probably because they are fairly open about their past affiliations with the intelligence community, though once in a while they do get a request that they're uncomfortable with. They have a privacy policy and terms of service and won't deal with organizations unwilling to sign such documents.

Every Glacier customer gets a consultation about their needs and possible threats to their privacy. After that, Glacier can provide custom solutions. If customers are willing, Glacier will set them up on one of CIS Mobile's AltOS devices and help manage it for them. And if they're Apple addicts too deep in the iPhone and Mac ecosystem to ever get out, Glacier has some custom ultra-secure Apple iPhones that it can set up—though Apple doesn't make it easy.

The most important thing Glacier has found is that people have to *want* to use the custom solution for their everyday needs. A secure phone that ends up in a desk drawer is of no use. This is why there are a litany of failed government efforts to create secure phones: they were so secure as to be unusable and forced their users to carry a second consumer-grade device around to access the apps and services that everyone relies on. Which, of course, defeats the purpose of a secure phone.

Glacier Security will serve you a fish—caught, gutted, filleted, grilled, and ready to be enjoyed with some butter and lemon. It will build a custom privacy solution tailored for your needs and manage it for you.

Michael Bazzell, on the other hand, will teach you how to fish.

Bazzell is a former law enforcement investigator who spent nearly two decades working on cybercrime for the FBI before turning privacy consultant, author, and evangelist. Like Glacier, Bazzell does consulting for clients. He estimates he probably helps hundreds of clients each year reclaim some aspect of their digital privacy. Some are celebrities trying to dodge stalkers or overly zealous fans. Some are billionaires looking to reduce their information profile. Some are law enforcement officers involved in sensitive investigations against dangerous criminal organizations. And many are ordinary people. Some of those people have urgent and legitimate needs, such as trying to escape an abusive partner. Others are just very private people who believe that the trade-offs of modern life aren't worth it and want to take steps to preserve their anonymity.

But Bazzell is also bringing the gospel of privacy to the masses—at least the masses who are interested in issues of privacy. He wrote the book *Extreme Privacy: What It Takes to Disappear,* which is now in its fourth edition, edits a digital privacy magazine called *Unredacted*, and hosts a popular podcast called *The Privacy, Security & OSINT Show.* He also served as a technical consultant to the popular USA Network show *Mr. Robot,* which ran between 2015 and 2019 and told the story of a brilliant, mentally ill hacker and his fight against a shadowy syndicate called the Dark Army. In his books, magazine, and weekly podcast, Bazzell also takes you deep down the rabbit hole, cataloging in eye-splitting detail what it takes to be invisible in America today. His techniques range from the basics like how to clean up your online presence and remove your data from data broker websites to the extremes. Bazzell can show you how to buy a house or rent an apartment anonymously, register a car without giving over your name, travel under aliases without showing ID at hotels, get all your mail at a private mail stop without ever revealing your true address, get cell phone service or utilities privately, and much, much more. He is even working on ways to do things like obtain private secondary passports with only a partial name from a privacy-friendly country.

When it comes to digital advice, Bazzell pushes clients to stop using computers running operating systems made by tech giants like Apple, Microsoft, and Google in favor of an open-source operating system called Linux. For a mobile phone operating system, he favors GrapheneOS, a free version of Android stripped of everything Google-related and not so dissimilar to AltOS. He encourages everyone to run virtual private networks and hardware-based home firewalls that obscure and encrypt their internet traffic as they browse the web. He urges clients to use throwaway voice over IP numbers instead of the number their carrier assigns them. He has people buy prepaid cell phone service under fake names.

Bazzell's bag of extreme privacy tricks includes tactics such as establishing "nomad residency" in a state like South Dakota—a designation usually given to allow full-time RVers to get a driver's license and establish a legal residency despite not being present in a state. He can tell you how to create "ghost addresses" consisting of private mailbox services and using anonymous LLCs to purchase cars and housing.

His book has detailed instructions about how to travel under an alias or get Amazon packages without ever giving over your true identity. Bazzell even has tips for how to establish alias identities for your pets. One recent issue of his digital magazine contained an anonymous article from an outside contributor detailing an almost certainly illegal scheme explaining how to board an airplane under an alias—a technique that the magazine made clear it was definitely not endorsing. Another described how to obtain a Massachusetts liquor ID in a fake name. Indeed, Bazzell is constantly fighting with his lawyers about which of his techniques are legal and which ones are not. And Bazzell practices what he preaches. He has said he doesn't even bring a cell phone into his house. It goes into a canvas-lined Faraday bag before he ever gets home, and that's where it stays until he's far away from his address.

Many of Bazzell's basic recommendations do not require being wealthy to implement. But they often require time, technological savvy, and in some cases sacrifice. I admire some of Bazzell's techniques and have wanted to implement many in my own life but find the up-front investment in time, cost, or technological know-how daunting.

And of course to truly disappear—to burn down your entire digital trail and start over—does require a great deal of time and money. It requires switching addresses and cars; changing every single digital identifier associated with you and rebuilding them in a more privacy-friendly way. It requires the creation of a sprawling array of shell corporations and fake digital personas and identifiers. And it requires constant vigilance in understanding the ever-changing threat landscape to our personal privacy and anonymity.

Will it ever become impossible to disappear? I asked Bazzell. Is it possible that in our lifetimes or our children's lifetimes data collection will become so ubiquitous and ever present that there will be no way to escape, as the intelligence community predicts?

"No," he said, but added, "It's that balance of convenience versus privacy. Can you disappear? Of course, that's not going away. Will you enjoy that life? Maybe not."

It shouldn't be a surprise that the ability to track people using commercially available location data wouldn't stay confined to secretive government programs. It would eventually become a shadowy market that anyone with a few thousand dollars could access. Private investigators have long taken advantage of data from companies like LexisNexis to find the addresses of their targets. But now they have a new tool: piles of geolocation data available on the open market.

One of the earliest examples of private actors gaining access to this data to track individuals came when PlanetRisk took the Southern Poverty Law Center on as a client. The SPLC, a civil rights group that tracks hate and white supremacy, wanted data on the identities of attendees at the 2017 Unite the Right rally in Charlottesville, Virginia, where neo-Nazis and far-right extremists marched against the removal of Confederate monuments. One woman, Heather Heyer, was killed after a white supremacist rammed his car into a crowd of counterprotesters. PlanetRisk was able to geofence the statue of Robert E. Lee and see whose phones were present at the infamous torch-lit rally that involved about a hundred right-wing extremists chanting "Jews will not replace us" while huddling around the Lee statue. After the rally, PlanetRisk was able to follow those protesters back to their homes around the country.

Since 2017, the ability of private parties to buy location data about one another has only grown. And I wanted to know how much it would cost to buy an individual's location history. So in the fall of 2022, I found someone willing to do it for me for $2,500 per person. He also offered me a discounted rate of $9,000 for four people. His company specialized in using data to answer questions on behalf of clients. It tries to vet its clients and avoid any truly odious uses. But the data is out there, floating around and completely unregulated. All this source needed from me was a name and an employer to try to track someone down. We set up a Zoom call to discuss my needs.

My first idea was to ask for an analysis on the movement of the CEOs of the companies brokering these location tracking capabilities. This seemed fair after all; these people were commercially brokering this data and claiming there was no privacy violation. How much was I obligated to respect their privacy? So I asked: Was Jeff White of Gravy Analytics in this data? Or was he using his knowledge of this market to opt himself out? Perhaps upon seeing the pained look of an exhausted first-time author weighing whether it was worth the equivalent of a mortgage payment for an anecdote that would take up a few paragraphs in this book, this source did me a favor and looked up White for free, waiving his usual $2,500 fee. What he found was that White or someone in his household *was* in the data. My source didn't dig deeper than that, but with enough time he probably could have figured out whose phone it was. Does the phone commute to Gravy's offices ever or take business meetings with other people in the data business? Does it go to Pilates class? White never struck me as a Pilates guy, so maybe it was another member of his household. As we've seen time and time again, our patterns of life give us all away. He never gave me a full report on White's movements; he only confirmed that White hadn't managed to remove himself or his family from the location tracking data sets that he was selling.

Next, I asked him to track me. I had invested a lot of time in reducing my digital signature. I hadn't quite gone as far as Michael Bazzell, but I had taken steps to reduce the amount of digital dust that comes off modern smartphones and computers. I had carefully curated the apps on my phone, revoked almost every location-based app's permission to follow me except in very limited circumstances. Whenever I wanted to take an Uber or Lyft anywhere, I'd ignore the prompt that asked for my location and typed my current location manually, for example. I was also running a virtual private network that was encrypting my internet traffic and was running a number of ad blockers on my computer and phone. So I was curious what a private firm with access to location data could find about me.

To my great relief, my source also waived the fee for this request. A few hours later, he replied that he could not find my movement data in the commercially available location records. He confirmed that I had successfully opted out. This is just basic digital hygiene for reporters; we try hard to protect our sources who ask us for anonymity. Being tracked through commercial data is not an abstract concern for journalists. Two government contractors who work on open-source data separately recounted to me stories about being approached by people close to President Trump and being asked to track critics of the president using their access to commercially available data. One person was asked by someone close to Trump to track a prominent White House reporter who had recently had a blockbuster scoop that had irked the president—seemingly hunting for the source that had leaked the reporter something. A second person independently recalled being asked by a Trump ally to help conduct an off-the-books leak investigation using an open-source intelligence tool. Both of these requests went to people outside the government and came from nongovernment officials but carried the imprimatur of being something that the president or people close to him wanted done.

Why would allies of the president's turn to commercial location data in an off-the-books effort to get answers about who was leaking about the president? The Justice Department is empowered to investigate leaks of classified material to journalists, though it is sometimes loath to do so because of concerns about the freedom of the press and the possibility of dramatic courtroom showdowns with reporters, who have sometimes chosen to sit in jail rather than reveal a source. But the Justice Department is not authorized to use tools like grand jury subpoenas or search warrants to investigate leaks that are merely politically embarrassing. Commercial data, on the other hand, is almost completely unregulated. It's available for purchase. There are vendors and private investigators who will give you the data or run queries for you if you have the money. From their point of view, why *not* use that data?

The consequences of being a data-rich society where so much of our lives is being collected and in some cases being put up for sale is only now coming into view for many.

On June 24, 2022, the U.S. Supreme Court handed down *Dobbs v. Jackson Women's Health Organization,* upending nearly fifty years of precedent and holding that the Constitution did not confer a right to obtain an abortion. The immediate impact of the decision meant that the United States would suddenly have a patchwork of laws regarding access to abortion services. It also raised at least the possibility that states where abortion is illegal might even try to reach beyond their borders to enforce their antiabortion laws against their residents traveling out of state.

The decision also prompted a flurry of public conversation about privacy among ordinary people, the likes of which hasn't been seen since Edward Snowden or the dawn of the war on terrorism. Out of necessity, the secretive, underground illegal abortion clinics that had existed in pre–*Roe v. Wade* America might make a return, but in our society awash in data those places might be much easier to detect and identify in 2022 than in 1972.

Our phones track our every location 24/7. There are search engines that capture our queries. Our entire message history is stored on our phone and in the cloud. Our maps apps collect and log our destinations. Our cars transmit an indecipherable package of data to who knows what parties. Today, fitness wearables and mobile phone apps even advertise the capability to track menstrual cycles and to analyze biometrics like heart rate and body temperature. If a state really did start cracking down on a person getting an abortion, all of this data could be used to identify and convict that person—or even anyone who aided them. Some of this data is already available for sale in bulk.

And nearly all of it would be obtainable by a state or local government with a court order.

Stewart Baker, an acerbic Republican lawyer who is often skeptical of the claims of privacy and civil liberties activists, put it this way: "Maybe *Dobbs* will do for location privacy what dope use did for the Fourth Amendment. It will turn into something where everyone says, 'That could be me.'"

Or in other words, the consequences of persistent tracking had largely fallen on *other people* for decades: terrorism suspects, unauthorized immigrants, criminals, and people living outside the United States. The suspicious patterns of life, or signatures, that the most powerful agencies in the U.S. government have been scanning for in huge piles of data have generally been ones that do not affect many middle-class Americans. But the *Dobbs* decision made data collection suddenly feel personal to hundreds of millions who had never felt vulnerable before.

The first few decades of the twenty-first century have been characterized by political and social tumult all around the world: 9/11, the wars in Iraq and Afghanistan, the rise of China to global power, Brexit, the election of Donald Trump, civil unrest over racial justice, reproductive health, and the fantasy that the 2020 election was stolen. In each of these crises, the central question in that conversation is, what does democracy look like—and can it even exist at all—in a world of ubiquitous data collection? Moreover, what happens when the two most powerful organizing forces in modern life, the corporation and the state, are in cahoots, intertwining their capabilities in ways that the ordinary person can't begin to fathom?

EPILOGUE

The Man Behind the Counter

There's a term that is popular among intelligence officers: "ubiquitous technical surveillance." It means that the sheer amount of data that is collected on a given person is now so vast that it makes it difficult to conduct spy operations in many parts of the world. Gone are the days when an agent could fish a fake driver's license out of their pocket to give to a police officer or present a forged passport at customs. No longer can an intelligence officer just swap out license plates after a close brush with a foreign spy service. The way that the intelligence community has come to cope with this problem is to ramp up its recruitment of people who have no discernible tie to the spy agencies and to conceal their affiliation at all costs.

But it's not just spies who must grapple with today's new surveillance norms. Citizens themselves—at least those fortunate to live in the world's democracies—must decide how much we want to be tracked and for what purposes. What does it mean to be unable to walk through the world without being observed, tracked, and analyzed and having that data sold to hundreds of thousands of strangers—in corporations and government security services alike?

The United States is not China, which is a one-party authoritarian state building a digital-techno surveillance structure. But our government's growing access to data is trending discomfortingly in the same general direction. How much data collection is too much data collection? What's the right balance to strike? These are not easy questions.

In China, the ruling Communist Party has long relied on surveillance, keeping extensive files on where people work, requiring residency registration, and building out political files of dissidents. But with the advent of digital technology, much of it invented in the West, China has dramatically ramped up its capabilities. And it's no coincidence that it is Xinjiang, the far western province home to millions of the Turkic Muslim minority group called the Uyghurs, that is at the center of the most invasive forms of mass surveillance that China has built out. The dismal situation in Xinjiang serves as a powerful cautionary tale of what the future could hold for the rest of us.

Remember, *information is power.* In a restive region like Xinjiang, surveillance offers the potential for social control on a grand scale, powered by the ubiquity of data collected by the terabyte or petabyte every day. In Xinjiang, "Chinese leaders have revived totalitarian techniques of the past and blended them with futuristic technologies in an effort not to eradicate a religious minority but to reengineer it," wrote Josh Chin and Liza Lin, two *Wall Street Journal* reporters who authored the 2022 book *Surveillance State: Inside China's Quest to Launch a New Era of Social Control.*

In Xinjiang, the Chinese government has a platform called the Integrated Joint Operations Platform. IJOP gathers information from sensors like cameras with facial recognition technology built in, or Wi-Fi "sniffers" that record unique identifiers. The system ingests travel and movement records, bank data, biographical data about millions of residents, including information about their families and social ties. Blood type, voice, and fingerprints are also collected in Xinjiang and integrated into IJOP. The system can even analyze things like unusual electrical use. All of it is tied together in one platform that gives public safety officials a 360-degree view of individuals and the society writ large.

As it turns out, the array of information being cataloged in Xinjiang is pretty much the exact same as data on Americans that already exists in disparate data banks. Unlike in China, we haven't yet taken the step of weaving all of it together and giving ordinary police officers unfettered access to it. It's scattered across corporate and government databases. And much of it requires a warrant to unlock.

But as this book shows, there is a growing hunger for bulk data at all levels of government. Underlying that hunger are very legitimate concerns: solving public health challenges like COVID-19; securing the United States against terrorism, hacking, and nation-state sabotage; and even transportation planning and a more efficient energy grid. All of this requires high-quality information to inform decision makers. And bringing new tools and techniques to bear in solving grisly crimes and delivering justice is an important mission, too. Corporate data collection is also often done with good intentions: it may reflect consumer resistance to paying for what they've grown accustomed to getting for free; the goal of delivering personalized content and understanding markets and industry better. Sensors, fleet telematics, and consumer behavioral data have brought efficiency and low-cost services to the world.

Where does that leave us? Today, what separates the United States from China is a thin membrane of laws, norms, social capital, and—perhaps most of all—a lingering culture of discomfort among both government officials and ordinary citizens about too much power and too much information in the hands of the state. It's a deeply American distrust of centralized power and of government authority. But much of that hangs in the balance: the United States is at a critical moment for deciding its technological future. We have functioning courts and checks and balances. We have freedom of speech and fair elections.

In China, the state wants you to know you're being watched. In America, the *success lies in the secrecy*. The government does not want you to notice the proliferation of license plate readers. It does not want citizens to understand that mobile phones are a surveillance system. It does not want people to realize that social media is being eavesdropped on and no group chat is truly private because on the internet no one knows whether you're a government agent or a sock puppet.

But if information is power, and America is a society that is still interested in the guarantee of liberty of its citizens by limiting the power of government, a serious conversation is needed about the kind of threat these data banks pose to us all. Historically, the difficulty of obtaining information is what kept surveillance limited. But in the twenty-first century, there is no shortage of data about everyone and everything. And that amalgamation of data is the greatest threat to limited government, personal dignity, and individual freedom. How societies answer the question of government access to private data streams is one of the single most important questions of the twenty-first century. The line separating techno-utopia from techno-dystopia is thin indeed. Telecommunications, advertising, social media, corporate data—these are *the technical means of control,* to borrow a line from Thomas Pynchon. What differentiates China and the United States is the *ends* to which they are deployed. But can a force that powerful be controlled?

"All data collected, regardless of the safeguards in place, will eventually be abused," warned Al Alborn, a retired army officer and intelligence community contractor who turned into a journalist and civil liberties activist after leaving government service. A privacy review that President Obama ordered after the Snowden leaks summarized the situation well: "At its core, public-sector use of big data heightens concern about the balance of power between government and the individual. Once information about citizens is compiled for a defined purpose, the temptation to use it for other purposes can be considerable, especially in times of national emergency."

During World War II, U.S. census data—collected under promises of confidentiality—was used to identify and round up Japanese Americans for internment.

Such a turn of events might strike you as unthinkable in the twenty-first century. But once-unimaginable scenarios have been occurring with frequency now in our polarized politics.

What's stopping history from repeating itself?

What motivated me to write this book was the sense that the public remains in the dark about the new world of surveillance their government and their business community have been building in tandem. I aim only to lift the veil on the amount of data and power ordinary consumers are handing over every day to people hidden behind a curtain—and to show that there is a high cost to the free digital services they have come to rely on. Secrets in a democracy are corrosive to public trust. In limited circumstances, such as the movement of troops about to deploy overseas or the names of spies, it might be justified to allow government to keep things from us. But the broad social choices about how much data and power we want our government to amass should be presented to the public for vigorous debate and discussion.

This book aims to remind everyone that in our role as both consumers and voters, we Americans still do have a say in what kind of society we want to build and live in. We have a choice in what we buy with our hard-earned money and whom we elect to represent us at all levels of government. And there are companies invested in building privacy into technology; there are business models other than advertising or data harvesting for consumer services and technologies. Take Signal. The app, originally launched in 2010 as a prototype called TextSecure, collects almost no data about its users. It built its platform from the ground up to provide complete messaging privacy to its millions of users. Signal cannot read anything you send or receive. It's built self-destructing messages right into its technology. And it's run by a nonprofit entity that collects donations. Services like Signal enable the ordinary person to reclaim their privacy.

And yes, there may be a price. That price may be paying for a service instead of getting it for free; a slightly longer commute; or a slightly elevated risk of something bad. Societies make these kinds of trade-offs and cost-benefit calculations all the time in determining what speed limits to set or what pandemic restrictions to put in place; it's no different in drawing lines between the balance of privacy, public safety, and ubiquitous data collection.

In the 1960 film *Inherit the Wind*, modernity meets tradition in a fictionalized portrayal of the Scopes monkey trial over the teaching of evolution in 1925. In it, Spencer Tracy's character—a lawyer defending a schoolteacher on trial for teaching the theory of evolution—addresses the nature of change in society in the climax of the film:

> Progress has never been a bargain. You have to pay for it. Sometimes I think there's a man who sits behind a counter and says, "All right, you can have a telephone, but you lose privacy and the charm of distance. Madam, you may vote but at a price: you lose the right to retreat behind the powder puff or your petticoat. Mister, you may conquer the air, but the birds will lose their wonder and the clouds will smell of gasoline."

What price citizens of a democracy are willing to pay the man behind the counter in the name of progress is a question only they can answer.

In April 2021, Senator Ron Wyden introduced a bill that he called the Fourth Amendment Is Not for Sale Act. He assembled a bipartisan coalition of strange bedfellows to co-sponsor the bill—just as he had two decades earlier when mobilizing against the Total Information Awareness program. Rand Paul, the Kentucky Republican senator with a libertarian bent, was the lead GOP co-sponsor. The bill would put a stop to U.S. law enforcement buying data that it would otherwise need a warrant to acquire. It would have ended Venntel and Babel Street contracts with the Department of Homeland Security and would ensure that no program like VISR could ever ingest data about Americans. It would have stopped Fog Data Science from marketing an adtech surveillance tool to local law enforcement. It would have also effectively stopped the U.S. government from doing business with facial recognition companies that scrape biometric data from social media photos and provide service to law enforcement or using hacked or leaked data bought from vendors that scrape the dark web for tantalizing leaks.

It was not a panacea to the problem of global data aggregation. For one thing, it doesn't stop private companies from collecting the data in the first place. For another, intelligence is increasingly becoming privatized. Spy agencies now recruit engineers and systems administrators to infiltrate companies like Twitter and Google, in the hopes of getting access to data. Nonprofit foundations filled with ex-spies or vigilante citizens groups, often with ties to the military or special forces, are increasingly springing up to do OSINT on a wide array of topics: combat sex trafficking, do analysis on the conflict in Ukraine, or track down the perpetrators of the January 6 assault on the U.S. Capitol. They provide their findings to their friends back in government as tips or reports—using investigative tactics or access to databases that would give government lawyers heartburn. Wyden's bill would not address any of that. Nor would it protect Americans from data collection by foreign governments that can and do buy data through shell companies and cutouts just as we do.

But, for many civil liberties activists, it was nevertheless an important start in tilting the balance of power and data away from the state. It would end the market for vendors selling specialized tools to law enforcement. It would reaffirm the idea that our government needs a warrant to access intimate and detailed information about us. And it would begin to address many of the glaring loopholes in our laws created by modern technology.

The bill bounced around Capitol Hill, lauded by activist groups like the American Civil Liberties Union and the Electronic Frontier Foundation. It won support even from top party leaders, such as the

Senate majority leader, Chuck Schumer—even as intelligence agencies quietly lobbied against the bill, arguing it would make their jobs more difficult.

And then, in the hot, sticky summer of 2023, amid a growing bipartisan chorus of concerns over surveillance and just as this book was going to press, the Fourth Amendment Is Not for Sale Act suddenly came up for a vote in the Republican-led House Judiciary Committee. The Judiciary Committee is famously partisan. It's a place where the most contentious issues in Congress land: presidential impeachments, civil rights, hot-button social issues. Most members who want to be on the Judiciary Committee are partisan brawlers in safe seats; unlike a seat on, say, the Appropriations Committee, it offers very little opportunity to bring any tangible deliverables back to constituents. You can't get a new bridge built back home from a perch on the Judiciary Committee.

Yet on July 19, 2023, the panel voted 30–0 to endorse the bill and send it to the full House. In the polarized modern Congress, 30–0 is the kind of lopsided vote reserved for uncontroversial things: renaming a post office or nonbinding resolutions praising motherhood. Yet the bill attracted support from everyone from conservative firebrands like Matt Gaetz to liberal progressive darlings like Pramila Jayapal. There was overwhelming bipartisan consensus that the government buying data on its citizens had gone too far. The bill still faces an uncertain future, and nobody ever went bankrupt betting on Congress doing nothing. But it was the start of a conversation in the halls of power that was long overdue.

Mike Yeagley—the veteran Washington security tech wise guy who had helped create this market in the first place—was unfazed by the public attention on these programs. Technology was moving so quickly, he explained, a capability like adtech was never going to be useful forever. The government got a few good years out of exploiting it in the shadows. But adversaries caught on, journalists had written front-page stories on these programs, and the public understood more about their consumer technology. Now it was on to something new.

So, what's the next crazy technology that government is going to exploit and a journalist like me is going to write about in five to seven years? I asked him.

He reached for a metaphor from an old Looney Tunes cartoon—the one that depicts Sam Sheepdog and Ralph Wolf as blue-collar workers who punch in every day, do their mutually antagonistic jobs, and then clock out. Ralph, the wolf, spends all day trying to eat the sheep, and Sam, the sheepdog, spends all day watching over the flock and trying to thwart Ralph. Then they walk home together.

"We're going to play this like Looney Tunes. I'm guarding the flock and you're trying to get it. Then we punch out and say, 'See you tomorrow, Sam,'" Yeagley said with a chuckle.

ACKNOWLEDGMENTS

This project would not have been possible without Paul Whitlatch at Crown Publishing, who took a chance on a first-time author with an ambitious but sprawling book topic. Without his vision, his support, and his deft editing, this book would not exist. Also, thanks to Katie Berry at Crown for her consistently valuable feedback and insight. This book also would not have been possible without my agent, Eric Lupfer, who took one look at a messy, half-formed book proposal and turned it into a viable project in a remarkably fast time. A few days after our initial phone call and before ever formally agreeing to work together, Eric on his own initiative had hammered my proposal into something he insisted he could sell. True to his word, he made it happen.

Though my name alone is on the book jacket, I came to discover that writing a book is more like managing a small business. Colleen Murphy was an invaluable sounding board throughout the process—acting as an editor and a writing coach who helped me with the structure, wordplay, and ideas in early chapter drafts. If anyone is looking for a book coach, they should hire Colleen. Ed Frost provided invaluable research assistance. Julie Tate was an expert fact-checker who saved me from myself many times over. A special thanks is also owed to two groups of attorneys who helped fight for access to public records that this book is drawn in part from. The Chicago-based firm Loevy & Loevy represented me in a wide-ranging Freedom of Information Act lawsuit where we sued several components of the Defense Department, the Department of Homeland Security, and the National Archives. Josh Loevy, in particular, represented me through the process and is owed a special thanks for handling the legal case. In addition, the nonprofit Reporters Committee for Freedom of the Press represented me pro bono in a separate matter to get some court records unsealed. Thank you to Gillian Vernick, Katie Townsend, and Jen Nelson for spearheading that effort. Also thanks to Lyndsey Wajert, now at Vedder Price, who tapped her contacts in the media bar to help me find legal help more than once. Attorneys who represent journalists in their quest to unlock information the government would prefer to keep under wraps are unsung heroes in our profession and contribute mightily to the mission of accountability and truth that our professions share.

Some of my closest friends in journalism read and gave important feedback in whole or in part on the first draft: Dustin Volz, Rebecca Ballhaus, Andy Thomason, Brian Dabbs, Tarini Parti, Tim Mak, Joel Schectman, and Miranda Green. They are owed a debt of gratitude and many future rounds at many future happy hours.

I was at *The Wall Street Journal* throughout most of the book reporting and writing process. My editors and colleagues there were nothing but supportive. The origin of this book was a series of stories published in the newspaper between 2020 and 2023. Viveca Novak, Jathon Sapsford, and James Graff all edited key pieces in that series and are owed a debt of gratitude for making my writing sharper and the reporting clearer. The *Journal*'s Jeanne Cummings has always been a cheerleader for me inside and outside the newspaper—and a special thanks to her for finding ways to submit my work to prize committees. The Washington bureau chief, Paul Beckett, has my everlasting thanks for his support and overall calm leadership of the D.C. operation during a very difficult time in history.

Paul never batted an eye when I told him I wanted to write a book and take six months off my day job. To my colleagues on the justice and judiciary team, I am in your debt for picking up the slack during that time. To Aruna Viswanatha, Sadie Gurman, Dave Michaels, Ryan Barber, Alexa Corse, Brent Kendall, Jess Bravin, and Jan Wolfe: For five years, I was lucky to get to come to work every day with such a talented and downright nice group of people. Jan, who is a recovering lawyer, did me the favor of reading over the legal language. I'm also in debt to Patience Haggin, a dogged and talented *WSJ* reporter on the advertising technology and digital marketing beat who had to deal with me constantly digging into topics that surely caused her sources much heartburn. Her Rolodex and her insight into the topic greatly expanded my horizons. Also, thank you to Michelle Hackman, the *WSJ*'s intrepid immigration reporter who was my partner on the initial story about Venntel and is always a generous colleague.

Thanks to Enid Zhou and Alan Butler of the Electronic Privacy Information Center for facilitating my access to troves of documents on TIA, ChoicePoint, and the CAPPS II system that EPIC has acquired over the years. The former *Wired* reporter Ryan Singel, now an Open Internet Fellow at Stanford Law School's Center for Internet and Society, generously provided me with FOIA documents from his former career as a journalist concerning the FBI's FTTTF. The ACLU, particularly Nathan Wessler, was instrumental in giving me access to material obtained under FOIA. Both the ACLU and the Electronic Frontier Foundation maintain valuable web archives that I drew heavily upon in drafting this book. The Canadian Journalists for Free Expression's compilation of documents released by Edward Snowden was invaluable. Zach Edwards, an independent researcher, provided key insights and research into the world of real-time bidding and advertising technology. Jack Poulson of Tech Inquiry was extremely generous in sharing material he'd obtain under FOIA and in trading tips and leads about the industry that we'd both become fascinated by. Jack also read a draft of this book and was a valuable peer reader. In the spirit of the generosity of everyone who provided documents they had obtained, I commit to make the research materials I gathered as part of this book available to any researcher who asks unless I have agreed with the source to keep them off the record.

Many people were instrumental in helping me understand this topic: Senator Ron Wyden and his staff (particularly Keith Chu and Chris Soghoian). After my initial story about the existence of Venntel in 2020, Wyden opened an investigation and used his perch in Congress to get answers from numerous location brokers and government agencies that shed important light on this topic. Mike Yeagley spent many hours answering my questions. Eliot Jardines was a very valuable source in understanding the history of OSINT. Brian Sharkey and Bob Popp were extremely helpful regarding the early history of data mining and the Total Information Awareness program. Sean Gorman was also a fountain of information. Many, many, many others have asked not to be named, but without them this book would not be possible.

A unique group of journalists would end up pursuing these stories with the same zeal and kept me on my toes. First, this book and my *Journal* series probably would not have existed without a pioneering investigation by Stuart A. Thompson and Charlie Warzel of *The New York Times* into the world of location brokers and the consequences for privacy. After that story published, I knew there was more to the government acquisition of these data sets and aimed to show it with my own series. Joseph Cox, formerly of *Vice* and now of 404 Media, is an immensely talented reporter who has been equally obsessed by stories about government access to private sector data. He published more than a dozen scoops on this topic, advancing my understanding of it and pushing me to be my best. Martin Gundersen and Henrik Lied of the Norwegian public broadcaster, NRK, did incredible work in using European data protection laws to examine the flow of data from mobile apps to Venntel. Charles Levinson wrote an early and comprehensive story about Babel Street's Locate X for Protocol just as I was digging into the company. While I was annoyed at the time to have been beaten to print, I built a lot of my own Babel Street reporting on the back of that story. Jon Keegan and Alfred Ng of the Markup also wrote important stories about data brokers and their collection of data off mobile devices. (Alfred later went to *Po-*

litico, where he continues to cover this topic.) Shoshana Wodinsky is the single best reporter who looks critically at the weirdness of the adtech and data broker world. Charlie Savage of *The New York Times* also broke an important story about the Defense Intelligence Agency's use of advertising data and has generally been a must-read reporter on the intersection of national security and law for more than two decades.

I owe my first big break in journalism to Debbie Bruno, who took a chance on hiring an intern with a résumé light on reporting experience at the height of a catastrophic global recession when she surely had better candidates. We had lunch shortly after I signed the contract to write this book, and detecting my anxiety about the scale of the project, she sagely pointed me to Anne Lamott's exhortation about writing to take things bird by bird. That's what I did with this book—slowly, painstakingly grinding out work on this manuscript in twenty-five- or fifty-minute increments for months on end until I had a whole book.

The first words of this book were written on an Amtrak train between D.C. and New York in the fall of 2021. A full chapter outline was completed at a rented farmhouse in Reisterstown, Maryland, in January 2022. The bulk of the text was written between May and August 2022 at a cabin on a beautiful piece of land in upstate New York. To my hosts David and Erika Rose and their lovely family, thank you for giving me a quiet and memorable place to focus. A special thanks to Zenith for tutoring me in upstate New York's wildlife and teaching this city slicker the difference between a beaver and a groundhog. An additional note of appreciation for Jackson's Old Chatham House, a quaint hole-in-the-wall down the street that always served a cold beer and a warm meal when I was too tired to cook. The final few weeks of writing the first draft were spent in New York City at the Work Heights on Franklin Avenue. After much procrastination, edits were done from the basement of my Washington, D.C., house in the winter of 2023 with a final sprint of editing and rewriting from a quiet cabin in Front Royal, Virginia.

Finally, a special debt is owed to my family and those closest to me. To my mother, it is no exaggeration to say I would not be in this profession without the fact that you raised me in a house full of books and nurtured an early interest in reading and the written word. To my father, I know you don't quite understand what I do and still think I should go work for the State Department, but I know you're proud of me in your own way. From you, I've inherited a certain stubbornness and obstinance that is a useful trait in a reporter. To my sister, it's been an honor to watch you climb the hardest, highest rock of all—adulthood—while doing it your own way. And finally, much love and appreciation to Alicia, who put up lovingly and (mostly) patiently with many hours of fretting, pacing, worrying, and typing furiously on my computer with furrowed brow for the better part of two years. The wrinkles will probably never fade, but at least I got a book out of it.

—Byron Tau
Washington, D.C.
Spring 2023

APPENDIX

AN ORDINARY PERSON'S GUIDE
TO DIGITAL PRIVACY

Many people in response to my stories on this topic in *The Wall Street Journal* or after reading early drafts of this book said they were disturbed by what they read but were left with a deep sense of pessimism and fatalism about what they could do about it. And so I offer this short guide in the hopes that it might help you implement some small changes to reclaim your own privacy.

Phone settings will change, some of the services named below will go out of business, and new products will be introduced that I can't imagine. But I hope these broader principles will always remain relevant.

1. Control your own data: Once upon a time, we kept our documents in file cabinets, drawers, or safes in our homes. At the dawn of the digital age, we stored files on our computer hard drives. But the past decades have seen an explosion of cloud storage options. To be sure, the cloud offers many real advantages. For one, you can access your data from anywhere and collaborate easily. And losing a phone or computer no longer means losing the data on that device.

But these services have come with tremendous privacy and security costs. For one, many of the most popular cloud services have access to your files. If those services get hacked, your data is vulnerable to being stolen or ransomed for bitcoin. If those services are compromised by a disgruntled engineer or an intelligence operative who managed to get a job at a cloud provider, your data is vulnerable. If you're under investigation by law enforcement or being sued in a civil lawsuit, your information could be obtained from these cloud services rather than from a computer you control.

To protect your data and privacy, store sensitive information on your device locally when possible and disable cloud backups. If you're going to use cloud services, pick those that are *end-to-end encrypted* whenever possible. This is also sometimes called *zero-knowledge end-to-end encryption*. This means that the service does not have access to your data. Today, there are zero-knowledge products for nearly every online use: cloud storage, photo storage, document sharing, messengers, email, and so on. None of them offer perfect security or privacy, but all will tilt the balance toward your privacy and away from backdoor access to your personal data by hackers, subpoena-wielding lawyers, and spies. Today, many of Apple's services can be made zero-knowledge if users enable an option called Advanced Data Protection. Email services like Proton Mail and Tutanota do the same for email, giving these companies no way to access your inbox. Signal, iMessage, and WhatsApp all offer similar protection for messages. And companies like pCloud and Tresorit offer similar options for cloud storage.

While law enforcement complains that these end-to-end encrypted services thwart their access to data, they actually restore the precomputer status quo. Once upon a time, police had to enter your home with a warrant to rifle through your papers, and corporations had no access whatsoever to your personal documents. Zero-knowledge services mean that anyone who wants your data has to seize or hack a device to get it.

2. Encrypt, but more important delete: The strongest, best encryption in the world is no good if your computer or phone is stolen, seized, or hacked. As such, you should also give serious attention to retention. Do you need ten years' worth of email, or can you set messages to delete after a year or two? Do you need every goofy chat you send to your friends, or can you set them to expire after a few hours or a few days? Can you move your communications to platforms that offer ephemeral disappearing message options by default or allow you to easily toggle them on? Some, like the messaging app Signal, are popular among cybersecurity professionals and journalists for providing these options. WhatsApp, Confide, and others offer similar encrypted and disappearing messaging services as of this writing.

Huge reservoirs of old data sitting around on cloud services or old devices are a serious threat to your privacy. Just ask John Podesta, the chairman of Hillary Clinton's 2016 presidential campaign. Russian-linked hackers broke into his email account and dumped thousands of emails online. There was nothing illegal in Podesta's emails, but there was plenty of private material that was put on the internet to embarrass him and the Clinton campaign.

The same thing plays out on social media. Over and over some ordinary person will find themselves in the public glare. Whenever they find themselves in the middle of a viral internet shitstorm—whether through their own making or not—they will encounter hordes of faceless, anonymous strangers eager to dig through their entire social media history for embarrassing or out-of-context material to feed the flames of viral social media outrage. Don't let them. Purge your old posts at regular intervals or sign up for a service that auto-deletes them for you.

You also see the same thing with criminals. They have increasingly moved their communications to encrypted messenger services like WhatsApp and Signal. They've done this because they think the encryption will protect them from the consequences, while giv-

ing no attention to retention. So every few months you see prosecutors quoting a criminal's Signal messages in some indictment or
arrest warrant—leading to a round of frenzied speculation online
that law enforcement has found a way to "crack" the encryption on
Signal and break into people's messages. This is not usually what's
happening. In most cases, law enforcement is arresting them, seiz-
ing their phones, opening them with a warrant, and reading all of
their super-secure "encrypted" messages right there on their phone
screen because they gave no thought to deletion.

To protect your privacy, even the law abiding should make it a
habit to delete old data aggressively. Not everyone can do this in all
cases, of course. Companies often require employees to retain messages in case they ever need to furnish them to comply with a lawsuit or a subpoena, and government officials would be evading
open-records laws by conducting official business on platforms that
do not retain records. And destroying records for the express purpose of covering up a crime is illegal. But for most people, it's a good
option to make it a habit to retain a lot less data and communicate
in ephemeral ways that do not leave a permanent record.

3. Review your settings and permissions to reduce your exposure:
Modern technology is incredibly customizable. Yet the vast majority
of users never even bother to check whether there are settings that
can be tweaked to increase their privacy. Your phone, your computer,
your internet browser, your smart TV, your smart doorbell and home
security system, and nearly every app and online service all have settings that can be tweaked to improve your privacy. But generally, the
default out of the box will maximize data collection. Apps that want
your location or access to your camera roll or all your contacts will
usually work just fine without such permissions. Finally, there are
often menu screens that let you opt out of targeted advertising or
personalized content buried deep in apps or on websites. Always
check the settings of every service you sign up for and be mindful of

the kinds of data you keep that could be of interest to spies or criminals based on who you are, what you do, and where you work.

4. Read the terms of service and privacy policy: You would be surprised how many services are fairly open about what they're going to do with your data. Privacy-respecting companies will use strong language like "we will never share any of your data with any third party unless legally required." Companies that are going to sell your data will use phrases like "we may disclose your information to third parties to deliver you personalized advertising, to make our service work or to comply with applicable law." Look for companies that write privacy policies in plain language and use clear, declarative, and unambiguous phrases when describing how they will handle your data and whom they share it with. "Never," "no one," and "only as required by law" are the best words to see in a privacy policy.

5. Take advantage of obscurity and anonymity technologies: There are a number of technology solutions that can improve your online privacy. None are perfect. But all may help you achieve better security and privacy as you move around the web. Consider using a reputable ad blocker, a privacy-friendly browser, a firewall service, or a trusted virtual private network service that can be paid for in cash.* Because these services are constantly changing, you should consult a reputable, up-to-date online privacy guide for the latest

---

* There is a major debate about the use of these services. For one, VPNs do hide your traffic from your internet service provider but also require you to trust that the VPN service is not logging your traffic. Likewise, ad blockers or privacy-friendly extensions can often be detected by web services, making users who take such steps look even more unique as they load web pages. None of these services is a perfect solution. It will depend on what is more important to the individual user: security, anonymity, or privacy. Sometimes those imperatives are in conflict. My personal view is that a paid VPN service with a no-logs policy based in a privacy-friendly country can confer some privacy benefits, especially if users pay in cash, which is an option that some allow.

best practices and recommended services. (See below for additional resources.)

6. Be smart: If something doesn't seem right, don't do it. Every time you download a new piece of software, ask yourself if it really needs your location or your browsing history. Say no as often as possible. If a piece of software seems suspect, don't install it. If a link seems unusual, don't click it.

7. Pay money: Finally, the single most important thing you can do is to pay money in exchange for software and digital services. Early internet techno-utopians believed that the network could be run by volunteers and computer software distributed for free—an attitude that has persisted among far too many people for too long. While that model can work in some instances (see Wikipedia), 99 percent of the time it usually obscures the true costs of the transaction.*

"Free" content or software is almost never actually free. The cost is usually your personal data. Software and content are expensive to produce: coders need to be paid salaries, servers need to be rented, data needs to be stored, lawyers need to be hired to draw up a privacy policy and a terms of service. None of this is free. All of it costs time and money that needs to come from somewhere.

Consumers who care about their privacy should push for a re-

---

*   There is a major split within the privacy community about using only what's called open-source software. This is software where the computer code is available to anyone who wants to inspect it. Many privacy activists and enthusiasts insist that only open-source software is secure whereas "closed source" proprietary software can never be secure because you can't understand what it's doing at any given time. Moreover, many privacy enthusiasts also insist on *free* and open-source software, sometimes abbreviated FOSS. My personal view is that enough vulnerabilities have been discovered in widely used open-source software, demonstrating that it's hardly a cure-all for security. In addition, the average person does not have the computer literacy skills to read the code and is still trusting that others have audited open-source code. Instead, I would encourage people to get software from large, reputable companies based in democratic countries with the rule of law whenever possible.

turn to the most basic economic exchange: paying money for a service, a piece of content, or a software program. Returning to that business model means that there is less incentive for companies to rely on behavioral advertising or personal data sales. Yet only a tiny percentage of internet users are willing to pay for a service, forcing even well-meaning developers to find other ways to monetize their apps, websites, and services. While it's not realistic to pay for everything, too many of us balk at paying 99 cents for an app while browsing the app store in line for our $7.99 latte. Most apps cost less than a cup of black coffee. But when developers can't count on money from the public for their time and efforts, they turn to selling data or monetizing their users in other ways.

It's time for the internet to grow up.

Further Resources

- Michael Bazzell's *Extreme Privacy: What It Takes to Disappear* as well as his podcast, *The Privacy, Security & OSINT Show* and his website, inteltechniques.com

- Bruce Schneier's book *Data and Goliath,* plus his web writing at www.schneier.com/

- April Falcon Doss's *Cyber Privacy: Who Has Your Data and Why You Should Care*

- Electronic Frontier Foundation's Surveillance Self-Defense, ssd.eff.org

- Privacy Guides, www.privacyguides.org/

- PrivacyTools, www.privacytools.io/

- The New Oil, www.thenewoil.org/

- The Privacy & Freedom in the Information Age subreddit, www.reddit.com/r/privacy/

- *The New York Times*'s Tech Fix column, www.nytimes.com /column/tech-fix

- *The New York Times*'s "How to Protect Your Digital Privacy," www.nytimes.com/guides/privacy-project/how-to-protect-your -digital-privacy

- The reporting of Joseph Cox, at 404 Media as of this writing

- The reporting of Kashmir Hill, at *The New York Times* as of this writing

- The reporting of Geoffrey Fowler and Drew Harwell, at *The Washington Post* as of this writing

- The reporting of Thomas Brewster, at *Forbes* as of this writing

- Finally, you can follow me on Twitter or LinkedIn at the handle @ByronTau, where I occasionally share my reporting on this topic and my thoughts on privacy and digital security, among other things

KEY CONCEPTS AND DEFINITIONS

Marketing, Advertising, and Technology

Ad exchange: The beating heart of the digital advertising industry, advertisement exchanges are how digital display ads are delivered to billions of smartphones. Developers partner with an ad exchange in order to monetize their app or website. At its most basic, an ad exchange seeks to connect an advertiser with a pair of eyeballs looking at a screen. Every time anyone opens a mobile website or app with ad space, the ad server is alerted to the available inventory. The user's phone then passes information about the user back to the ad exchange. This mainly includes an identifier called a mobile advertising ID, or MAID, which is how consumers are identified to the ad exchange—a pseudonymous alphanumeric identifier that allows advertisers to target consumers.

RTB, or real-time bidding: This term refers to the instantaneous ad auctions that result in data being sent from the phone to the ad exchange, the bidding by advertisers to display an ad.

SDK: An SDK is a software development kit—pre-written lines of code from third parties that app developers can download and embed in their apps. A game developer could use an SDK, for example, to get analytics information about who is using the app and how much it crashes. And the third-party SDK maker would also get that information—giving the company a wider visibility into the world of app makers. Location data companies have developed SDKs to collect location information from apps. In exchange, they often pay the app a small amount for every user whose data they can collect. This allows location companies to obtain data from apps they do not own, and it allows app makers to monetize their apps.

Types of location data: There are several different methods of collecting location data from consumer cell phones: SDK, RTB, server-to-server, and cell tower data.

SDK, RTB, and server-to-server data are all sourced from cell phone applications and are derived primarily from GPS, a system of satellite navigation. Cell tower data is collected by the carriers and is derived from cell tower triangulation.

With *SDK-derived data,* a location broker partners with an app, sends the app maker an SDK to install, and collects location data directly from its code running inside the developer's app. This is actually fairly easy to track because anyone looking at an app's source code can see that it is transmitting data to web domains owned by the broker. The app maker knows who is collecting it, has its users consent to the collection, and discloses in the privacy policy that third parties are collecting the data.

RTB data, on the other hand, is data that is secretly siphoned off the advertising exchanges. This is possible because, when placing a bid, any participant can see the data that billions of phones are transmitting back to the ad exchange. They can save that data, clean it up, and offer it as a location data product. This can often be a violation of the terms of service of the advertising exchange— it doesn't require consent from the maker or the users of an app—but the exchange has no way of policing it and little incentive to.

Server-to-server data: Some app makers are sophisticated enough to collect and save their own location data and simply share it from their own servers with brokers. Data sales in this market are impossible to track. Apple and Google can only see that the developer is receiving location data. After that, nobody knows where it goes.

Finally, with *cell tower data* the carriers can calculate the approximate location of your phone because phones constantly ping off multiple towers. In navigation, relative distance from three points is enough to determine a precise location. This is called triangulation. Cell carriers record and store the location of users at certain intervals using triangulation. In the early days of cell phones, cell tower triangulation was far less precise than GPS because there weren't enough cell towers, and carriers could get only a loose approximation of phone location—usually down to about a three-quarter-square-mile area. In urban areas, where cell towers are more common, the location is more precise. And with 5G, location is extra precise because 5G requires lots of smaller towers everywhere rather than just a few large towers in a few spots. Today, 5G cell carrier data is as precise as GPS in most places.

Mobile advertising ID (MAID): Called the identifier for advertisers (IDFA) on Apple phones and the Android Advertising ID (AAID) on phones running Google's Android operating system, this is the primary identifier that advertisers use to target consumers. It is a pseudonymous alphanumeric identifier created by Apple and Google to allow advertisers to target consumers without knowing personal information about them such as their name or email address. Most of the privacy protections it offers are purely theoretical. Advertisers can cross-match a MAID to widely available demographic information about consumers to figure out who is who. While it's resettable and rotatable, advertisers can easily match your new MAID with your previous MAID based on behavior attributes or movement patterns. Apple in recent years has sharply limited the use of the MAID, and as a result Apple users are increasingly harder to see with targeted advertising. Google has not taken similar steps.

Legal Concepts

Fourth Amendment to the U.S. Constitution: Foundational constitutional right establishing that the government may not conduct searches without probable cause of a crime in the United States. The amendment, passed in 1791, reads, "The right of the people to be secure in their persons, houses, papers, and effects, against unreasonable searches and seizures, shall not be violated; and no Warrants shall issue but upon probable cause, supported by Oath or affirmation, and particularly describing the place to be searched, and the persons or things to be seized." It is a key pillar in limiting the American government's reach.

Executive Order 12333: This executive order directs the U.S. intelligence community to provide the president and the National Security Council "with the necessary information on which to base decisions concerning the conduct and development of foreign, defense and economic policy, and the protection of United States national interests from foreign security threats. All departments and agencies shall cooperate fully to fulfill this goal." It directs them to use "all reasonable and lawful means" in pursuit of that aim. This order serves as the legal basis for most intelligence activity undertaken by the United States. It was signed in 1981 by Ronald Reagan and has been modified several times. Notably, U.S. intelligence gathering is governed largely by an executive order, not a law passed by Congress.

Personally identifiable information (PII): Information linked to a specific individual. It is only loosely defined under American privacy law. In federal law, the 1974 Privacy Act hinges on a similar concept and forbids disclosure by the federal government of "personally identifiable records" maintained by government agencies. In most instances, commercial entities that claim to have non-PII data sets are actually sitting on pseudonymized or de-identified data that could be reidentified and linked to a specific individual. An example is location data: an anonymized data set of phone location may be stripped of personal information, but it can usually be linked to a specific individual based on their movements in the world. Or a person's browsing records could be de-identified, but their unique search patterns and interests could link back to them.

Third-party doctrine: A foundational concept in American law, establishing that information you freely share with a third party does not get protection under the Constitution. It was fully articulated in the 1979 U.S. Supreme Court case *Smith v. Maryland*. That case found that records provided to another party did not fall under the scope of the Fourth Amendment. The case dealt with the placement of a pen register (which records whom a person dials using their telephone) and determined that it was not a search, because in dialing, the suspect voluntarily provided numerical information to the telephone company to dial the call and therefore had no reasonable expectation of privacy—meaning the government could without a warrant monitor and store all the phone numbers a person dials, simply because she shared them with the telephone company. The court held that "a person has no legitimate expectation of privacy in information he voluntarily turns over to third parties." In another case dealing with metadata, *Katz v. United States* from 1967, the court held, "Although petitioner's conduct may have been calculated to keep the contents of his conversation private, his conduct was not and could not have been calculated to preserve the privacy of the number he dialed." In recent years, the doctrine has begun to be revisited by the Supreme Court.

U.S. person: A legal concept in American national security law. A U.S. person encompasses anyone with U.S. citizenship or U.S. permanent residency or any U.S. corporation, company, or trust. U.S. persons have additional privacy protections when it comes to intelligence collection. In most cases, the explicit targeting of U.S. persons for collection by intelligence agencies or the U.S. military is forbidden without a warrant. The general policy is that the United States does not "knowingly collect" intelligence on its citizens, but it does "incidentally" collect it. Let's say there is a terrorist target overseas who is being monitored and that terrorist calls an American. The call to the American is "incidentally collected" because she or he was communicating with a valid U.S. intelligence target overseas.

Intelligence and Law Enforcement Concepts

The "INTs": *SIGINT, HUMINT, MASINT, GEOINT, OSINT, and so on.* Intelligence community jargon for the source of a particular piece of information in an intelligence report. SIGINT refers to "signals intelligence," or covertly intercepting signals—such as using the radio transmissions of a ship at sea to determine its position in the ocean and extrapolate its course. HUMINT is "human intelligence"—the classic spy game of developing a human source or mole somewhere and receiving inside information from them. MASINT refers to "measurement and signature intelligence" and includes intelligence from highly technical detection methods like radar, acoustics, nuclear, chemical, or biological signatures: for example, specialized sensors set up to detect nuclear material coming across a bridge, or radars that try to see where a specific entity is located and where it might be heading. GEOINT usually refers to overhead imagery collected by spy planes, drones, or space-based satellites. See below for the definition of OSINT.

Metadata versus content: Metadata refers to information about information. Consider an email: the "To," "From," "CC," "BCC," and "Date" fields are metadata. They tell you whom the email is going to, who sent it, when it was sent, but not what the email is about. Content refers to the body of the email. Metadata about a phone call could include the number dialed, the date and time of the call, the length of the call. Metadata about a smartphone could include its GPS coordinates, its battery level, and so on.

OSINT, or open-source intelligence: Open-source intelligence is intelligence derived from unclassified or "open" sources—contrasted with intelligence derived from secret or classified sources. This kind of data is the primary focus of this book. It once referred mostly to monitoring press reports from around the globe but has come to encompass a wide range of data collection, as well as unclassified material available online or for purchase—often through commercial services. That can include social media sites like Twitter and Facebook. It can also be posts on more obscure web forums or even Airbnb listings. It can mean commercially available data collected by technology giants, advertising entities, and consumer-facing companies. It also includes a huge category of obscure data that modern electronic devices and consumer technologies emit as part of moving through the world. These are often collected without much consumer awareness and include precise geolocation, IP addresses, wireless identifiers associated with cars, and modern Bluetooth devices.

Publicly available information, or PAI: A related concept to OSINT. Publicly available information has been defined by the Pentagon as "information that has been published or broadcast for public consumption, is available on request to the public, is accessible online or otherwise to the public, is available to the public by subscription or purchase, could be seen or heard by a casual observer, is made available at a meeting open to the public, or is obtained by visiting a place or attending an event that is open to the public." PAI is only information. When it is incorporated into an intelligence report by a trained analyst, it becomes OSINT.

Pattern of life: A type of analysis that looks at behavioral attributes, transactions, or patterns to determine information about a target. Pattern of life analysis is data agnostic; anything can be used to try to identify an actor. Often people's patterns in data are highly specific to them.

Government Offices and Agencies

Director of National Intelligence (DNI) or the Office of the Director of National Intelligence (ODNI): Office created in 2004 by the Intelligence Reform and Terrorism Prevention Act. The office was created to direct and oversee the national intelligence program—basically all intelligence priorities that could affect the country as a whole. This responsibility was taken away from the CIA director, who also simultaneously held the title of director of central intelligence. *The 9/11 Commission Report* recommended the creation of this position to better coordinate the members of the intelligence community.

The intelligence community (IC): The community consists of eighteen agencies that are responsible for collecting, processing, analyzing, and disseminating intelligence reports. They are spread out across the Departments of State, Justice, Defense, Energy, Treasury, and Homeland Security plus the Central Intelligence Agency (an independent agency under no cabinet department). In theory, they are supposed to coordinate with each other through the director of national intelligence.

U.S. Special Operations Command (SOCOM): A combatant command of the Department of Defense. Headquartered at MacDill Air Force Base in Tampa, Florida, the U.S. Special Operations Command is the umbrella military command for all U.S. special forces and special operators. Increasingly, U.S. special forces conduct the bulk of U.S. military activity, even though they represent only a tiny fraction of the military budget. In the post-9/11 world, the United States was not fighting peer or near-peer nations; it was arrayed against a small group of terrorist actors hiding in remote areas of the globe. As a result, light, mobile, clandestine special operations forces became an integral part of how the United States conducted the war on terrorism.

Joint Special Operations Command (JSOC), technically a part of SOCOM, and part of the Department of Defense: A highly specialized, secretive arm of SOCOM. The most specialized and highly trained special operators—including Delta Force and SEAL Team 6—are supervised by JSOC. Unlike most parts of the military, JSOC also can sometimes operate under the protection of U.S. law intended for intelligence agencies—meaning that its activities can be designated covert and could be officially denied, if necessary.

The National Geospatial-Intelligence Agency (NGA): A military intelligence agency responsible for GEOINT. Traditionally, this has meant interpreting photographs from spy satellites and aerial surveillance. The CIA was very territorial about its right to conduct ground-level surveillance (surveillance cameras, on-the-ground photography), and as a result that has traditionally not been part of the NGA's mission or responsibilities.

The Defense Advanced Research Projects Agency (DARPA): A research and development agency within the Department of Defense that funds and directs advanced research projects into topics that could have military or national security relevance.

Combating Terrorism Technical Support Office (CTTSO): Like DARPA, CTTSO is a research arm of the Pentagon. Its aim is to fund research and development into terrorism-related capabilities. It got its start in the 1980s under the purview of the Department of State. It has gone through a number of name changes. It was once called the Technical Support Working Group and is currently named the Irregular Warfare Technical Support Directorate. Throughout the events described in the book, it was known as CTTSO.

NOTES

Most of the interviews for this book were conducted between January 2020 and the spring of 2023. Many of the best sources I interviewed more than once. My interviews were mostly conducted on the phone or in person, though I occasionally had lengthy exchanges or running dialogue with people on Signal, WhatsApp, or iMessage. Some agreed to speak with me only for fact-checking purposes or merely to listen to what I was prepared to report before declining to comment. Among those interviewed were two former directors of U.S. intelligence agencies, several cabinet-level officials, and numerous high-level Pentagon officials both civilian and uniformed, as well as current and former members of Congress and the executive branch. In total, the people interviewed for this book have worked at nearly every agency inside the U.S. government with a law enforcement, military, intelligence, or national security function—CIA, NSA, FBI, NGA, DOD, DOJ, DHS, CBP, ICE, SOCOM, JSOC, the National Security Council, and many more. Overwhelmingly, the best information came from the mid-level intelligence analysts, uniformed service members, special operators, program managers, lawyers, and contractors who worked directly on these programs or issues. As part of my reporting, I also sought out the perspectives of those outside government: in civil society, private industry, and the legal bar. I did not just seek out critics; in fact, I often went looking for people who would make the best possible case for these tools and techniques. Though they often could not provide me with insider information, their diverse perspectives helped inform this book and my thinking on the topic.

In general, the vast majority of the conversations were conducted on "background," which does not allow me to identify the source by name but generally permits quotation, or on "deep background," which requires the promise of the maximum protection of the source's confidentiality and identity and generally does not permit direct quotations but allows the information to be used.

I also did an extensive review of documents and other printed material. Much of it was released to either me or other researchers, lawyers, activists, or journalists under the U.S. Freedom of Information Act (FOIA), the bedrock open-records law, or similar state-level public records statutes. Other documents were found as part of lawsuits or court dockets at all levels of government. Another invaluable source was the thousands of pages of contracting documents that the federal government posts annually, which describe in detail many of the government's activities. Finally, I reviewed an array of published books about intelligence, military operations, advertising, digital technology, and the law. All are cited below whenever possible.

Introduction: The Grindr Problem and a Wine-Soaked Dinner

I interviewed Mike Yeagley at length probably about half a dozen times in person, and we had numerous other shorter interviews by phone or messenger. In some instances, he showed me documents that corroborated his account. I also interviewed numerous people familiar with the programs he helped run as an outside contractor and reviewed documents that others provided to me to cross-check the information.

The account of how digital ad exchanges work was the result of many hours of conversations with people in the advertising technology world, as well as published accounts. Particularly helpful was Antonio García Martínez's *Chaos Monkeys: Obscene Fortune and Random Failure in Silicon Valley* (Harper, 2016) and Mike Smith's *Targeted: How Technology Is Revolutionizing Advertising and the Way Companies Reach Consumers* (AMACOM, 2014). I'm also indebted to Shoshana Zuboff's landmark work, *The Age of Surveillance Capitalism: The Fight for a Human Future at the New Frontier of Power* (Profile Books, 2019), which gave us the language to describe how the modern digital landscape is dominated by technology companies that are largely in the business of collecting reams of data about their users and how that business model was essentially a form of surveillance. I also am indebted to daily news coverage of the advertising industry from trade publications like *Ad Age, Digiday, Street Fight,* and *AdExchanger,* all of which proved invaluable resources in understanding this technology.

xv   **"It's no longer necessary"** Tom Capon, "How Growing Up with Grindr Taught Me an Important Lesson About Dating," GayStarNews.com, March 25, 2019.

xix   **an "anonymized" advertising ID** Trevor Testwuide, "What Is IDFA (Identifier for Advertisers) and Is IDFA Going Away?," Measured.com, June 23, 2022.

xxi   **Technically, we can reset this number** Bennett Cyphers, "How to Disable Ad ID Tracking on iOS and Android, and Why You Should Do It Now," Electronic Frontier Foundation, May 11, 2022.

xxi   **Understanding the movement of phones** Jon Keegan and Alfred Ng, "There's a Multibillion-Dollar Market for Your Phone's Location Data," The Markup, Sept. 30, 2021.

xxii **cannot truly be anonymized** Yves-Alexandre de Montjoye et al., "Unique in the Crowd: The Privacy Bounds of Human Mobility," *Scientific Reports,* March 25, 2013.

xxiii **a lawsuit against the U.S. government** Complaint, *Tau v. U.S. Department of Defense et al.,* Case No. 1:21-cv-03329 (D.D.C., filed 2021), ECF No. 1.

xxiv **personal lives are being mined** Brooke Auxier et al., "Americans and Privacy: Concerned, Confused, and Feeling Lack of Control over Their Personal Information," Pew Research Center, Nov. 15, 2019.

xxiv **Government lawyers have invoked** Hamed Aleaziz and Caroline Haskins, "DHS Authorities Are Buying Moment-by-Moment Geolocation Cellphone Data to Track People," BuzzFeed, Oct. 30, 2020; Treasury Inspector General for Tax Administration (TIGTA), Letter in Response to Sens. Ron Wyden and Elizabeth Warren Regarding Concerns About the Internal Revenue Service (IRS) Criminal Investigation's (CI) Use of a Database Provided by a Contractor Named Venntel, Feb. 18, 2021.

Chapter 1: The Bad Guys Database

This account of data brokers in the days after 9/11 was based on interviews with numerous former Acxiom and Seisint employees as well as government officials who had direct interaction with both companies between 2001 and 2010. It also draws upon documents released under FOIA and a review of the press coverage of Acxiom over its more than fifty-year history. I also drew from the former Acxiom CEO Charles Morgan's self-published book, *Matters of Life and Data: The Remarkable Journey of a Big Data Visionary Whose Work Impacted Millions (Including You)* (Morgan James, 2015), and Robert O'Harrow Jr.'s *No Place to Hide: Behind the Scenes of Our Emerging Surveillance Society* (Free Press, 2005). Finally, I heavily relied on the numerous official reports into the 9/11 attacks to detail the activities of Waleed al-Shehri and his associates before and during the attacks.

3   **Acxiom consumer No. 254-04907-10006** Richard Behar, "Never Heard of Acxiom? Chances Are It's Heard of You," *Fortune,* Feb. 23, 2004.

3   **al-Shehri had been busy** Federal Bureau of Investigation, "Working Draft Chronology of Events for Hijackers and Associates, Parts 1 and 2," fbi.gov.

4   **checked in to the 144-room Park Inn** James C. McKinley Jr. and Kate Zernike, "After the Attacks: The Hijackers; F.B.I. Traces Path of 5 in New England," *New York Times,* Sept. 13, 2001.

4   **al-Shehri was flagged for additional screening** National Commission on Terrorist Attacks upon the United States, *The 9/11 Commission Report: Final Report of the National Commission on Terrorist Attacks upon the United States* (Washington, D.C.: National Commission on Terrorist Attacks upon the United States, 2004).

4   **under the security procedures** National Commission on Terrorist Attacks upon the United States, "The Aviation Security System and the 9/11 Attacks, Staff Statement No. 3."

5   **al-Shehri shouldn't even be in the country** National Commission on Terrorist Attacks upon the United States, "Monograph on 9/11 and Terrorist Travel."

5   **"We have some planes"** National Commission, *9/11 Commission Report.*

6   **Khalid al-Mihdhar and Nawaf al-Hazmi** Ibid.

6   **That was the thirty-sixth time** Ibid.

6   **There was a memo** U.S. Department of Justice Office of the Inspector General, "A Review of the FBI's Handling of Intelligence Information Prior to the September 11 Attacks," Nov. 2004.

6   **"reports of possible near-term terrorist operations"** National Commission, Aviation Security Staff Statement.

7   **"Hammza, whatever you do"** FBI, Working Draft Chronology.

8   **Charles Ward happened to have access** Morgan, *Matters of Life and Data.*

8   **Ward was also a Democratic Party activist** Natasha Singer, "Mapping, and Sharing, the Consumer Genome," *New York Times,* June 16, 2012.

9   **Acxiom was sitting on marketing data** Morgan, *Matters of Life and Data.*

12   **"Looks promising"** Acxiom, "Acxiom / Homeland Security" presentation given to Vice President Dick Cheney. On the document, Cheney scribbled a note: "Dean—did Ridge operation ever do anything with this—looks promising -D." Released under the Freedom of Information Act by the National Archives.

13   **brief stint as a drug smuggler** Michael Shnayerson, "The Net's Master Data Miner," *Vanity Fair,* Dec. 2004.

13   **Asher was drinking** Asher, interview by Robert O'Harrow, *No Place to Hide* (audio documentary), produced by American Public Media.

13   **"I know how to find these guys"** The quotation differs slightly between Shnayerson's *Vanity Fair* article and Asher's interview with Robert O'Harrow. I've gone with the O'Harrow version because as a transcript it's a primary source, but it's clear that Asher has been consistent in saying *something* like this.

13   **About 120,000 people had elevated risk scores** Shnayerson, "Net's Master Data Miner."

Chapter 2: The Supersnoop's Dream

The account of the creation and legacy of the Total Information Awareness program relies heavily on Shane Harris's *Watchers: The Rise of America's Surveillance State* (Penguin Books, 2011) and O'Harrow's *No Place to Hide.* I also drew from two histories of DARPA: Annie Jacobsen, *The Pentagon's Brain: An Uncensored History of DARPA, America's Top-Secret Military Research Agency* (Little, Brown, 2015), and Sharon Weinberger, *The Imagineers of War: The Untold Story of DARPA, the Pentagon Agency That Changed the World* (Knopf, 2017).

I conducted several on-the-record interviews with top officials who were involved in the program, including Bob Popp and Brian Sharkey. I had conversations with others who prefer to remain anonymous. John Poindexter and I had only a brief email exchange; he declined to be interviewed at length. I also reviewed hundreds of pages of documents about the program. Some of them were provided to me directly by sources involved, while others were obtained by civil society groups or journalists. All were invaluable in understanding the history of the TIA program.

Finally, Senator Ron Wyden participated in two lengthy phone interviews with me in 2022. I also spoke to several congressional staff members who were directly involved in the negotiations over TIA, many of
whom were reluctant to identify themselves on the record due to the classified nature of the annex to the 2004 omnibus appropriations bill, even
two decades later. I also reviewed the contemporary news coverage of the
TIA controversy and the FY 2004 funding debate, as well as a transcript
from Wyden's January 2003 event with Senators Feingold and Corzine.

16 **like the Soviet nuclear submarines** John Poindexter, "Remarks as Prepared for
Delivery by Dr. John Poindexter, Director, Information Awareness Office of DARPA"
(DARPA Tech 2002 Conference, Anaheim, Calif., Aug. 2, 2002).

17 **The signature of a terrorist** Ibid.

17 **TIA was born out of the personal friendship** Harris, *Watchers.*

18 **tools could be built, tested, and evaluated quickly** Poindexter, "Remarks."

19 **"The US may need huge databases"** Doug Dyer, email to Poindexter and Robert
Popp, May 21, 2002, in the Electronic Privacy Information Center FOIA collection.

19 **But the TIA team thought they could do it better** Ibid.

19 **Poindexter had publicly announced** Poindexter, "Remarks."

20 **In dire language** William Safire, "You Are a Suspect," *New York Times,* Nov. 14,
2002.

20 **"How is this not domestic spying?"** Victoria Clarke, David A. Gove, and
Edward C. Aldridge, "Department of Defense Press Briefing," U.S. Department of
Defense News Transcript, Nov. 20, 2002.

21 **Ron Wyden strode into the room** Jon Corzine, Russell Feingold, and Ron Wyden,
"News Conference on Legislation Suspending the Total Information Awareness Program," Federal News Service, Jan. 16, 2003.

21 **"Our country must fight terrorists"** Ibid.

24 **Congress had sought to strike** Stephen P. Mulligan, Wilson C. Freeman, and
Chris D. Linebaugh, "Data Protection Law: An Overview," Congressional Research
Service, Report No. R45631, March 25, 2019.

25 **technology that would test the boundaries of law** U.S. Congress, "S. Doc.
103-6—Constitution of the United States of America: Analysis and Interpretation—
1992 Edition, Fourth Amendment—Search and Seizure," June 29, 1992.

26 **delivering . . . a 102-page document** Department of Defense's Defense Advanced
Research Projects Agency, "Report to Congress Regarding the Terrorism Information
Awareness Program in Response to Consolidated Appropriations Resolution, 2003,
Pub. L. No. 108-7, Division M, § 111(b)," May 20, 2003.

26 **were spelled out in a classified annex** "Pentagon's 'Terror Information Awareness'
Program Will End," Associated Press, Sept. 25, 2003.

26   **"caused a significant amount of uncertainty"** Shane Harris, "TIA Lives On," *National Journal,* Feb. 25, 2006.

27   **"TIA has been terminated"** Ibid.

27   **that agency's tentacles would be nearly inescapable** Barton Gellman, *Dark Mirror: Edward Snowden and the American Surveillance State* (Penguin Press, 2020).

Chapter 3: The Gordian Knot

The bulk of this chapter comes from several hours I spent interviewing Paul Rosenzweig over the phone. I also did a review of his writing and testimony during this time period. I conducted numerous interviews with aviation security experts and government officials involved in security civil aviation for a chapter that I intended to write about airlines after 9/11 that was later scrapped. Much of that material was repurposed into this chapter. I also read widely on the history of the Fourth Amendment, including some of the important case law, law review overviews, and legal journalism. Because I am not a lawyer, I asked several friends and colleagues who are attorneys to read drafts of this chapter to offer perspective and guidance on whether my legal history was correct. None of the people who were shown the draft for their legal views are subjects of the reporting in this chapter or any other.

30   **"most polite way of standing out"** Michael Arnone, "Conservative at Helm of Privacy Panel," FCW, June 6, 2005.

34   **envelope can be scanned and saved** Ron Nixon, "U.S. Postal Service Logging All Mail for Law Enforcement," *New York Times,* July 3, 2013.

35   **A 2016 Stanford study** Jonathan Mayer et al., "Evaluating the Privacy Properties of Telephone Metadata," *Proceedings of the National Academy of Sciences of the United States of America* 113, no. 20 (2016).

35   **"We kill people based on metadata"** Lee Ferran, "Ex-NSA Chief: 'We Kill People Based on Metadata,'" ABC News, May 12, 2014.

36   **corporate data conveyed voluntarily** Orin S. Kerr, "Buying Data and the Fourth Amendment," Hoover Institute, Aegis Series Paper No. 2109.

37   **Congress had mandated** Department of Homeland Security, "Authorities and Responsibilities of the Chief Privacy Officer," dhs.gov.

37   **composed of academics and industry and other outside experts** Department of Homeland Security, "Privacy Office—DHS Data Privacy and Integrity Advisory Committee Membership," dhs.gov.

38 **The committee's first report** Department of Homeland Security's Data Privacy and Integrity Advisory Committee, "The Use of Commercial Data to Reduce False Positives in Screening Programs," Report 2005-01, Oct. 6, 2005.

38 **The second was about the use** Department of Homeland Security's Data Privacy and Integrity Advisory Committee, "Recommendations on the Secure Flight Program," Report 2005-02, Dec. 6, 2005.

39 **And the third was something** Department of Homeland Security's Data Privacy and Integrity Advisory Committee, "The Use of Commercial Data," Report 2006-03, Dec. 6, 2006.

Chapter 4: Electronic Footprints

The account of the manhunt for Agha Ali Abbas Qazalbash was drawn heavily from the court documents in the federal cases against Humaira Jawed and Hamid Sheikh. Hundreds of pages of transcripts and other material were filed on the public court docket as part of the government's case against the pair, enabling me to reconstruct in great detail Qazalbash's life in the United States and the manhunt for him. The account of the work of the FTTTF was in large part drawn from FBI documents released under FOIA, though a small number of former FBI officials were willing to speak to me. In addition, the former *Wired* reporter Ryan Singel did pioneer reporting on the program while at the magazine and generously dug up many of his archives to share with me. This chapter and all others involving the FBI also drew from Garrett Graff's *Threat Matrix: The FBI at War in the Age of Global Terror* (Little, Brown, 2011), an indispensable history of the bureau after 9/11.

42 **It was about 7:30 p.m.** Transcript of Sentencing Hearing, *USA v. Jawed,* Case No. 2:03-cr-510 (E.D. Pa., filed 2003), Doc. No. 27.

42 **more than fifty federal agents** Ibid.

42 **ties to a Pakistani militant group** Criminal Complaint, *USA v. Jawed,* Case No. 2:03-cr-510 (E.D. Pa., filed 2003), Doc. No. 1.

43 **Qazalbash would tell family members** *USA v. Jawed,* Transcript.

44 **both had lied** Criminal Complaint, *United States v. Sheikh,* Case No. 2:03-cr-00514-AB, Doc. No. 1 (E.D. Pa.); *USA v. Jawed,* Complaint.

46 **"When we identify someone"** Jerri Williams, "Kathy Lambert—Counterterrorism, Joint Terrorism Task Forces, and Jihad Jane," *FBI Retired Case File Review,* podcast, episode 010, March 26, 2016.

46 **went on a data binge** Ben Worthen, "Data Privacy: What to Do When Uncle Sam Wants Your Data," *CIO,* April 15, 2003.

47   **started showing up at scuba shops** Karen Brandon, "FBI Puts Scuba Dive Shops, Schools on Terrorism Alert," *Chicago Tribune*, June 6, 2002.

47   **turned over its entire list** Worthen, "Data Privacy."

47   **"In the year and a half since Sept. 11, 2001"** Ibid.

47   **the FBI began to lean heavily** Dustin Volz, "U.S. Government Reveals Breadth of Requests for Internet Records," Reuters, Dec. 1, 2015.

47   **A national security letter is similar** Charles Doyle, "National Security Letters in Foreign Intelligence Investigations: Legal Background," Congressional Research Service, report No. RL33320, July 30, 2015.

47   **FBI's use of national security letters soared** U.S. Department of Justice Office of the Inspector General, "A Review of the Federal Bureau of Investigation's Use of National Security Letters Oversight and Review," Feb. 2016.

48   **Four data brokers would end up** Federal Bureau of Investigation, "Current FTTTF and IDW Dataset List & Details." Documents released under FOIA to Ryan Singel.

48   **"monitor the electronic footprints"** Federal Bureau of Investigation, "Fiscal Year (FY) 2008 Internal Planning and Budget Review, Program Narrative Summary for BASE RESOURCES," Feb. 19, 2008. Documents released under FOIA to Ryan Singel.

48   **major role in the case of Russell Defreitas** Federal Bureau of Investigation, "Foreign Terrorist Task Force (FTTTF) Input to Office of Congressional Affairs Concerning Reference Below," June 15, 2007. Documents released under FOIA to Ryan Singel.

48   **had been a cargo handler** Department of Justice United States Attorney's Office for the Eastern District of New York, "Four Individuals Charged in Plot to Bomb John F. Kennedy International Airport," June 2, 2007.

49   **"not classified but sensitive"** Federal Bureau of Investigation, "CTD—Senate Questions; Responses Due COB Friday," Feb. 16, 2007. Documents released under FOIA to Ryan Singel.

51   **would also become government contractors** FBI, FTTTF and IDW Dataset List.

52   **small, secretive elite special operations units** Mark Bowden, "American Special Ops Forces Are Everywhere," *Atlantic*, April 2021.

52   **"We also have to work"** Dick Cheney, "The Vice President Appears on Meet the Press with Tim Russert," White House, Sept. 16, 2001, georgewbush-whitehouse .archives.gov.

Chapter 5: The Dots Guys

The account of the role U.S. special operations played in the war on terror is heavily drawn from two books: Stanley McChrystal's memoir *My Share of the Task* (Portfolio, 2014) and Sean Naylor's *Relentless Strike: The Secret History of Joint Special Operations Command* (St. Martin's

Press, 2015). I also consulted Mark Ambinder and D. B. Grady's *Command: Deep Inside the President's Secret Army* (Wiley, 2012). Also invaluable were the many hours spent listening to archived episodes of Jack Murphy and Dave Parke's podcast *The Team House*, which, among other things, is essentially a fantastic ongoing oral history of U.S. special operations and intelligence.

Patrick Biltgen and Stephen Ryan's *Activity-Based Intelligence: Principles and Applications* (Artech House, 2016) was also a critical source in understanding the data-driven approach taken by the NGA and intelligence agencies during this time period. I also interviewed several senior intelligence community officials, including two NGA directors, as part of my reporting and numerous mid-level former intelligence analysts at data-driven counterterrorism organizations such as SKOPE, the Joint Improvised-Threat Defeat Organization, and the interagency joint task forces that were responsible for hunting terrorists.

54 **It was exactly 6:12 p.m.** McChrystal, *My Share of the Task.*

54 **Overhead, American F-16s circled** "U.S. Military: Al-Zarqawi Was Alive After Bombing," CNN.com, June 9, 2006.

55 **public enemy number one** Mary Anne Weaver, "The Short, Violent Life of Abu Musab al-Zarqawi," *Atlantic,* July/Aug. 2006.

56 **"Find—Fix—Finish"** McChrystal, *My Share of the Task.*

56 **F3EAD strategy had an immediate impact** Charles Faint and Michael Harris, "F3EAD: Ops/Intel Fusion 'Feeds' the SOF Targeting Process," *Small Wars Journal,* Jan. 31, 2012.

56 **In August 2004, McChrystal's special operations** McChrystal, *My Share of the Task.*

56 **they executed three hundred raids** "Generation Kill: A Conversation with Stanley McChrystal," *Foreign Affairs,* March 1, 2013.

57 **One was called the SKOPE Cell** Henry Kenyon, "A Mandate to Innovate in Intelligence Analysis," FCW, March 28, 2011.

58 **NGA had decided that it wanted** Barry Harris, "Stabilizing Iraq: Intelligence Lessons for Afghanistan," Washington Institute for Near East Policy, May 28, 2009.

59 **owed an intellectual debt** Patrick Biltgen and Sarah Hank, "ABI in Policing," in Biltgen and Ryan, *Activity-Based Intelligence.*

60 **pattern of life analysis** Naylor, *Relentless Strike.*

61 **That day they had actually been stalking** McChrystal, *My Share of the Task.*

Chapter 6: The Firehose

Sean Gorman generously agreed to be interviewed multiple times for this chapter on the record. I also reviewed several issues of the NGA's *Pathfinder* magazine that covered Zezima's project, which required a FOIA request to obtain. I also spoke to numerous former employees at Gnip and Twitter. The interviews were conducted in a mixture of on the record and on background. These interviews helped inform internal conversations about the early days of social media. Dave Troy, the man who invented geotagged coordinates on Twitter, also agreed to be interviewed on the record. Finally, I covered a lot of the early days of social media use in politics as a young reporter at *Politico*. I was particularly interested in the use of email marketing, social media, and data analytics in political campaigns and spent a good deal of time back then trying to understand how politicians and eventually government agencies were tapping this technology.

66   **impressed by the power of the internet** M. Karen Walker, "Disaster Response Efforts Highlight Value of Relationships, Nontraditional Partners," *Pathfinder* 10, no. 4 (July/Aug. 2012).

66   **a PhD candidate in Boston** Hannah Bloch, "When Disaster Strikes, He Creates a 'Crisis Map' That Helps Save Lives," NPR, Oct. 2, 2016.

66   **allowed various forms of data** Josh Halliday, "Ushahidi Launches Simplified Crisis-Mapping Service," *Guardian*, Aug. 11, 2010.

68   **"tedious and unimportant"** Laura Blumenfeld, "Dissertation Could Be Security Threat," *Washington Post*, July 8, 2003.

69   **"Dissertation Could Be Security Threat"** Ibid.

70   **CIA-backed venture capital firm, In-Q-Tel** Jason Moll, "Tool Proves Value of NGA, In-Q-Tel Relationship," *Pathfinder* 2, no. 1 (Spring 2013).

70   **what was being called Web 2.0** Jamin Brophy-Warren, "The Good, the Bad, and the 'Web 2.0,'" *Wall Street Journal*, July 18, 2007.

72   **"Grand Central Station for the social web"** Marshall Kirkpatrick, "Gnip: Grand Central Station for the Social Web," Readwrite.com, July 1, 2008.

72   **about 5,000 tweets a day in 2007** Twitter, "Measuring Tweets," Twitter.com (blog), Feb. 22, 2010, blog.twitter.com/official/en_us/a/2010/measuring-tweets.html.

72   **By 2008, it was up to 300,000** Twitter, "200 Million Tweets per Day," Twitter.com (blog), June 30, 2011, blog.twitter.com/official/en_us/a/2011/200-million-tweets-per-day.html.

72   **"What you say on Twitter"** Twitter, "Terms of Service," Version 4, effective Nov. 2010 to June 2011, twitter.com/en/tos/previous/version_4.

72   **huge sums of money online** Kenneth P. Vogel, "Obama Fundraising Slips from 2008," *Politico,* March 20, 2012.

73   **the most transparent administration** Josh Gerstein, "Obama's Muddy Transparency Record," *Politico,* March 5, 2012.

73   **the prevailing sentiment** Jonathan Allen and Michelle Quinn, "Arab Spring: Tech as Tinder," *Politico,* Sept. 14, 2012.

74   **"We had become too accustomed"** Michael Morell, *The Great War of Our Time: The CIA's Fight Against Terrorism—from al Qa'ida to ISIS* (Twelve, 2015).

76   **Athar fired off a series of tweets** Megan Chuchmach, "Man Unknowingly Live Tweets About Raid on Osama Bin Laden's Compound," ABC News, May 2, 2011.

Chapter 7: The Ugly Stepchild

Eliot Jardines was extremely helpful in recounting the history of open-source intelligence. We sat in his office near D.C. for several hours discussing the topic in a lengthy on-the-record interview, and he was always available by email to answer follow-ups. I also drew heavily on Jardines's public writings to draft some of this chapter. He was not the only one. Several other intelligence community officials involved in open-source intelligence efforts gave interviews on the condition that their words not be attributed to them, as did several analysts assigned to military task forces in this time period. Finally, numerous people confirmed the levels of PAI, which had been classified for a long time. At this point, I'm told they have been declassified, but the federal government still refuses to discuss them, at least with me.

78   **Norman Schwarzkopf had a plan** Eliot A. Jardines, "Open Source Intelligence," in *The Five Disciplines of Intelligence Collection,* ed. Mark M. Lowenthal and Robert M. Clark (CQ Press, 2015).

79   **In 1941, President Franklin D. Roosevelt** Ibid.

80   **"defiant, hostile tone"** Ibid.

80   **"I don't want to be in the position"** George Tenet, "Nomination of George J. Tenet to Be Director of Central Intelligence," Hearing before the Senate Select Committee on Intelligence, May 6, 1997.

80   **"we only pay for secrets"** Ronald Marks, "The Fog of Cyber War," *Newsweek,* June 15, 2015.

80   **The 9/11 Commission floated the idea** National Commission on Terrorist Attacks upon the United States, *9/11 Commission Report.*

80   **"The Cold War notion"** Michael T. Flynn et al., "Fixing Intel: A Blueprint for Making Intelligence Relevant in Afghanistan," Center for a New American Security, Jan. 2010.

81   **the Open Source Center** Office of the Director of National Intelligence, "Intelligence Community Directive Number 301," effective July 11, 2006.

83   **2005 *New York Times* story** James Risen and Eric Lichtblau, "Bush Lets U.S. Spy on Callers Without Courts," *New York Times,* Dec. 16, 2005.

84   **a tenuous reading of the U.S. Constitution** L. Rush Atkinson, "The Fourth Amendment's National Security Exception: Its History and Limits," *Vanderbilt Law Review* 66, no. 5 (2013).

84   **Church Committee revelations spurred Congress** James Risen, *The Last Honest Man: The CIA, the FBI, the Mafia, and the Kennedys—and One Senator's Fight to Save Democracy* (Little, Brown, 2023).

86   **Facebook, Twitter, Instagram, and others have rules** Melissa Holzberg, "Facebook Banned 1.3 Billion Accounts over Three Months to Combat 'Fake' and 'Harmful' Content," *Forbes,* March 22, 2021.

Chapter 8: The Berber Hunter

The history of SUNet and the development of the Berber Hunter Tool Kit was described to me by numerous people who worked on the program both inside the government and as contractors or subcontractors on the various contract vehicles that funded the computer network and the acquisition of the tools. Brian Sharkey sat with me for a lengthy interview that was on the record, but numerous others directly involved in the program also spoke at length on the condition that their words not be attributed to them. I also obtained numerous documents under FOIA that shed light on the SUNet program or the Berber Hunter Tool Kit. Most were contracting records, which show the basics of the program. I tried to sue to obtain policy documents, such as training manuals and safety procedures. But unfortunately, despite the lawsuit, SOCOM entirely withheld nearly all public documents about the program, citing the need to protect U.S. critical infrastructure and intelligence sources and methods. The matter is still in court as of the deadline for this book, highlighting the broken nature of FOIA to unlock even unclassified information about military and intelligence programs.

I also often found myself in conversation with Jack Poulson, a technologist and computer science PhD turned independent journalist and surveillance researcher. Some of this chapter was drawn on conversations or tips from him that were verified by other sources or were based on documents that he provided, including the fact that the SUNet/Berber Hunter users all had a 761link.net email domain. Poulson often obtained documents either under the Freedom of Information Act, by scouring open sources, or by pulling from the millions of pages of contracting documents the government posts online. His report "Easy as PAI" (techinquiry.org/EasyAsPAI/) was also an instructive source on the contracting history of SUNet and the Berber Hunter Tool Kit. Poulson was incredibly generous in sharing tips, leads, and ideas with an ostensible "competitor," and I tried to return the favor whenever I could.

88 **the Darién Gap** Carolyn McCarthy, "Silent Darien: The Gap in the World's Longest Road," BBC, Aug. 14, 2014.

88 **a popular migrant route** Nick Paton Walsh et al., "On One of the World's Most Dangerous Migrant Routes, a Cartel Makes Millions off the American Dream," CNN, April 17, 2023.

89 **half a dozen or so Somali migrants** Todd Bensman, *America's Covert Border War: The Untold Story of the Nation's Battle to Prevent Jihadist Infiltration* (Bombardier Books, 2021).

89 **He was quickly arrested** "Costa Rica Detains Somali with Alleged Terrorism Links," Reuters, March 23, 2017.

90 **ECS Federal, served as the gatekeeper** Complaint, *Babel Street Inc. v. Brendan Huff, Jeffrey Heinz, et al.*, Case No. 2018 16334 (Fairfax County Cir. Ct. Va., filed 2018).

91 **Poindexter had a lofty vision** Poindexter, "Remarks."

93 **developed a way to share data** "Combating Terrorism Technical Support Office 2013 Review Book," Combating Terrorism Technical Support Office, 2013.

94 **sold their business** "ECS Federal Acquires Information Systems Worldwide," Mergr.com.

94 **Conflict Zone Tool Kit** "Combating Terrorism Technical Support Office 2015 Review Book," Combating Terrorism Technical Support Office, 2015.

95 **"The explosion of social media"** Department of Defense, "Federal Contract Opportunity for Secure Unclassified Network (SUNet) Infrastructure W911QX19R0005," Oct. 16, 2018, sam.gov.

96 **as many as 400 accounts** Department of Defense, "01.26.2021 Questions RFI Architecture" as part of "HQ USSOCOM Architecture Solution 21-0001," Jan. 26, 2021, sam.gov.

Chapter 9: Decipher Your World

The history of Babel Street is sourced to numerous former Babel Street employees, including those who held senior positions inside the company. I also interviewed numerous Acxiom employees who were familiar with the Harbinger product and acquisition. I talked to analysts and operators who were frontline users of Babel Street's products. I also obtained thousands of pages of documents under FOIA and state open-records laws related to Babel Street. Finally, I consumed a wide variety of open-source media about Jeff Chapman and Babel Street, including transcripts and videos of him and other executives appearing in other media interviews, podcasts, panels, and other public events. The list of Babel's sources was released to me by Mississippi State University. In answering one of my open-records requests, the university tried to redact the document describing Babel's sources, but the text was still extractable.

The history of Twitter's approach to government access to its data feeds is based on interviews with employees of Twitter, Gnip, Geofeedia, Topsy, and other companies that were in the social media monitoring space. I also spoke to a wide variety of voices in civil society about the issues raised by social media surveillance.

99 **Prior to going to Babel** Brendan Huff, Co-Founder / Security Consultant / Instructor / U.S. Army Senior CI Technician, LinkedIn profile, accessed June 6, 2023, www.linkedin.com/in/brendanhuff/.

99 **A classic example of the genre** Charlie Warzel, "It's Not Cancel Culture—It's a Platform Failure," Galaxy Brain, Substack, April 13, 2021.

100 **When the FBI director, James Comey, let slip** Ashley Feinberg, "This Is Almost Certainly James Comey's Twitter Account," Gizmodo, March 30, 2017.

100 **Keith Urbahn, would take to Twitter** Alex Eichler, "Meet Keith Urbahn, First to Tweet News of Bin Laden," *Atlantic,* May 4, 2011.

101 **pattern that would repeat** "Factbox: News That Broke on Twitter," Reuters, July 7, 2011.

101 **Harbinger was founded by** Acxiom, "Acxiom Acquires Harbinger Technologies Group," March 30, 2007, archived at insidearm.com.

102 **operates in long acquisition cycles** Alec C. Blivas et al., "Cycle Times and Cycles of Acquisition Reform," CSIS.org, Aug. 5, 2020.

102   **ending up in the Treasury Department** Jeffrey Chapman, Founder of Babel Street, LinkedIn profile, accessed June 6, 2023, www.linkedin.com/in/jeffrey-chapman-3a012a8/.

102   **Chapman, a Starkville, Mississippi, native** James Carskadon, "MSU Continues to Boost Mississippi's Advanced Technology Manufacturing Economies," *Alumnus,* Mississippi State University, Spring 2023.

103   **it would allow users to search** Mississippi State University, "Providing Actionable Intelligence to Increase the Capabilities of the Warfighter by Use of MSU Open Source Exploitation Systems (MOSES)," status reports and deliverables, 2019–20. Released to the author under the Mississippi Public Records Act.

103   **Babel really came into its own** Jordan Novet, "Babel Street Picks Up $2M to Serve as Your International Data Interpreter," *Venture Beat,* Feb. 28, 2014.

104   **Twitter authorized four companies** Alex Hern, "Twitter Buys Gnip, One of Only Four Companies with 'Firehose' Access," *Guardian,* April 16, 2014.

105   *The Wall Street Journal* **reported in 2016** Christopher S. Stewart and Mark Maremont, "Twitter Bars Intelligence Agencies from Using Analytics Service," *Wall Street Journal,* May 8, 2016.

106   **the ACLU of Northern California** Jonah Engel Bromwich et al., "Police Use Surveillance Tool to Scan Social Media, A.C.L.U. Says," *New York Times,* Oct. 11, 2016.

106   **also received an In-Q-Tel investment** Lee Fang, "The CIA Is Investing in Firms That Mine Your Tweets and Instagram Photos," *Intercept,* April 14, 2016.

107   **Chapman participated in a single** Aaron Gregg, "For This Company, Online Surveillance Leads to Profit in Washington's Suburbs," *Washington Post,* Sept. 10, 2017.

110   **"I like making fun of our own people"** Sam Biddle and Jack Poulson, "American Phone-Tracking Firm Demo'd Surveillance Powers by Spying on CIA and NSA," *Intercept,* April 22, 2022.

Chapter 10: The Network of Death

This account of the U.S. government's counter-ISIS campaign was drawn from interviews with people familiar with the matter who served in the military, in civilian government jobs, or as government contractors or were familiar with ISIS as independent experts or analysts. It also involved an extensive review of the published literature, especially the academic literature around terrorism and social media. Finally, some parts of this chapter were drawn from my previous reporting experience. I was a White House reporter from late 2014 through the end of Barack Obama's term in office, and though I was a generalist who did not specialize in foreign policy or national security at the time, it was frequently a topic that was addressed at the highest levels of the White House during this period. Also Joby Warrick's *Black Flags: The Rise of ISIS* (Doubleday, 2015) was an instructive bit of background reading.

The history of Operation Gallant Phoenix was not easy to piece together. Most people refused to discuss the intelligence fusion cell with me, even though the ISIS threat has receded, much of it is no longer classified, and the U.S. efforts were a positive story. There are very few media mentions of it, even years later. In short, it has been well kept under wraps. In recent years, there has been slightly more openness to talking about it. And if you carefully read enough government documents, you can piece together an idea of its operations. However, this was the most challenging part of reporting the book and significant gaps remain in the public's understanding of this important chapter in U.S. counterterrorism operations.

111 **Mark John Taylor was one** "Kiwi Jihadi Mark Taylor Not So 'Bumbling'—Law Expert," RNZ, March 6, 2019.

111 **Born in New Zealand's North Island** Stacey Kirk and Tracy Watkins, "Mark Taylor's Former Wife Gives Portrait of Kiwi Jihadist Jailed in Kurdish Prison," *Stuff,* March 5, 2019.

111 **"a lost little lamb"** "Kiwi Jihadi Mark Taylor Not So 'Bumbling.'"

112 **"Now is the time to commence"** Tracy Watkins, "Police in Anzac Security Boost After Jihadist Video," *Stuff,* April 24, 2015.

112 **included GPS coordinates** Denver Nicks, "New Zealander ISIS Fighter Accidentally Tweets Secret Location," *Time,* Jan. 1, 2015.

112 **"bumbling Jihadist"** Australian Associated Press, "New Zealand's 'Bumbling Jihadi' Isis Recruit Caught in Syria," *Guardian,* March 4, 2019.

113 **The Brookings Institution in Washington** J. M. Berger and Jonathon Morgan, "The ISIS Twitter Census: Defining and Describing the Population of ISIS Supporters on Twitter," Center for Middle East Policy at Brookings, Analysis Paper No. 20, March 2015.

113 **quietly stood up a secretive intelligence cell** Jim Garamone, "Dunford Asks Defense Chiefs to Guard Against Complacency," Defense.gov, Oct. 16, 2018.

114 **a slickly produced video surfaced online** Rukmini Callimachi, "Militant Group Says It Killed American Journalist in Syria," *New York Times,* Aug. 19, 2014.

114 **By December 2015, thirty thousand people** Les Picker, "Where Are ISIS's Foreign Fighters Coming From?," National Bureau of Economic Research, *Digest,* no. 6 (June 2016).

114 **At its height, ISIS** Cameron Glenn et al., "Timeline: The Rise, Spread, and Fall of the Islamic State," Wilson Center, Oct. 28, 2019.

115   **143 attacks across twenty-nine countries** Tim Lister et al., "ISIS Goes Global: 143 Attacks in 29 Countries Have Killed 2,043," CNN, Feb. 12, 2018.

115   **The group circulated a document** Charlie Winter, "What I Learned from Reading the Islamic State's Propaganda Instruction Manual," *Lawfare*, April 2, 2017.

115   **derisively refer to secular "moderns"** Graeme Wood, "What ISIS Really Wants," *Atlantic*, March 2015.

115   **"network of death"** Carol E. Lee and Jay Solomon, "Obama Addresses Islamic State Threat in United Nations Speech," *Wall Street Journal*, Sept. 24, 2014.

116   **Operation Inherent Resolve** Department of Defense, "Iraq and Syria Operations Against ISIL Designated as Operation Inherent Resolve by U.S. Central Command," press release, Oct. 15, 2014.

116   **recounted in a 2015 speech** Brian Everstine, "Carlisle: Air Force Intel Uses ISIS 'Moron's' Social Media Posts to Target Airstrikes," *Air Force Times*, June 4, 2015.

117   **described in a podcast interview** Dave Park and Jack Murphy, "Jade Parker, Cyber Special Reconnaissance," *The Team House*, podcast, episode 105, July 31, 2021.

119   **a device with the IP address 122.61.118.145** Government of New Zealand, "Report of the Royal Commission of Inquiry into the Terrorist Attack on Christchurch Masjidain on 15 March 2019," vol. 2.

Chapter 11: Like a Real Person

My material about the Loren Reed case was drawn from police records and court documents. The police records were released to me under Arizona's open-records law. The court documents were part of the public record in the case. I also obtained or reviewed thousands of pages documenting police and other government use of social media. Some were released directly to me as part of public record requisitions; others were obtained by civil society groups such as the American Civil Liberties Union and the Brennan Center. Finally, my work on this chapter was informed by a wide variety of conversations with former employees of social media companies, vendors who sold social media analytic tools, and government contractors who specialize in social media matters. I also spoke with people in civil society to understand the perspective of those who want the monitoring of social media curtailed.

121   **inviting others to join him in a "riot"** "Supplemental Narrative—Miller, C," Page, Arizona, Police Department, Incident 20-04964.

121   **Facebook group called Fuck 12** Miller Narrative, Page Police.

121   **yell, "ACAB"** Affidavit in Support of Complaint, *USA v. Reed*, Case No. 3:20-cr-8098 (D. Ariz., filed 2020), Doc. No. 1.

121   **burning down the local courthouse** Affidavit, *USA v. Reed.*

122   **"Arson, Assault, Conspiracy"** Ibid.

122   **Reed was arrested** U.S. Department of Justice, "Page Man Charged with Threatening to Burn Page Magistrate Court," June 4, 2020.

122   **"Loren oscillated between saying"** Motion to Dismiss All Charges, *USA v. Reed,* Case No. 3:20-cr-8098 (D. Ariz., filed 2020), Doc. No. 51.

122   **"I really wanna remain peaceful"** Ibid.

123   **running an account with the name Bob Smith** Daniel Connolly, "Police Surveillance Trial: White Official Ran 'Bob Smith' Account, Called Himself Man of Color," *Memphis Commercial Appeal,* Aug. 20, 2018.

123   **"My party, the Democrat party"** Ibid.

124   **"You have to make this look"** Ibid.

124   **extensive contact between the FBI, DHS, and Twitter** Aaron Terr and Matthew Harwood, "Yes, You Should Be Worried About the FBI's Relationship with Twitter," Foundation for Individual Rights and Expression, Dec. 23, 2022, thefire.org.

124   **to obtain bulk Twitter user data directly from the company** Michael Shellenberger (@shellenberger), Twitter, Dec. 19, 2022, 12:14 p.m., twitter.com/shellenberger/status/1604888013422485505.

124   **"If you're not wearing a mask"** Claire Foster (@ClaireFosterPHD), Twitter, Nov. 3, 2022, 8:01 a.m., twitter.com/ClaireFosterPHD/status/1588139398402609154.

124   **"For every negative comment"** Claire Foster (@ClaireFosterPHD), Twitter, Nov. 3, 2022, 9:00 a.m., twitter.com/ClaireFosterPHD/status/1588154067011997699.

126   **The industry estimated it would have to pay** Jennifer A. Kingson, "Exclusive: $1 Billion–Plus Riot Damage Is Most Expensive in Insurance History," *Axios,* Sept. 16, 2020.

127   **It would purchase five thousand licenses** John Hewitt Jones, "FBI Purchases 5,000 Licenses for Babel X Social Media OSINT Tool," FedScoop.com, April 5, 2022.

127   **"provide critical information"** Aaron Schaffer, "The FBI Is Spending Millions on Social Media Tracking Software," *The Cybersecurity 202* (newsletter), *Washington Post,* April 5, 2022.

128   **a company called Echosec** Department of Defense, Documents Related to Task Order 47QFCA19F0040, in the Tech Inquiry FOIA Collection.

129   **"due to the fact that searching"** Ibid.

Chapter 12: They Know How Bad You Are at *Angry Birds*

This account of the impact of the Snowden disclosures was in large part drawn from contemporaneous coverage of leaks by the news media. Especially helpful was the work of *The Washington Post, The Guardian, Der*

Spiegel, ProPublica, and *The New York Times.* My account of these events was also informed by interviews with former officials with the FBI, the NSA, and the CIA. Finally, I drew on my own personal experience covering the Obama administration on and off between 2011 and 2017 as a White House reporter first for *Politico* and then for *The Wall Street Journal* in my understanding of the political fallout and the president's handling of the situation. I also drew on Edward Snowden's own memoir, *Permanent Record* (Metropolitan Books, 2019), and Barton Gellman's account of his role in the disclosures, *Dark Mirror.* I also reviewed Laura Poitras's *Citizenfour* film and a wide array of Glenn Greenwald's writings. I also interviewed a number of senior government officials involved in intelligence matters who were serving at the time of the disclosures.

133   **For a few minutes on January 28, 2014** John Leyden, "Angry Anti-NSA Hackers Pwn Angry Birds Site After GCHQ Data Slurp," *Register,* Jan. 29, 2014.

133   **claimed on Twitter** Syrian Electronic Army (@Official_SEA16), "A friend hacked and defaced @Angrybirds website after reports confirms its spying on people," Twitter, Jan. 28, 2014, https://twitter.com/Official_SEA16/status/428301730581737472.

134   **was buried in several slide decks** GCHQ, "Mobile Apps Doubleheader: Badass Angry Birds: From 6 Weeks to 6 Minutes: Protocols Exploitation in a Rapidly Changing World. Exploring and Exploiting Leaky Mobile Apps with BADASS." From the collection of Edward Snowden, published by *Der Spiegel.*

134   **metadata from the Verizon telephone network** Glenn Greenwald, "NSA Collecting Phone Records of Millions of Verizon Customers Daily," *Guardian,* June 6, 2013.

134   **a coordinated barrage of stories** James Ball, "Angry Birds and 'Leaky' Phone Apps Targeted by NSA and GCHQ for User Data," *Guardian,* Jan. 28, 2014; James Glanz, Jeff Larson, and Andrew W. Lehren, "Spy Agencies Tap Data Streaming from Phone Apps," *New York Times,* Jan. 27, 2014; Jeff Larson, "Spy Agencies Probe Angry Birds and Other Apps for Personal Data," ProPublica, Jan. 27, 2014.

135   **"BEGAL Automated Development"** GCHQ, "Mobile Apps Doubleheader."

135   **"Abusing BADASS for Fun"** Ibid.

135   **"effectively means that anyone"** Ball, "Angry Birds and 'Leaky' Phone Apps Targeted by NSA and GCHQ for User Data."

137   **"It was not shocking to discover"** David Anderson, *A Question of Trust: Report of the Investigatory Powers Review,* June 2015.

137   **"Mo-ther fuckers . . . I've spent years"** Gellman, *Dark Mirror.*

138   **"It's time that the post-Snowden pendulum"** James Comey, "FBI Director James Comey on Technology, Law Enforcement, and 'Going Dark'" (speech to the Brookings Institution, Oct. 16, 2014).

139 **a speech on the Senate floor** Ron Wyden, "Statement on Patriot Act Reauthorization, as Prepared for Delivery," May 26, 2011.

139 **James Clapper** Hearing of the Senate Select Intelligence Committee, Subject: "Current and Projected National Security Threats to the United States," March 12, 2013.

140 **"least untruthful manner"** Glenn Kessler, "James Clapper's 'Least Untruthful' Statement to the Senate," *Washington Post,* June 12, 2013.

142 **"The challenges to our privacy"** Barack Obama, "Remarks by the President on Review of Signals Intelligence," Jan. 17, 2014.

142 **"was disappointed to see"** John Eggerton, "President Launches Review of Big Data and Privacy," NextTV.com, Jan. 17, 2014.

Chapter 13: Location and Motive

As mentioned previously, Yeagley sat for numerous interviews with me. I also interviewed other people familiar with PlanetRisk's work. I also interviewed dozens of people who worked at location brokers or used the data offered by such brokers in business, government, or nonprofit work. I spoke to nearly two dozen people familiar with UberMedia, all of whom asked to remain anonymous.

144 **in government circles as adtech data** Office of the Director of National Intelligence, Senior Advisor Group Panel on Commercially Available Information, "Report to the Director of National Intelligence," Jan. 27, 2022.

145 **an overland driving race** Bruce Rogers, "Journey Through Minefield Sparks Idea for Mobile Marketing Platform," Forbes.com, July 27, 2015.

147 **technology executive Bill Gross** Erick Schonfeld, "UberMedia CEO Bill Gross: Twitter Turn-Off 'Took Us by Surprise,' but 'We Will Change,'" *TechCrunch,* Feb. 18, 2011.

147 **helped invent keyword-targeted ads** Will Oremus, "Google's Big Break," *Slate,* Oct. 13, 2013.

147 **a social-media-focused company called TweetUp** Paul Boutin, "Bill Gross Buys His Way onto Twitter," VentureBeat, July 6, 2010.

152 **published an explosive story** "Pillar Investigates: USCCB Gen Sec Burrill Resigns After Sexual Misconduct Allegations," *Pillar,* July 20, 2021.

153 **"This was something that was obtained"** J. D. Flynn and Ed Condon, "Let's Talk About It," *The Pillar Podcast,* episode 28. I lightly cleaned up Condon's quotation.

Chapter 14: Where You Go Is Who You Are

The description of Ivan Lopez's arrest was drawn from police reports and court documents. The police reports were obtained under Arizona's open-records law; the court documents were public records. I also visited the KFC in 2021 on a trip through Arizona. The history of Gravy Analytics was based on numerous people familiar with the company and its work. I also did a review of all of the interviews and speeches that I could find given by Jeff White and other top Gravy and Venntel executives.

157   **Ivan Lopez was driving his pickup** "Officer Vasquez Narrative," San Luis Police Department Report, Case No. 2018-00017162, Aug. 14, 2018. Lopez's full name is Jesus Ivan Lopez Garcia, according to the charging documents, but he appeared to be known as Ivan per media reports and police documents.

157   **The dog, Laika, circled** "Officer Cardenes Narrative," San Luis Police Department Report, Case No. 2018-00017162, Aug. 14, 2018.

158   **later revealed in lab testing** United States' Memorandum for Detention, *United States of America v. Jesus Ivan Lopez Garcia,* Case No. 2:18-mj-01760 (D. Ariz., filed 2018), ECF No. 5.

158   **sentenced to eighty-four months** "Judgment and Commitment of Probation Issued," *USA v. Lopez Garcia,* Case No. 2:18-cr-01212 (D. Ariz., filed 2018), ECF No. 43.

158   **press conference announcing the arrest** Amy B. Wang, "Drug-Smuggling Tunnel to Mexico Found Under Abandoned KFC in Arizona," *Washington Post,* Aug. 24, 2018.

159   **shared a first glimpse** Byron Tau and Michelle Hackman, "Federal Agencies Use Cellphone Location Data for Immigration Enforcement," *Wall Street Journal,* Feb. 7, 2020.

159   **Both *The Washington Post* and *The New York Times*** "Apps Are Selling Your Location Data. The U.S. Government Is Buying," *Washington Post,* Feb. 9, 2020; Editorial Board, "The Government Uses 'Near Perfect Surveillance' Data on Americans," *New York Times,* Feb. 7, 2020.

160   **Jeff White just wanted to help** Steven Overly, "Even Serial Entrepreneurs Face Capital, Customer Struggles; Three Longtime Entrepreneurs Share Insights on the Challenge of Finding a First Customer, Raising Money," *Washington Post,* July 28, 2013.

160   **White grew up in the Washington, D.C., area** Alejandro Cremades, "Jeff White on Selling Two Startups for Millions and Now Raising $20M to Take On the $270B Big Data Industry," Alejandro Cremades podcast, episode 137.

160   **But he struggled to balance** Ellen Schneider, "This Exec Keeps His Balance with Workouts and a Rural Lifestyle," *Washington Business Journal,* Aug. 16, 2018.

160   **chock-full of technologists** Lindsay Ellis and Kailyn Rhone, "Silicon Valley Layoffs Mean Washington, D.C., Is a Hotter Tech Hiring Market," *Wall Street Journal,* Feb. 7, 2023.

161   **Upwards of 70 percent** Ginger Woolridge, "How Ashburn, VA Became the Co-location Mecca Known as Data Center Alley," *Lightyear,* accessed Sept. 3, 2023.

162   **a company called TimeRazor** Steven Overly, "Smartphone App Gravy Raises $3M from Investors," *Washington Post,* Dec. 16, 2012.

162   **raised a few million dollars** Sarah Perez, "Stealthy Startup timeRAZOR Raises $3.4M Pre-launch, Partners with Major Household Brands," *TechCrunch,* Feb. 8, 2012.

162　**In a breathless press release** Gravy Analytics, "Gravy App Raises Additional Funding Bringing Total Capital to $6.4 Million," press release, Dec. 13, 2012.

162　**raised a combined $6.4 million** Overly, "Smartphone App Gravy Raises $3M from Investors."

162　**"not this thing that dominates your plate"** Ibid.

164　**a deal with the newspaper publisher Gannett** Kasra Kangarloo, "A Leesburg Marketing Analytics Company Has Landed $7.6 Million in Funding," *Washington Business Journal,* April 8, 2015.

164　**fuse its detailed calendar of goings-on** "Location Intelligence for Social Good," YouTube video, posted by Northern Virginia Technology Council, June 25, 2021.

164　**Gravy's belief was that where a person went** Jeff White, "Going Beyond Demographics with Jeff White," YouTube video, posted by MCNY INFO, July 29, 2019.

165　**"Half my advertising spend is wasted"** Darren Woolley, "Which Half of My Advertising Is Wasted—and It Is Only Half?," MediaVillage.com, Sept. 4, 2019.

166　**"We felt the most powerful signal"** Cremades, "Jeff White on Selling Two Startups."

167　**able to collect the location data** Ibid.

167　**"geo-signals cloud"** Gravy Analytics, "Gravy's Open Geo-Signals Cloud Breaks 200 Million Mobile-Device Mark Within Two Months of Launch," press release.

168　**"This data could eventually be used"** Gravy Analytics, "Gravy CTO's Point of View: Privacy in an 'Always-On' World."

169　**"privacy-friendly"** Cremades, "Jeff White on Selling Two Startups."

Chapter 15: The Fun House of Mirrors

This chapter is based on interviews with several Department of Homeland Security officials, as well as people directly familiar with the internal operations of Gravy, Venntel, and Babel Street at the time the events in question occurred. It is also based on thousands of pages of documents released by DHS and its components under FOIA. Some were released to me, but most were released to the American Civil Liberties Union, which generously made them available to me as part of my research for this book.

171　**"At this time, due to the unanswered privacy"** Lindsay Lennon Vogel, email to DHS S&T Office, June 19, 2019, in the American Civil Liberties Union FOIA collection. Note: I made a small alteration to Vogel's email. The original email capitalizes "Privacy." It's unclear whether Vogel was referring to the DHS privacy office, or privacy concerns in the abstract and capitalized the word out of habit. Given that the word "legal" is not capitalized, I understood her to be referring to privacy as a concept and not the office, but obviously the office also had concerns. For readability, I did not capitalize "privacy," but the sentence could be read in two ways.

171   **how effective the company's data** Department of Homeland Security, Market Research document, undated and highly redacted, in the American Civil Liberties Union FOIA collection. The unredacted portion of the email states, "ERO's Alternatives to Detention (ATD) program, participated in a pilot project with the personnel from the Combined Intelligence Unit (CIU); the project's objective was to locate and apprehend ATD Absconders. The CIU evaluated two of the most commonly accessed geospatial intelligence web-based platforms utilized in support of law enforcement activities, Locate X, sold by Babel Street and Venntel, a subsidiary of location-based marketing company Gravy Analytics."

172   **attempt to respond to the nationwide opioid crisis** DHS email, May 14, 2019, in the American Civil Liberties Union FOIA collection. The email chain appears to be about a privacy threshold assessment for Hamilton, where at one point in the chain someone says, "We are looking forward to helping to counter the Opioid epidemic."

173   **"I understand that S&T has purchased"** Vogel, email to DHS.

173   **upended nearly fifty years** Jess Bravin and Brent Kendall, "Police Need Warrant for Cellphone Location Data, Supreme Court Rules," *Wall Street Journal,* June 22, 2018.

173   **It was a huge shift** Orin Kerr, "Understanding the Supreme Court's Carpenter Decision," *Lawfare,* June 22, 2018.

173   **A meeting was set for late summer** DHS email from an attorney in the Technology Programs Law Division in the Office of the General Counsel, Aug. 30, 2019, in the American Civil Liberties Union FOIA collection. Highly redacted, but shows a proposed date for a meeting for fifteen to twenty people including Venntel staff proposed for September 5, 2019.

174   **Tijuana kidnapping victim** Customs and Border Protection's National Targeting Center, Counter Network Division slideshow, stamped CBP-2020-033428-0000092. Released to me under the Freedom of Information Act. A redacted slide has the title "NTC Exploits AD ID to Help DEA-SOD Locate Tijuana Kidnapping Victim."

174   **shooting of a Border Patrol agent** DHS email, June 14, 2018, in the American Civil Liberties Union FOIA collection. The "to" and "from" fields are redacted, but the body of the email reads, "A few days ago a Border Patrol Agent was shot while patrolling a remote area in Arizona. CBP asked [Redacted] Data Analytics team to use the VennTel [*sic*] cell phone app location data aggregator to identify possible uses of cell phones in the area of the shooting."

174   **bombing in Sri Lanka** Venntel employee, email to DHS, April 29, 2019, in the American Civil Liberties Union FOIA collection. The "to," "from," and "CC" fields are redacted, but the body text reads, "We just had a call with [Reacted] at CBP/NTC regarding a request for information from the events in Sri Lanka and wanted to speak with you about this request. I understand that you currently don't have the 'Rest of the World' data but we are inclined to do a data pull for [Redacted] but we don't have the bandwidth to do the analytics and thought we could pass this off you [*sic*] your group." I am inferring, because of the date, that they are referring to the widely reported 2019 Sri Lanka Easter bombing, but in the spirit of full disclosure that is an inference.

174   **"were able to identify specific stash houses"** U.S. Immigration and Customs Enforcement, "Homeland Security Investigations—Office of Intelligence. Commercial Digital Data Location Tool," n.d., in the American Civil Liberties Union FOIA collection.

174 **a host of local police and sheriff's departments** U.S. Immigration and Customs Enforcement, Homeland Security Investigations Chief Intelligence Officer, email to ICE-HSI-INTEL_SIP-Washington D.C., in the American Civil Liberties Union FOIA collection. The email is partially redacted, but one sentence reads, "SAC DC was one of the major users of the system supporting our state and local partners. Prince William County, Fairfax, Richmond PD, Newport News, Northern Virginia Gang Task Force, Chesterfield PD, Henrico County, Norfolk PD, Fauquier County Sheriff Department and some smaller agencies requested our assistance with VENNTEL."

177 **The existence of Locate X** Charles Levinson, "Through Apps, Not Warrants, 'Locate X' Allows Federal Law Enforcement to Track Phones," Protocol, March 5, 2020.

177 **mirrored the history of an earlier technology** Spencer McCandless, "Stingray Confidential," *George Washington Law Review* 85, no. 3 (May 2017).

178 **"I have a silly question"** LaCicero, email to Margaret Giles, Nov. 13, 2019, in the American Civil Liberties Union FOIA collection.

179 **Venntel claims to derive data** DHS email, Jan. 25, 2019, in the American Civil Liberties Union FOIA collection. Unknown senders and recipients, but an unredacted paragraph reads, "The vendor collects data from 80,000 application providers globally, totalling over 40 billion signals a day and cleans the data to ensure accuracy. The data is available to ICE continually via a web portal but usually 24 hours delayed."

179 **Venntel also claims the data** Venntel, Marketing Material, n.d., in the American Civil Liberties Union FOIA collection.

179 **A *Washington Post* reporter tried in 2022** Geoffrey A. Fowler, "I Tried to Read All My App Privacy Policies. It Was 1 Million Words," *Washington Post,* May 31, 2022.

180 **"*the terms of service*"** Department of Homeland Security, "Privacy Impact Assessment Update for the Border Surveillance System (BSS)," DHS/CBP/PIA-022(a), Aug. 21, 2018.

181 **NRK, had the same idea** Martin Gundersen, "My Phone Was Spying on Me, So I Tracked Down the Surveillants," NRK, Dec. 3, 2020.

Chapter 16: Success Lies in the Secrecy

185 **"the aggregate of individuals"** Department of Defense, "Strategy for Operations in the Information Environment," June 2016.

185 **Aspects of this conflict** Nicole Perlroth, *This Is How They Tell Me the World Ends: The Cyberweapons Arms Race* (Bloomsbury, 2021).

186 **The United States is routinely accused** Nancy A. Youssef, "The Number of People the US Is Accused of Killing While Fighting ISIS Keeps Rising," BuzzFeed News, March 27, 2017.

187 **packaged up Venntel's data** Garance Burke and Jason Dearen, "Tech Tool Offers Police 'Mass Surveillance on a Budget,'" Associated Press, Sept. 2, 2022.

188 **"Picture getting a suspect's phone"** Ibid.

190 **helped a Philadelphia performing arts venue** "Case Study: Kimmel Cultural Campus," ncontext.com.

192 **"should appear to be based in Iraq"** Defense Department, U.S. Special Operations Command, "Atmospheric Reporting and PAI: Solicitation RFIs & Answers," Federal Contract Opportunity for Atmospheric Reporting and PAI H9227720R0010, archived by GovTribe.com.

Chapter 17: Going Gray

The ability of the government to track people based on their car tires' pressure readings was confirmed by more than half a dozen intelligence officials. It wasn't even a particularly secretive or classified capability— just an amusing aside to them about how little the public knows about the technology they rely on and how clever intelligence agencies are at finding vectors to exploit that technology. Also, a special thanks to Fairfax Hyundai for putting up with me as a customer.

200 **those aren't hardwired sensors** Bridgestone, "What Is TPMS & How Does It Work?," April 1, 2021.

200 **never bothered to secure the transmission** Kenneth L. Hacker, "Preserving Privacy in Automotive Tire Pressure Monitoring Systems" (master's thesis, Air Force Institute of Technology, March 2019).

200 **Tero Mononen placed a digital radio** Corrafig, "Sniffing Car Tire (TPMS) Data (and Tracking Cars)," corra.fi, Aug. 29, 2021, corra.fi/posts/sniffing-tpms-data/.

201 **One contractor** Weathered Security, "New Products," accessed July 29, 2023, weatheredsecurity.com/new-products.

201 **The same vendor sold** Department of Homeland Security, Award PIID 70B06C21P00000535, "Purchase Order for Emerging Radio Frequency Sensor Nodes for Use by the U.S. Border Patrol Tactical Unit (BORTAC)," USAspending.gov.

201 **Bjørn Martin Hegnes** Martin Gundersen, "Someone Could Be Tracking You Through Your Headphones," NRK, Sept. 2, 2021.

203 *Politico* **reported in 2022** Alex Thompson, Ruby Cramer, and Tina Sfondeles, "Kamala Harris Is Bluetooth-Phobic," *West Wing Playbook* (newsletter), *Politico*, Dec. 6, 2021.

203 **Retailers have started embedding** Kelly Hill, "Four Predictions for the Indoor Location Market," RCR Wireless News, Dec. 22, 2021.

203 **Wi-Fi-enabled trash cans** Richard Trenholm, "London Tosses Out Wi-Fi-Sniffing 'Smart Bins,' " CNET, Aug. 12, 2013.

204 **device called the Nemo Handy** "The Secret Surveillance Catalogue," *Intercept*, legacy.theintercept.com/surveillance-catalogue/.

204 **called the Ulysses Group** Joseph Cox, "Cars Have Your Location. This Spy Firm Wants to Sell It to the U.S. Military," *Motherboard* (blog), *Vice*, March 17, 2021.

205   **Otonomo is the Gravy Analytics of car data** Joseph Cox, "Class-Action Lawsuit Targets Company That Harvests Location Data from 50 Million Cars," *Motherboard* (blog), *Vice*, April 15, 2022.

205   **"We may share Covered Information"** Hyundai USA, "Vehicle Technologies and Services Privacy Notice," effective date Jan. 1, 2023, accessed June 18, 2023.

206   **Nissan's privacy policy states** Felix Salmon, "Your Car Has 'Unmatched Power' to Spy on You—and Share the Data," Axios.com, Sept. 8, 2023.

207   **company called Vigilant** Byron Tau, "License-Plate Scans Aid Crime-Solving but Spur Little Privacy Debate," *Wall Street Journal*, March 10, 2021.

207   **a hacker who identified himself** Ben Yakas, "Is Your E-ZPass Being Tracked Around NYC? Probably," Gothamist, Sept. 13, 2013.

Chapter 18: We're All Signal Collectors Now

This account of X-Mode's rise and fall was drawn from interviews with numerous people familiar with the history of the company. All were conducted on background. Anton gave several on-the-record interviews to *The Wall Street Journal* that I drew from prior to embarking on this book project. I spoke to other X-Mode employees, investors, and advisers from various stages of the company's history as well. I also did an exhaustive review of all of the material published about X-Mode and Anton. Anton had a prolific internet and social media presence, which I reviewed in great detail. Particularly helpful were several talks and lectures he did that remain available on his YouTube channel. I also reviewed documents about X-Mode's government work. Some were released under FOIA; others were shared with me by sources. I also spoke with numerous people familiar with SignalFrame's national security work and reviewed documents about their efforts that were provided to me by sources.

209   **"condom for your phone"** Andrew Trotman, "'A Condom for Your Phone': New App Stops You Drunk-Calling Your Ex," *Telegraph*, Nov. 25, 2014.

209   **Before a person set out for a night** Madeline Roth, "This Amazing App Will Recover Your Snapchats and Prevent Drunk Dialing . . . AMEN!," MTV.com, Nov. 22, 2014.

209   **Anton spent his formative years growing up** Joshua Anton, "Leaving the Cave Barefoot Isn't a Bad Thing," YouTube video, posted by TEDx Talks, May 15, 2015.

210   **"not the greatest idea"** Ibid.

210   **he misspelled the name of the business school** Ibid.

210   **His first fall on campus** Alexandra Svokos, "This App Can Track Your Drunk Night Out and Recover Snapchats," *Huffington Post,* Nov. 14, 2014.

210   **self-publishing e-books with titles** Joshua Anton, author page, Amazon.com, accessed July 30, 2023, www.amazon.com/stores/Joshua-Anton/author/B00BC9G4A8.

210   **to keep his classmates safe** Svokos, "This App Can Track Your Drunk Night Out and Recover Snapchats."

210   **He didn't drink in college** X-Mode, "What Is X-Mode?"

211   **later found murdered** Meghan Keneally, "Hannah Graham: A Look Back at UVA Student's Disappearance," ABC News, Feb. 10, 2015.

211   **thought the app could be a way** Svokos, "This App Can Track Your Drunk Night Out and Recover Snapchats."

211   **launched in 2013 and cost 99 cents** Lalita Clozel, "Why This Sober UVA Grad Created an App for His Drunk Peers," *Technical.ly,* June 11, 2015.

211   **job offers from Google and Unilever** Ibid.

213   **"Congrats on finishing your first mile!"** Casey Russell, "Sophomore's Work with Startup Helps Launch Alternative App," *Daily Orange,* Feb. 7, 2017.

213   **partnering with other apps** X-Mode, "So You Want to Build an App: Tips and Wisdom from the Team Behind Drunk Mode."

219   **And it would get plenty of takers** X-Mode, "Trusted Partners," archived on the Internet Archive, web.archive.org/web/20200409092626/https://xmode.io/trusted -partners/.

Chapter 19: Mini-spies

The account of Premise Data's transformation from international development work to defense contractor has been drawn from interviews with more than two dozen people who were directly involved in the company over its ten-year history, including some senior leaders. I also reviewed hundreds of pages of documents—some obtained from sources, some government documents, and some filed as part of various lawsuits. Because of Premise's litigiousness against its former employees, only a single person other than Lanny Davis and Maury Blackman was willing to speak to me on the record. I also interviewed Blackman twice during the course of this reporting and spent uncountable hours on the phone with Davis.

Numerous people confirmed Blackman's remark about throwing up on the homeless the way I wrote it, though Blackman through Davis claimed that he warned staff *against* throwing up on homeless people.

Two of them brought it up completely unprompted by me and both remembered the quotation exactly the same way. Both of those people were present when he said it.

Premise's lawsuits against its own employees were a gold mine in reporting this chapter. I examined hundreds of pages from the legal filings in these cases, which told the story of the company's internal drama and strife in 2018. These hundreds of pages of filings provided invaluable information about the internal workings of the company. Let that be a lesson to companies: sue employees at your own risk, because court dockets are public and are often the greatest source of information that exists when a reporter is interested in a company.

221 **This rumor had gone viral** Byron Tau, "Premise Mobile-Phone App Suspends Ukraine Activities After Accusations Fly," *Wall Street Journal,* Feb. 26, 2022.

221 **The reports had been given legitimacy** Louise Matsakis, "California-Based App Premise Battles Accusations of Helping Russian Military," NBC News, Feb. 26, 2022.

225 **Premise had become an intelligence** Premise Data, "Capability Overview for CJSOTF-A," May 31, 2019, published by *The Wall Street Journal,* s.wsj.net/public /resources/documents/premise-doc.pdf.

226 **wagering real money on terrorist attacks** Nicole Duran, "Dorgan, Wyden Decry DOD's Terrorism Futures Market," *Roll Call,* July 28, 2003.

226 **Red Balloon Challenge** "MIT Wins $40,000 Prize in Nationwide Balloon-Hunt Contest," CNN, Dec. 5, 2009.

226 **one U.S. intelligence community project** Authentic8, OSINT Insider "Episode 4, GEOINT" Thom Kaye. Authentic8 removed this web video from YouTube after I contacted several participants in the discussion to ask for details on some of their claims; however, I saved a copy.

227 **a punk rock musician** Soloff's punk rock history is mentioned a few places, including on his personal website and his LinkedIn profile. See David Soloff, Founder, LinkedIn Profile, accessed June 18, 2023, www.linkedin.com/in/davidsoloff.

227 **deep-pocketed Silicon Valley investors** Alexander Davis, "Premise Data Taps New CEO for Gig-Based Data Collection Startup," *Wall Street Journal,* Feb. 6, 2018.

227 **Premise also got glowing write-ups** David Baker, "Photos Are Creating a Real-Time Food-Price Index," *Wired,* April 2016; Vijith Assar, "A New Premise to Capture Prices Around the World," *New Yorker,* Oct. 14, 2013.

228 **Its website still boasted** Premise.com, archived on the Internet Archive, web .archive.org/web/20201101001232/https://www.premise.com/.

228 **It would advertise itself** Premise Data, "Capability Overview."

233 **staff morale was sinking rapidly** Complaint, *Premise Data Corporation v. Steffen Weiss,* Case No. CGC-19-576127 (Cal. Super. Ct., filed 2019).

234 **stew of toxic dissatisfaction** Cross-Complaint of Steffen Weiss, *Premise Data Corporation v. Steffen Weiss,* Case No. CGC-19-576127 (Cal. Super. Ct., filed 2019).

234 **People began resigning en masse** Ibid.

234 **called Dark Slack; another, Axiom** Exhibit C, Declaration of Dhaivat H. Shah in support of Premise Data Corporation's Motion to Compel Moorea Brega to Produce Documents Pursuant to Subpoena and Request for Sanctions, *Premise Data Corporation v. Steffen Weiss,* Case No. CGC-19-576127 (Cal. Super. Ct., filed 2019).

234 **Prexit and yet another called lesmiserables** Memorandum of Points and Authorities in Support of Premise Data Corporation's Motion for an Order Compelling Further Responses to Subpoena for Appearance and Production of Documents and Things to Angela Jo and for Sanctions, *Premise Data Corporation v. Steffen Weiss,* Case No. CGC-19-576127 (Cal. Super. Ct., filed 2019).

234 **Signal group chat titled Dumpster Fire** Memo to Compel Angela Jo, *Premise v. Weiss.*

234 **nearly thirty people would leave** Memorandum of Points and Authorities in Support of Defendant's Motion to Compel Plaintiff Premise Data Corporation to Further Respond to Requests for Production of Documents and for Monetary Sanctions, *Premise Data Corporation v. Steffen Weiss,* Case No. CGC-19-576127 (Cal. Super. Ct., filed 2019).

234 **Premise had become a very different** Complaint, *Premise Data Corporation v. Alex Pompe,* Case No. 19CV346678 (Cal. Super. Ct., filed 2019).

Chapter 20: Rhamnousia, the Goddess Who Punishes Hubris

The story of Rodney Joffe, Neustar, and the buying and selling of large amounts of internet data was told largely through court records and public records requests, as well as a review of archived clips going back to the 1980s. I reviewed eleven days of trial transcripts in *USA v. Sussmann,* which contained a huge amount of detail on what unfolded, as well as tens of thousands of pages of emails released by Georgia Tech. I also spoke to numerous people familiar with Joffe's work and the technical issues raised by the buying and selling of internet data. This chapter was in many ways a team effort. Aruna Viswanatha, Robert McMillan, and Dustin Volz were essential partners in doing the reporting on this story for *The Wall Street Journal* that would eventually help inform this chapter. Our Georgia-based correspondent Cameron McWhirter is also owed a debt of gratitude. He made several public records requests on our behalf. In addition, an unusual mix of anonymous/pseudonymous researchers who call themselves sleuths made public a large number of documents they obtained under public records requests. While I do not always endorse the conclusions these sleuths drew about the case, the documents they made available were useful contributions to the public's understanding of this matter—particular Margot Cleveland, a lawyer and writer for *The Federalist,* and Ryan Milliron and Paul Anderson.

236 **transmitted a message between one computer** UCLA, "The Internet's First Message Sent from UCLA," 100.ucla.edu/timeline/the-internets-first-message-sent -from-ucla.

237 **cybersecurity lawyer named Michael Sussmann** Sadie Gurman and Byron Tau, "Lawyer Michael Sussmann Indicted on Charges of Lying to FBI," *Wall Street Journal,* Sept. 16, 2021.

238 **combing through a massive trove** John H. Durham, "Report on Matters Related to Intelligence Activities and Investigations Arising out of the 2016 Presidential Campaigns," May 12, 2023.

238 **Certain telecommunications companies** Transcript of Jury Trial, Afternoon Session, *USA v. Sussmann,* Case No. 1:21-cr-582 (D.D.C., filed 2021), Doc. No. 172, Testimony of Jared Novick.

238 **done in the shadows** Manos Antonakakis, email to Angelos D. Keromytis, June 15, 2018. In it, Antonakakis writes about Keromytis, "Due to potential national security implications from the results of his research, the publication of the attribution analysis is slower than normal."

239 **cybersecurity executive named Rodney Joffe** Evan Perez and Katelyn Polantz, "Durham Issues Fresh Round of Subpoenas in His Continuing Probe of FBI Investigation into Trump, Russia," CNN, Sept. 30, 2021.

239 **under consideration for a cybersecurity job** Durham, Report.

239 **Trump as a national security risk** Joffe, email to Manos Antonakakis, David Dagon, and April D. Lorenzen, Aug. 25, 2016. Released under the Georgia Open Records Act to *The Wall Street Journal.*

239 **producing a white paper** Government Trial Exhibit 200, *USA v. Sussmann,* Case No. 1:21-cr-582 (D.D.C., filed 2021).

239 **"I'm coming on my own"** Government's Motion in Limine, *USA v. Sussmann,* Case No. 1:21-cr-582 (D.D.C., filed 2021), Doc. No. 61.

239 **"It appears abnormal that a presidential candidate"** Defense Trial Exhibit 523, *USA v. Sussmann,* Case No. 1:21-cr-582 (D.D.C., filed 2021).

241 **peddling cheap grandfather clocks** "Rhode Island Authorities Ring Bell on Clock Scam," Associated Press, May 4, 1988.

242 **Joffe dropped out of college** Plaintiff's Final Motion for Extension of Time to Serve Process on Defendant, *AO Alfa Bank v. John Doe et al.,* Case No. 50-2020-CA-6304 (Fla. 15th Cir. Ct., filed 2020).

242 **"world famous Bentley IX"** Paul Sperry, "The Checkered Past of the FBI Cyber Contractor Who 'Spied' on Trump," Real Clear Investigations, Feb. 17, 2022.

242 **"You say grandfather clocks"** "Rhode Island Authorities Ring Bell on Clock Scam."

242 **he started an internet service provider** MAAWG-Messaging, Malware, and Mobile Anti-abuse Working Group, "Rodney Joffe Shares Industry's Anti-abuse History for 2016 Litynski Award," YouTube, June 9, 2015.

242 **the source of the email spam** Ibid.

243 **marketing opt-out list** Ibid.

243 **lawsuits against fax spammers** Ibid.

243 **rail on a private industry listserv** Joffe, email to NANOG email list, June 13, 2017. Released under the Georgia Open Records Act to Ryan Milliron.

243 **"Rodney, What do you suggest?"** Mel Beckman, email to NANOG email list, June 13, 2017. Released under the Georgia Open Records Act to Ryan Milliron.

244 **UltraDNS was acquired by Neustar** Neustar, "NeuStar Announces Agreement to Acquire UltraDNS, a Recognized Industry Leader of DNS and Directory Services," press release, April 19, 2006.

244 **Neustar was spun out** "Neustar Is Splitting into 2 Publicly Traded Companies," Reuters, June 21, 2016.

244 **he was part of a working group** Aruna Viswanatha, Robert McMillan, and Byron Tau, "Trial of Clinton Lawyer Michael Sussmann Puts Spotlight on a Veteran Tech Executive," *Wall Street Journal,* May 16, 2022.

244 **prestigious award by the FBI** Neustar, "Neustar's Rodney Joffe Receives Prestigious FBI Director's Award," press release, Oct. 29, 2013.

245 **He started numerous other companies** Transcript, Jared Novick testimony, *USA v. Sussmann.*

246 **machine learning framework called Rhamnousia** Danielle Gambino, email to Antonakakis, July 12, 2016, "Clarification Requested on HSR in 'Rhamnousia' Proposal (DARPA-BAA-16-34 Enhanced Attribution)."

246 **about 150 billion DNS lookups a day** Transcript of Jury Trial, Afternoon Session, *USA v. Sussmann,* Case No. 1:21-cr-582 (D.D.C., filed 2021), Doc. No. 162. Testimony of Steve DeJong.

246 **Comcast and Cox were initially planning** Department of Defense, Amendment of Solicitation/Modification of Contract P00003 to HR001118C0057, April 30, 2018. Released under Georgia Open Records Act to *The Wall Street Journal.*

246 **CenturyLink, offered to turn over** Angelos Keromytis, email to Antonakakis, June 19, 2018. Released under the Georgia Open Records Act to Ryan Milliron.

247 **he would field calls** Antonakakis, email to William Ware, et al., Jan. 30, 2020. Released under the Georgia Open Records Act to Ryan Milliron.

247 **was also an FBI source** Transcript of Jury Trial, Morning Session, *USA v. Sussmann,* Case No. 1:21-cr-582 (D.D.C., filed 2021), Doc. No. 173. Testimony of Thomas Grasso.

247 **"fraud and manipulation"** Hillary Clinton, "Remarks at the OSCE First Plenary Session," Dec. 6, 2011.

248 **"I'm not the smart guy"** MAAWG-Messaging, Malware, and Mobile Anti-abuse Working Group, "Rodney Joffe Shares Industry's Anti-abuse History for 2016 Litynski Award."

249 **"Rodney, you do realize"** Motion in Limine, *USA v. Sussmann.*

249 **"I would preface the whitepaper"** Ibid.

250 **Joffe left Neustar in 2021** Verified Complaint for Advancement and, in the Alternative, Indemnification, *Rodney Joffe v. Neustar Inc. and Security Services, LLC,* Case No. 2022-1041-KSJM (Del. Ch., filed 2023).

250 **enmeshed in a criminal investigation** Ibid.

250 **totaled more than $2.5 million** Ibid.

250 **"indisputable evidence that my campaign"** Statement by Donald J. Trump, 45th President of the United States of America, Feb. 12, 2022.

250 **"Nearly four months after I 'received'"** Antonakakis, email to Christian Fuller and Ling-Ling Nie, Sept. 28, 2021. Released under the Georgia Open Records Act to Margot Cleveland.

251 **"It seems possible that the U.S. government"** Dexter Filkins, "The Contested Afterlife of the Trump–Alfa Bank Story," *New Yorker,* Oct. 7, 2020.

251 **"Some of the most trusted DNS specialists"** Franklin Foer, "Was a Trump Server Communicating with Russia?," *Slate,* Oct. 31, 2016.

252 **"kinda bonkers"** Joseph Cox, "How Data Brokers Sell Access to the Backbone of the Internet," *Motherboard* (blog), *Vice,* Aug. 24, 2021.

253 **"As Congress debates important legislation"** Joseph Cox, "Pentagon Surveilling Americans Without a Warrant, Senator Reveals," *Motherboard* (blog), *Vice,* May 13, 2021.

254 **Georgia Tech's Enhanced Attribution project** Kirk McConnell, email to Victor Oppleman, Joffe, Antonakakis, Christian Cook, Lisa Patel, and Lily Kim, July 31, 2019. Released under the Georgia Open Records Act to Paul Anderson.

Chapter 21: The Apps Are Not What They Seem

Special thanks to Joel Reardon and Serge Egelman for bringing me this story back in 2022 and for helping me understand the mobile app ecosystem.

255 **more than ten million times** Joel Reardon, "The Curious Case of Coulus Coelib," AppCensus, April 6, 2022.

255 **It used the GPS locations** Google Play Store, "Al-Moazin Lite (Prayer Times)," accessed July 30, 2023, play.google.com/store/apps/details?id=com.parfield.prayers .lite&hl=en_US&gl=US.

260   **"The technology we are using"** Ryan Singel, "Law Enforcement Appliance Subverts SSL," *Wired,* March 24, 2010.

262   ***Vice* reported on the source** Joseph Cox, "How the U.S. Military Buys Location Data from Ordinary Apps," *Motherboard* (blog), *Vice,* Nov. 16, 2020.

263   **It stoked outrage among many Muslims** Johana Bhuiya, "Muslims Reel over a Prayer App That Sold User Data: 'A Betrayal from Within Our Own Community,'" *Los Angeles Times,* Nov. 23, 2020.

265   **intermittent outbreaks of bipartisan alarm** Stu Woo, "Why Is the U.S. Threatening to Ban TikTok?," *Wall Street Journal,* March 16, 2023.

265   **federal judges ruled against the administration** Bobby Allyn, "U.S. Judge Halts Trump's TikTok Ban, the 2nd Court to Fully Block the Action," NPR, Dec. 7, 2020.

266   **Inside that data were the internal layouts** Alex Hern, "Fitness Tracking App Strava Gives Away Location of Secret US Army Bases," *Guardian,* Jan. 28, 2018.

266   **"This is where I politely remind"** Dr. Jeffrey Lewis (@ArmsControlWonk), Twitter, Jan. 28, 2018, 6:20 p.m., twitter.com/ArmsControlWonk/status/957755184876109824.

267   **revealed the presence of sensitive information on an app called Untappd** Foeke Postma, "Military and Intelligence Personnel Can Be Tracked with the Untappd Beer App," Bellingcat, May 18, 2020.

Chapter 22: The Privilege of Disappearing

CIS Mobile's former president Bill Anderson met me on the sidelines of a Defense Department conference in late 2021 to brief me on the product. He was kind enough to connect me to Paul Litva, who helped develop AltOS. Litva briefed me on the product once, and we communicated several times afterward. Also special thanks to the two executives of Glacier Security and to Michael Bazzell, whose podcast I have been listening to for several years. The bulk of this chapter is drawn from those interviews. The history of Sky Global is drawn from the court documents in the Sky Global case as well as other media reports.

269   **that it calls AltOS** CIS Mobile, "CIS Mobile Data Sheet," CIS Secure, May 27, 2023.

270   **Founded in Canada in 2010** Joseph Cox, "Crime Boss or Tech CEO? An Encrypted Phone Company Sues the Government to Save Itself," *Motherboard* (blog), *Vice,* Nov. 18, 2021.

271   **was indicted in 2021** Indictment, *USA v. Eap et al.,* No. 3:21-cr-00822-GPC (S.D. Cal., filed 2021), ECF No. 1.

272   **"allegedly provided a service"** Department of Justice, "Sky Global Executive and Associate Indicted for Providing Encrypted Communication Devices to Help International Drug Traffickers Avoid Law Enforcement," press release, March 12, 2021.

272 **propose a legislative measure** Joseph Cox, "UK Proposes Making the Sale and Possession of Encrypted Phones Illegal," *Motherboard* (blog), *Vice,* Feb. 8, 2023.

272 **sales reps offered Canadian law enforcement officials** Byron Tau, "Encrypted-Phone Company Says U.S. Improperly Shut It Down," *Wall Street Journal,* Nov. 18, 2021.

275 **served as a technical consultant** Matthew Giles, "The Unusually Accurate Portrait of Hacking on USA's *Mr. Robot,*" *Vulture* (blog), *New York,* July 23, 2015.

276 **One recent issue of his digital magazine** Anon E. Mouse (pseudonym), "How (Not) to Fly Anonymously," *Unredacted,* no. 004 (Q4 2022).

280 **"Maybe *Dobbs* will do for location privacy"** *The Cyberlaw Podcast,* episode 420, Sept. 7, 2022.

Epilogue: The Man Behind the Counter

A special thank-you to Preet Bharara for reminding me of the quotation from *Inherit the Wind* in one of his 2022 podcast episodes. The quotation stuck with me as I was writing this book. I liberally borrowed the observation about surveillance in America being hidden versus surveillance in China being open from a 2023 Aspen Institute event conducted under Chatham House rules that ban me from citing its original source. But thank you to that person for the wisdom and the astute observation, because it neatly distilled a lot of my thinking on the topic of surveillance in the West versus China.

284 **"Chinese leaders have revived totalitarian techniques"** Josh Chin and Liza Lin, *Surveillance State: Inside China's Quest to Launch a New Era of Social Control* (St. Martin's Press, 2022).

284 **Integrated Joint Operations Platform** Maya Wang, "China's Algorithms of Repression," Human Rights Watch, May 1, 2019.

287 **collects almost no data** "Grand Jury Subpoena for Signal User Data, Central District of California (Again!)," Signal, Oct. 28, 2021.

INDEX

ABOUT THE AUTHOR

BYRON TAU is an author and a journalist based in Washington, D.C., where he writes about law, courts, and national security. In more than a decade in the nation's capital, Tau has reported on all three branches of the federal government, with stints as a White House correspondent, a Capitol Hill reporter, and a legal journalist. He's also covered two presidential campaigns as well as the lobbying and campaign-finance beat. He now works at the Allbritton Journalism Institute, a nonprofit launched in 2023 that trains and mentors early-career reporters, and writes for *Notus*, the institute's publication. He previously worked at *The Wall Street Journal* and *Politico*. He received his undergraduate degree in political science and American history from McGill University and a master's degree in journalism from Georgetown University. Byron is a native of Holliston, Massachusetts. He's a voracious reader, a mediocre runner and cyclist, and an atrocious chess and poker player. His superpower is starting arguments on neighborhood listservs.

ABOUT THE TYPE

———

This book was set in Caslon, a typeface first designed in 1722 by William Caslon (1692–1766). Its widespread use by most English printers in the early eighteenth century soon supplanted the Dutch typefaces that had formerly prevailed. The roman is considered a "workhorse" typeface due to its pleasant, open appearance, while the italic is exceedingly decorative.